STUDIES IN IMPERIALISM

general editor John M. MacKenzie

When the 'Studies in Imperialism' series was founded more
than twenty years ago, emphasis was laid upon the conviction that 'imperialism as a cultural phenomenon had as significant an effect on the dominant as on the subordinate
societies'. With more than fifty books published, this
remains the prime concern of the series. Cross-disciplinary
work has indeed appeared covering the full spectrum of cultural phenomena, as well as examining aspects of gender
and sex, frontiers and law, science and the environment,
language and literature, migration and patriotic societies,
and much else. Moreover, the series has always wished to
present comparative work on European and American
imperialism, and particularly welcomes the submission of
books in these areas. The fascination with imperialism, in
all its aspects, shows no sign of abating, and this series will
continue to lead the way in encouraging the widest possible
range of studies in the field. 'Studies in Imperialism' is fully
organic in its development, always seeking to be at the
cutting edge, responding to the latest interests of scholars
and the needs of this ever-expanding area of scholarship.

Ireland, India and empire

MANCHESTER
1824

Manchester University Press

Ireland, India and empire

INDO-IRISH RADICAL CONNECTIONS, 1919–64

Kate O'Malley

MANCHESTER
UNIVERSITY PRESS
Manchester and New York

distributed in the United States exclusively by
PALGRAVE MACMILLAN

Published by Manchester University Press
Oxford Road, Manchester M13 9NR, UK
and Room 400, 175 Fifth Avenue, New York, NY 10010, USA
www.manchesteruniversitypress.co.uk

Distributed in the United States exclusively by
Palgrave Macmillan, 175 Fifth Avenue,
New York, NY 10010, USA

Distributed in Canada exclusively by
UBC Press, University of British Columbia, 2029 West Mall,
Vancouver, BC, Canada V6T 1Z2

British Library Cataloguing-in-Publication Data is available

Library of Congress Cataloging-in-Publication Data is available

ISBN 978 0 7190 8171 2 paperback

First published in hardback 2008

This paperback edition first published 2009

The publisher has no responsibility for the persistence or accuracy of URLs for any external or third-party internet websites referred to in this book, and does not guarantee that any content on such websites is, or will remain, accurate or appropriate.

Printed by the MPG Books Group in the UK

For my Mother and Father
In memory of Brian, Rita, Joe and Mamie

CONTENTS

GENERAL EDITOR'S INTRODUCTION

It is increasingly apparent that scholars should be adopting a 'four-nation' approach not only to the pasts of the British and Hibernian Isles, but also to the history of the so-called British Empire. The separate strands of Irish, Scottish, Welsh and English influences and responses run through empire in highly illuminating ways. In many respects, the efforts to constitute a supposedly integrated set of 'British' institutions and territories transparently failed. These strands were of course inter-woven with indigenous histories and made up a range of developing identities which were, like all identities, constantly in a state of flux and never fully constituted. The identities of the four 'home' nations were themselves modified in the process and, in the twenty-first century, still show marks of that imperial experience.

The affinities between Ireland and India have been much com-mented upon in the nineteenth-century context. Modes of governance, tenancy laws, famines, migrations, policing and military matters have all received attention. Rudyard Kipling was clearly fascinated by the role of the Irish in India and the relationship between the two, one small and the other vast, runs through his writings. He considered that they shared an adherence to the emotions, a sense of the supernatural, notions of a romantic sensibility, as well as powerful religious affilia-tions. In all of these they contrasted with the rational restraint and pragmatic practicality of the English. But what he considered to be their attractive characteristics could also be their undoing. For Kipling, there was a constant tension between good and bad Ireland and Irish, good and bad India and Indians. Yet he considered that each (notably the Irish in the military) could lead the other in the direction of what he con-sidered to be the path of imperial righteousness. For him, the Irish were certainly both imperial and colonial.

Needless to say, they were much more likely to lead each other in quite another direction, that of nationalism and resistance. By the time of Kipling's death in 1936, he was inconsolably beached on the shores of hostile territories shaped by the political earthquakes of Anglo-Irish treaties and Government of India Acts. Meanwhile, polit-ical nationalism, as so often happens, had its precedents in literary connections. The phenomenon sometimes called 'Celtic Orientalism' had been represented in the relationship between W.B. Yeats and Rabindranath Tagore, only the most prominent of a range of similar reciprocal influences.

All of this is well enough known, but Kate O'Malley moves these studies forward in new and exciting directions. The twentieth century, particularly the period after the First World War, has been much less studied. Using the remarkable files of the Indian Political Intelligence (IPI) department (barely noticed in studies of the secret services) she reveals an extraordinary set of connections among the personnel of Irish and Indian nationalism. Many prominent politicians viewed themselves as sharing similarities in historical tribulation and nationalist aspirations. They not only indulged in the emotional satisfaction of shared experiences, as they saw it, but also proposed the sharing of techniques (boycott for example), methods of agitation, the use of publications and the press, and the encouragement of joint organisations like the League Against Imperialism, the Indian-Irish Independence League, and the Friends of India Society. They also both recognised the significance of calling overseas settlements and ideologies to their aid – American Irish, South African Indians, communism, and the Axis powers.

Yet when all that has been said, we have to be cool in our assessment of the importance of all of this. Secret service organisations suffer in their nature from the paranoia that gives their activities meaning. As O'Malley reveals, the British services, including IPI, were much more obsessed with communism than with nationalism and were sometimes confused as a result. Gandhi was deeply suspicious of the Irish precedent because he saw it as representing a violent nationalism which he abjured. The connections between Irish political figures, including de Valera, and Subhas Chandra Bose were extensive and thoroughly intriguing, but the latter's connections with Germany, Russia and Japan during the Second World War have rendered his reputation controversial. Moreover, the two nationalist movements often seem to throw up a succession of shifting groups and alliances whose relative influence has to be assessed dispassionately. All this is covered eminently successfully and in addition, the book's highly original research demonstrates just how significant 'intra-colonial' relationships were. Very often, the really important developments in the associations of the British Empire were actually taking place outside of the direct, metropolitan imperial loop. This book adds a great deal to our understanding of these processes.

John M. MacKenzie

ACKNOWLEDGEMENTS

My greatest debt is to my former supervisor Professor Eunan O'Halpin for his guidance, encouragement and belief. This all happened during a difficult period in his life and his good humour in the face of adversity was never failing. I am also very grateful to Dr Deirdre McMahon and Dr Michael Kennedy for their help at various stages and for their ongoing support. I thank also the editors of the Documents on Irish Foreign Policy series: Catriona Crowe, Professor Ronan Fanning and Professor Dermot Keogh, as well as the Ambassador of India to Ireland His Excellency P. S. Raghavan and the former Ambassador, Saurabh Kumar and his wife Sulekha. This project was aided by the conversations and correspondence I was lucky enough to have had with Aideen Austin, née Woods, Anna Austin, Eithne Frost and Lal Wright, née Dey, whose recollections about their fascinating families greatly supplemented the primary source material. I wish to thank everyone at Manchester University Press, particularly Alison Welsby, Emma Brennan, Rachel Armstrong, Stephanie Matthews, Ron Price and Professor John MacKenzie. Thanks are also due to Helen Litton for providing the index and to Dave O'Grady for final proof reading.

My research in India was made all the more enjoyable by the kindness and assistance extended to me by the Irish Embassy staff and Ambassador Kieran Dowling. I am especially grateful to Pat Bourne and his family for making me feel so welcome and for ongoing correspondence on all things Indo-Irish. I also thank Grainne Morrissey, Dr Manoj Joshi, Dr Indivar Kamtekar and especially Gurpreet Singh Bindra and family, who were extremely hospitable and kind. My first trip to Kolkata was both memorable and stimulating due to the welcome I received from the Netaji Research Bureau. I was lucky enough to have presented a paper in the very house in which Subhas Chandra Bose had lived and from which he famously escaped while under house arrest in 1941. Special thanks go to the Bose family, Professor Sugata Bose and Krishna Bose, for their interest in my research and for their hospitality.

I wish to thank the following historians and fellow researchers and friends who have assisted or supported me in various ways: Agnes and Sean Aylward, Dr Anna Bryson, Dr Garret FitzGerald, Professor Tom Fraser, Patrick French, Dr John Gibney, Dr Brian Hanley, Dr Tara Keenan-Thomson, Professor Seán McConville, Dr Fearghal McGarry, Dr Barry McLoughlin, Dr Éamonn O Ciardha, Dr Donal O'Drisceoil, Rosemary O'Halpin, Colonel (retired) Dr Terry O'Neill, Dr Susannah

Riordan, Kevin O'Sullivan, Dr Malcolm Sen, Dr Michael Silvestri, Dr Brian Thomson, Professor Tadhg Foley, Professor Luke Gibbons, Dr Maureen O'Connor and everyone involved in the Fourth Galway Conference on Colonialism. I also thank the Centre for Contemporary Irish History and the Department of History, Trinity College Dublin, especially Professor Jane Ohlmeyer and Professor David Dickson.

Thanks are due to the staff of the various libraries and archives in which I have worked, in particular Mary Mackey, Elizabeth McEvoy and the staff of the National Archives of Ireland, Seamus Helferty and the staff of the UCD Archives, Commandant Victor Laing and the staff of the Irish Military Archives, Jill Geber and everyone at the British Library's Oriental and India Office Reading Room, the Gilbert Library, the National Library of Ireland, the National Photographic Archive of Ireland, the National Archives of the United Kingdom, the Public Record Office of Northern Ireland, the Women's Library at the University of London, the Hull University Archives, the National Archives of India and the Nehru Memorial Library.

I am grateful to Trinity College for granting a Faculty Postgraduate Award from 2001 to 2003, to the Bank of Ireland for the award of a Research Studentship in Contemporary Irish History from 2003 to 2005 and to Trinity College's Grace Lawless Lee Fund and Graduate Studies Travel Fund for research travel and conference grants.

I am grateful for the support I have received from my close friends and extended family in both Galway and Dublin, especially Finian O'Shea and the O'Grady family. Thanks are extended to the various O'Malley dogs, especially Failbhe and Taz, who walked over manuscripts and kept me company during writer's block coffee breaks.

This book would not have been possible without the help and support of Mick, Dolores, and Tony O'Malley and my partner, Dan O'Grady, to whom I am eternally grateful.

ILLUSTRATIONS

ABBREVIATIONS

BL	British Library
Comintern	Communist International
CPGB	Communist Party of Great Britain
CPI	Communist Party of India
DIB	Delhi Intelligence Bureau
DT	Department of the Taoiseach
FOIS	Friends of India Society
G2	Irish Army Intelligence
ICS	Indian Civil Service
IFL	Indian Freedom League
IIL	Indian Independence League
IIIL	Indian–Irish Independence League
ILP	Independent Labour Party
IMA	Irish Military Archives
INA	Indian National Army
IPI	Indian Political Intelligence
IRA	Irish Republican Army
ISC	Irish Situation Committee
LAI	League Against Imperialism
NAI	National Archives of Ireland
NAUK	National Archives of the United Kingdom
NLI	National Library of Ireland
NML	Nehru Memorial Library
RDS	Royal Dublin Society
SPI	Socialist Party of Ireland
TCD	Trinity College Dublin
TD	Teachta Dála, a member of Dáil Éireann
UCD	University College Dublin

Introduction

In January 1954 Erskine Childers Jr[1] and his wife, Rita, stood on the deck of a ferry from Ceylon and watched the low landline of India come up on the horizon. As the vista unfolded before him he could not help but think of Ireland's physical and cultural remoteness from the vast exotic country they were approaching. He expected to find very few Indians 'other than the national leaders who would know anything more about Ireland than its geographical location – a tiny country thousands of miles and a world of civilisations away, not even linked to India by a diplomatic mission in New Delhi.'[2] He was soon proved wrong when, on landing on 26 January, India's Republic Day, a customs official examining his passport glanced up at him and with a smile said: 'Ah – the land of de Valera and MacSwiney: we are remembering your struggle too on this day.' Childers was struck by that phrase and surprised

> not that he should know the name of Ireland's then Taoiseach but that he should couple it with the name of Terence MacSwiney, who died so many years ago. And when, an hour later in the train to Madras, the second Indian of our chance acquaintance used the very same phrase on learning my nationality, I became still more curious.[3]

That curiosity was one I shared with Childers when I set about researching this topic. In both Irish and Indian historiography subtle references to an innate affinity between the two countries on the back of their shared imperial history are often to be found. Further research, by scholars from a variety of disciplines, has scratched the surface of that affinity. Work has been carried out on nineteenth-century data relating to famines and the land question in India and Ireland, and on literary connections and the relationship between Yeats and Tagore.[4] More relevant to this study is the work of historians like Nicholas Mansergh, Deirdre McMahon and T. G. Fraser in considering how Irish precedents influenced British policy-making in India and how partition has affected both countries.[5] The post-colonial, theoretical issue of whether Ireland was subject to colonialism or imperialism and is as such a relevant candidate for comparison with India in the first place has also been teased out by several academics.[6] However, that is an area which I do not wish to explore, save to say that the very foundations of this thesis, the numerous primary source documents that I have worked through in a variety of archives, demonstrate that in the first half of the twentieth century British, Indian and Irish elites alike believed that fundamental parallels between the two countries' historical experiences formed the basis of a developing Indo-Irish political nexus, one which the British authorities thought warranted monitoring. Childers concluded his reflections by saying:

> What I learned in an all too cursory enquiry reveals a record of indirect influence from Irish nationalism on India's own freedom struggle which, while small in the sum total of recent Indian history, must some day take its rightful place in the annals of the two nations.[7]

This study aims to contribute to that process.

The book examines the relationship between Indian and Irish nationalists in the period between 1919 and the late 1940s, and culminates in documenting the establishment of formal diplomatic ties between the two countries. It takes in the Irish and Indian independence struggles, placed respectively at the start and the end of the period in question, with neither route a peaceful one. It does not address all of the political developments which led to independence in the two countries, focusing rather on those necessary to the cogency of the Irish–Indian narrative, as for example when the two countries became republics within a year of one another, one outside of and the other within the Commonwealth.

There are earlier instances of an Irish–Indian discourse: for example, during Ireland's Home Rule movement in the late nineteenth and early twentieth centuries Irish MPs had an obvious interest in Indian affairs and two of the most vocal in the House of Commons on India's interests were Frank Hugh O'Donnell and Michael Davitt.[8] Ireland as an inspiration can of course be identified elsewhere in the Empire, perhaps most notably in Egypt in the aftermath of the 1916 Rising. Nationalist unrest in Egypt in the spring of 1919 and the search for a constitutional settlement inevitably drew comparisons with Ireland.[9] It was nationalists in India, however, who exhibited a sustained interest in the Irish freedom struggle. There are many reasons why this was so. The nationalist elite spoke English; many of them were educated in Britain, bringing them in closer touch with Ireland; and coverage in the British national press of developments in Ireland may have had a lasting impact on them. Equally, the existence in London and other centres of Irish and Indian migrant communities, presented radicals from both with plenty of opportunities to interact and exchange ideas.

I rarely address the career of Mohandas Gandhi, the various civil disobedience campaigns or his many associates, some of whom happened to be Irish or had Irish connections, like Annie Besant and Margaret Cousins.[10] I again call upon Childers to clarify Gandhi's absence:

> So decisive was [Gandhi's] influence in shaping nationalist policy from 1920 forward that the role of armed revolution in India's fight for freedom is now officially regarded as a somewhat immature and minor phase. Yet the fact remains that many of the leading figures in Indian politics today supported and participated in acts of violent rebellion . . . Moreover right up to the end of World War II influential groups continued to dissociate themselves from the Gandhian approach. . . Before and after Gandhi, these groups drew both moral inspiration and guidance in method from Ireland's revolutionaries.[11]

Gandhi did not think that Ireland was a useful, or indeed a healthy, model for India's struggle for independence, and he had dismissed Sinn Féin as an example after the party's adoption of violent methods. While Gandhi was radical in his own right and though the methods he adopted were undoubtedly unique, the figures I deal with were radical in the physical force they were prepared to use, and many, as Childers remarked, did distance themselves from the Mahatma. Most famously, Subhas Chandra Bose, who quite readily adopted physical-force methods during the Second World War, believing the end justified the means. (Bose's extensive contacts with Ireland are discussed in chapter three.) Many others, while not as overtly extremist, acknowledged that resort to force was not necessarily to be ruled out. There is a more basic reason why Gandhi is not a focus of this study. While the Indian nationalists I deal with deliberately sought association with Irish republicans, and many of them visited Ireland at some stage, Gandhi did not.

This study also throws further light on Irish republicanism in the inter-war period, a field in which quite a lot of work has, of late, been carried out. Recent studies have revealed fascinating facets of Irish republicanism, a movement previously considered somewhat insular in outlook, in the period after the establishment of the Irish Free State, from its social republicanism to right-wing and Irish Republican Army (IRA)–Nazi connections to the divergent nature of Irish participation in the Spanish Civil War.[12] More recently, Emmet O'Connor has illuminated the area of Irish left-wing republican connections with the Communist International (Comintern) through study of previously unavailable archival material in Moscow.[13] This study of Indo-Irish connections adds a further international dimension to the history of

Irish republicanism, as well as contributing to a better understanding of the nature of republicanism and its self-perception in the post-colonial era.

It is also evident, however, that no previous study of this area has considered Irish connections with Indian nationalism in any great depth.[14] This seemed strange given the fact that there are several obvious indicators in that direction. For instance, when, in the late 1940s, de Valera visited India on his anti-partition world tour and Nehru reciprocated with a visit to Dublin, they both spoke of a long-standing relationship. In India in 1948 de Valera speaking to a radio audience said:

> For more than 30 years some of us in Ireland have followed with the deepest sympathy the fortunes of the people of India in their efforts to secure freedom. It was a source of the greatest joy to us when the right to that freedom was fully acknowledged. The two peoples have regarded themselves as allies and co-workers in a common cause.[15]

In April 1949 Nehru said:

> For many years [Ireland's] past history has been interlinked with ours because of our struggles for freedom. We have tried to learn much from the experience of the Irish struggle . . . I come here to meet the leaders of this country, and to renew old contacts.[16]

What did they mean exactly? What was the nature of this long-established relationship and to whom were they referring? Moreover, given the significant amount of coverage that India received in the republican press during the period, the lack of research into this particular phenomenon seemed somewhat anomalous. There had to be more to it than an imagined relationship with little substance, where using India as a rhetorical device and an imperial analogy merely provided effective hyperbole for the dramatic pages of the republican press. Besides there was extensive coverage – detailed reports, in-depth interviews, entire front pages and graphic pictures – all dealing with the Indian situation in the late 1920s and early 1930s. What were the sources of so much information? Could there have been Indian contributors? Finally, in the pages of *An Phoblacht* in 1932 an overt reference to the setting up of an Indian–Irish Independence League (IIIL) spawned further questions. Who had been associated with the IIIL? What functions did it have and what became of it? These questions are addressed in chapter two.

The main source materials used in this study are the Indian Political Intelligence (IPI) files of the Oriental and India Office Collection in the British Library. An introduction to this little known organisation and its collection is necessary. IPI was formally established as a consequence of Indian nationalist activities at the turn of the century. The collection was released as a result of the British 'open government' policy of the late 1990s (the Waldegrave initiative). There has been no extensive study carried out of IPI files, nor is there a publication available detailing their contents. The collection provides a rich source of material spanning several decades of intelligence-gathering. It should also be noted that a lot of material available in IPI files is more than likely contained in numerous as yet unreleased files of the Security Service (MI5) and the Secret Intelligence Service (SIS or MI6) as IPI's role was essentially that of a 'catch-all' coordinator of all information relating to India and to Indians within the Empire and it relied heavily on MI5 and SIS reports to supplement its data. IPI shared premises with MI5 from 1924 and had access to its registry.

This study seeks to support a more general argument about British intelligence in the interwar period: that there was an over-emphasis on monitoring the actions of communist or Bolshevik suspects and organisations at the expense of other, perhaps more menacing, threats to Empire, such as the development of right-wing organisations, radical nationalism and anti-imperialist nationalist alliances of a non-communist variety. Material contained in IPI files supports this view. IPI had particular Irish links as for most of its existence it was headed by a Trinity College Dublin (TCD) man, Philip Crawford Vickery, a graduate in Modern Languages, who was seconded to it from the Indian Police during the First World War and became its chief from 1926 until its closure in 1947 (when India became independent, and IPI was absorbed as a section in MI5). Another key IPI officer was Charles Tegart, also a TCD man, who refused the headship of the organisation in 1923 and instead became Chief Commissioner of the Calcutta Police. These Irish links merit attention when information about Irish nationalists presents itself in IPI records, and they give rise to the question of the impact of these officers' own Irish loyalist backgrounds on their analysis of the potential threat that Indian revolutionary activity generally, and on Irish–Indian collaboration more specifically, could provide.

But why was IPI, which was essentially a separate and non-avowed intelligence agency, although one that worked closely with MI5, SIS and Scotland Yard's Special Branch, established at all? For the British, a surprising feature of the Indian revolutionary movement, in the wake of the unpopular partition of Bengal in 1905, was its rapid growth; and an even more alarming feature was the emergence of revolutionary centres abroad. By 1907 Indian revolutionary groups were active in London and Paris. In London a group of Indian students set up 'India House' in Highgate and began publishing *The Indian Sociologist*. One of the more famous Indian activists associated with India House was

Veer Savarkar, who later became the President of the hard-line Hindu Mahasabha group which was implicated in Gandhi's murder in 1948.[17] In Paris, the Indians who had established the revolutionary centre there were also suspected of supplying explosives and revolvers to India. Among the activists there at the time were Sarat Chandra Bose, brother of Subhas, and Madam Cama, both of whom had established contact with the Irish nationalist Maud Gonne MacBride.

By the eve of the First World War the British authorities were alarmed that Indian radicals were active also in the United States and Canada. This group became known as the revolutionary Ghadr movement, its figurehead was Lala Har Dayal who in 1914 had sought German support for the liberation of India. Richard Popplewell has documented the activities of the Ghadr movement and British monitoring of them from 1904 to 1924 in *Intelligence and Imperial Defence*, but at the time of his book's publication the IPI files remained closed.[18] In fact de Valera had met with this group of Indian activists during his own tour of America, seeking recognition of the Irish Republic in 1919. They presented him with a Sikh sword which he kept throughout his life and would later take out to show to visiting Indian dignitaries.

As a result of this increase in international activity, IPI was established through the secondment of John Wallinger from the Indian Police to the India Office in 1909.[19] His brief was to monitor Indian nationalists throughout Europe but also to co-ordinate the activities of a non-declared operation against Indians on the Pacific coasts of North America, which was run under the cover of the Canadian Immigration Department. The Delhi Intelligence Bureau (DIB) continued to run operations there. That same year, 1909, an Indian student, Madan Lal Dhingra, shot dead Sir William Curzon Wyllie, the political *aide-de-camp* of the Secretary of State for India, Lord Morley, on the steps of the India Office in London. Three years later, in 1912, there was an unsuccessful attempt on the life of the Viceroy Lord Hardinge. As Popplewell succinctly put it, 'in the period 1907–1917 the Raj faced a serious threat from Indian revolutionaries; this threat was a major stimulus to the growth of British intelligence operations on a global level'.[20] Arguably it was this which provided the impetus for the very formation of IPI. Viewed from this standpoint IPI has a contemporary resonance, as the 'war on terrorism' has seen Western governments seek to confront transnational threats that evaded traditional, national based intelligence strategies.

In 1915 as a result of this increased demand for the monitoring of Indian revolutionary activities, Philip Vickery joined Wallinger, who in the meantime had managed to recruit the writer Somerset Maugham as an agent. Maugham subsequently portrayed Wallinger as the cold-blooded 'R' in his Ashenden spy stories. Vickery was charged with expanding and developing the network, and in 1919 was deployed to the United States and Canada where he ran operations for five years. Back in India, however, the expansion of IPI throughout Europe and America was not without its critics. To the annoyance of the Government of India, London, rather than Calcutta, Delhi or Shimla was to remain the clearing-house for all intelligence relating to India right up until independence. In 1922 the Home Department of the Government of India even suggested to the India Office that IPI be merged with SIS. The response was unequivocal and also illuminates some other difficulties that the existence of IPI threw up for the British intelligence services, as well as the importance that the India Office placed on its new separate agency:

> The suggestion that the IPI might be amalgamated with the SIS is not practicable or likely to result in economy . . . SIS is not allowed to work in the United Kingdom or the United States of America, where IPI *must* have agents. Difficulties of housing in London would be raised; and differences in direction and policy as between the objects of the SIS and those of the IPI might easily cause friction between the Foreign Office and this office.[21]

Sir Cecil Kaye of the Home Department (and father of the writer M. M. Kaye) was unconvinced:

> I must admit that I feel rather sceptical regarding both the India Office arguments: and am inclined to doubt whether, if they could really be examined in detail, from this end, they would hold water. As it is, of course, they cannot be challenged.[22]

After the First World War IPI's activities were concentrated on the communist threat, on suspected Indian subversives and, as the introduction to the collection's catalogue itself surprisingly states, 'to a lesser extent on mainstream Indian nationalism'. A quick breakdown of the files relating to various topics shows that 'Personal Files' encompass 17 per cent of the overall collection, but larger than that again are files devoted to communism, in all its various guises, which amount to 20 per cent of the collection. Other topics include, for example, 'Islam and the Kalifat Movement' (1.9 per cent), 'North America' (5.6 per cent) and the 'Indian National Congress' (which amounts to only 2.2 per cent). However, surprisingly, what IPI describe as 'Revolutionary and Terrorist Activities' comprises only 3.5 per cent and 'Arms Smuggling' only 2.8 per cent. With the subsequent rise of and threat supplied by Subhas Chandra Bose and his Indian National Army, even though Bose himself was monitored closely from an early stage, this seems with hindsight to be quite an anomaly. Perhaps surprisingly, numerous notable Irish figures crop up on the pages of these files, sometimes in the most unlikely places, like the veteran 1913 Lock-Out leader Captain Jack White, who in the 1930s was noted by IPI as liaising with Philip Rupasangha Gunawardena in London, a Ceylonese communist.[23] The files also shed welcome light on British perceptions of the communist menace in the interwar period and their perceptions of and attempts to infiltrate Moscow-controlled bodies like the League Against Imperialism (LAI). Indo-Irish contacts within the confines of this body, and other communist-inspired associations, are addressed in chapter one.

IPI's files are a crucial aspect of this study as they demonstrate how the monitoring of Indian nationalists' activities throughout Europe revealed radical contacts previously less evident to the British authorities in the form of Indo-Irish collaboration. As Indian elite activists fled their country for Europe or America, either for further study or because of the danger of imprisonment, they found themselves in a geographical arena more conducive to practical collaboration with fellow anti-imperialists, Irish or otherwise. As already alluded to, one of the biggest challenges for the British intelligence services during the First World War was unravelling the emergent Indian Ghadr conspiracy in the United States, in which Irish Americans also played a part.[24]

The monitoring of Indian radicals' activities after the war, as already noted, was stepped up a notch, especially as an increasing number of Indian nationalists found a safe haven in Germany. Before Hitler came to power, Berlin was at the apex of international communist organisation and was the base of the LAI. On the other side of the ideological spectrum, Indian nationalists later found the Nazi regime sympathetic, at least in principle, to their separatist aspirations. In London, too, Indian nationalists were watched closely, and IPI files from this period indicate just how uneasy the British authorities became when faced with evidence of Indo-Irish separatist collaboration, particularly where communist influence was suspected. This was a relationship that proved beneficial to both sides, a contra-imperial, nationalist alliance of which the British Government was both aware and apprehensive.

The Second World War, the final years of British rule and the formal establishment of diplomatic ties between Ireland and India are discussed in chapters four and five. This was a dramatic period for both Ireland and India: India became independent through the relatively peaceful transfer of power in 1947, although the creation of Muslim Pakistan and the accompanying partition of the sub-continent saw appalling communal violence. Indian independence was an unavoidable consequence of the decline of British power and imperial resolve as a result of the Second World War. In Ireland's case, the war provided an opportunity to demonstrate independence in foreign policy through the maintenance of neutrality, previously described as a 'psychological necessity' on the road to complete independence.[25] Given the swift developments in these few years it is significant to note how contacts between the two countries were maintained, matured and indeed formally established, as erstwhile radicals became statesmen and diplomats. De Valera's high profile anti-partition tour in 1948 (in the aftermath of losing his first general election in sixteen years) took in the newly partitioned India. His visit was a concern for the British Government, with the Dominions Office being kept abreast of his actions and utterances, as significantly India had yet to decide its own fate in relation to Commonwealth membership. The visit however was more of a long awaited meeting and the beginning of a fond friendship between the one-time revolutionaries, Nehru and de Valera.

To date, Irish, Indian and British imperial historiography often neglects to cite, let alone expand on, the significance that Indo-Irish radical connections had on the Indian nationalist movement, British policy making in relation to India, or Irish republicanism. Rozina Visram's *Asians in Britain* is arguably the only book that records the activities of Indians in Britain in any great depth.[26] While Visram's thoroughly researched work fills a long-vacant void in Indian historiography it covers a vast span of 400 years, and a lack of further material in this vein means that in detailing the conduct of those who were politically active in the twentieth century, her work fails to address the deeper implications that the very existence of such radicals in the metropole had on British policy-making. This is especially significant in relation to the development of British security and intelligence policy as the Indian independence movement was gaining momentum.

Thus the emergence of radical Indian nationalism at the very heart of the Empire eventually resulted in the emergence of an intelligence agency devoted entirely to nationalist actions, and again, the resonance of these developments in relation to the security issues facing some of today's Western governments is clear. Significantly, the progress of IPI remains entirely undocumented in British intelligence historiography even though the collection has been open to research for almost a decade. The importance of using IPI material in the documentation of the Indian nationalist movement abroad becomes all the more significant having reflected on the nature of the collection. IPI material and India Office files can be found side by side, while most other intelligence and security material in the UK's National Archive have been removed from various series. Therefore the way in which IPI influenced policy-making is clearly visible.

[9]

In relation to Indian nationalism and terrorism, Peter Heehs has observed that 'coverage of the terrorist campaigns of 1907 to 1934 focuses largely on personalities . . . the standard approach was commemorative . . . treated in isolation from political developments, anti-British terrorism ends up looking like a heroic but futile display of pyrotechnics'.[27] That is a fitting observation to describe the existing literature on Indian physical-force nationalism, most of which is by now quite dated,[28] yet in his promisingly titled *Nationalism, Terrorism, Communalism* there is but one passing reference to Ireland. The notable exception, however, is the more recently published *Do and Die: The Chittagong Uprising 1930–34* by Manini Chatterjee.[29] The author explains how the Easter Rising had a direct influence on the Chittagong Armoury Raid some fourteen years later, the latter even timed by Hindus to coincide with the Christian festival. Those involved grouped together under the banner of the Indian Republican Army, named after the IRA. But Chatterjee presents us with a brief and somewhat basic overview of Ireland as an influence in this isolated example, affecting only one particular set of Indian revolutionaries.

Given that many of the Indians detailed in this study travelled to Ireland, spent time there and moved in Irish nationalist and republican circles, how does Irish historiography hold up when scrutinised this way? The answer is unfortunately a similar one, with very few Irish historians apparently aware that those Indians frequented their shores at all. Those who have drawn attention to the nexus, however briefly, have concluded that the relationship 'seems to have been largely rhetorical'[30] or 'helped in the creation of an "imagined community" of anti-colonial nationalist movements'.[31] The content of the following chapters confounds that conclusion. Historians of British imperialism are also guilty of what I would term the 'fleeting reference phenomenon': in many cases the Irish independence movement's influence on the Indian nationalist elite is reduced to merely a sentence, if not a footnote, if indeed referred to at all. This book will not only supplement the relevant historiographies mentioned above, but will redefine accepted paradigms of decolonisation.

Notes

1   Son of the Irish nationalist Robert Erskine Childers, who was executed in the Civil War in 1922. Childers Jr was first elected to Dáil Éireann in 1938, served as Tánaiste from 1969 to 1973 and became the fourth President of Ireland in 1973. He died in office on 17 Nov. 1974.
2   *Irish Press*, 10 Aug. 1954, see also National Archives of Ireland (hereafter NAI) Department of the Taoiseach (hereafter DT), S 15740. The Irish Embassy in Delhi was not established until 1964.
3   *Ibid*.

4   Cormac Ó Gráda, *Markets and Famines: Some Evidence from India and Ireland* (Dublin, 1977). S. B. Cook, *Imperial Affinities: Nineteenth-Century Analogies and Exchanges Between India and Ireland* (London, 1993). Roy Foster, *W. B. Yeats: A Life*, vol. 1 (Oxford, 1996), pp. 469–73. Margaret Kelleher, 'Literary connections: cultural revival, political independence and the present', in Michael Holmes and Denis Holmes (eds), *Ireland and India: Connections, Comparisons, Contrasts* (Dublin, 1997).

5   Nicholas Mansergh, *Nationalism and Independence: Selected Irish Papers* (Cork, 1997); Deirdre McMahon, 'A larger and noisier Southern Ireland: Ireland and the evolution of dominion status in India, Burma and the Commonwealth, 1942–49', in Michael Kennedy and Joseph Morrison Skelly (eds), *Irish Foreign Policy 1919–66: From Independence to Internationalism* (Dublin, 2000); and Deirdre McMahon, 'Ireland, the Empire and the Commonwealth', in Kevin Kenny (ed.), *Ireland and the British Empire: The Oxford History of the British Empire Companion Series* (Oxford, 2004); T. G. Fraser, *Partition in Ireland, India and Palestine: Theory and Practice* (London, 1984).

6   See Keith Jeffery (ed.), *'An Irish Empire'? Aspects of Ireland and the British Empire* (Manchester, 1996); and Stephen Howe, *Ireland and Empire: Colonial Legacies in Irish History and Culture* (Oxford, 2002).

7   *Irish Press*, 10 Aug. 1954.

8   McMahon, 'Ireland, the Empire and the Commonwealth', p. 188.

9   Jeffery, *Irish Empire*, p. 13. Also for examples of contemporaneous commentary drawing attention to the similarities between the situations in Ireland and Egypt, see *The Times*, 19 April 1919 and 20 Dec. 1920.

10 There are some sections that look at Gandhi and Cousins, if briefly, in chapter two.

11 *Irish Press*, 10 Aug. 1954.

12 Richard English, *Radicals and the Republic* (Oxford, 1994); Brian Hanley, *The IRA: 1926–36* (Dublin, 2002); Eunan O'Halpin, 'British intelligence, the republican movement and the IRA's German links, 1935–45', in Fearghal McGarry (ed.), *Republicanism in Modern Ireland* (Dublin, 2003); and Fearghal McGarry, *Irish Politics and the Spanish Civil War* (Cork, 1999).

13 Emmet O'Connor, *Reds and the Green: Ireland, Russia and the Communist Internationals 1919–43* (Dublin, 2004).

14 There is one chapter on this topic: Sarmila Bose and Eilis Ward, ' "India's cause is Ireland's cause": elite links and nationalist politics', in Holmes and Holmes (eds) *Ireland and India*. It deals with some, but not all, material available in the National Archives of Ireland and does not draw on any other depository.

15 Radio talk by de Valera from New Delhi, 15 June 1948, University College Dublin Archives (hereafter UCDA), De Valera Papers (hereafter P150) P150/2955.

16 *Irish Press*, 29 April 1949.

17 For further reading see Vidya Sagar, *Savarkar: A Study in the Evolution of Indian Nationalism* (London, 1967).

18 Richard Popplewell, *Intelligence and Imperial Defence: British Intelligence and the Defence of the Indian Empire, 1904–24* (London, 1995).

19 British Library, Oriental and India Office Collections, India Office Records (hereafter BL, OIOC, IOR), Indian Political Intelligence files (hereafter L/P&J/), Catalogue introduction notes.

20 Popplewell, *Intelligence and Imperial Defence*, p. 1.

21 Ferrard to O'Donnell, 23 Aug. 1922, Home Department Political 12, 1922 Poll, Indian National Archives. My thanks to Deirdre McMahon for this reference.

22 *Ibid.*

23 See chapter one.

24 For further reading on British intelligence and the monitoring of Indian radical activity in this earlier period see Popplewell, *Intelligence and Imperial Defence*.

25 J. J. Lee, *Ireland 1912–85* (Cambridge, 1985), pp. 262–4.

26 Rozina Visram, *Asians in Britain: 400 Years of History* (London, 2002).

27 Peter Heehs, *Nationalism, Terrorism, Communalism: Essays in Modern Indian History* (Oxford, 1998), p. 1.

28 See for example: Arun Coomer Bose, *Indian Revolutionaries Abroad: 1905–22: In the Background of International Developments* (Allahabad, 1971); Mihir Bose, *The Lost Hero* (London, 1982); Sagar, *Savarkar.*
29 Manni Chatterjee, *Do and Die: The Chittagong Uprising 1930–34* (New Delhi, 1999), pp. 55–61.
30 Hanley, *The IRA*, p. 173.
31 Bose and Ward, ' "India's cause is Ireland's cause" ', p. 69.

CHAPTER ONE

The communist menace

> Bukharin, too, though acknowledging that national or colonial revolutions were an aspect of the 'great revolutionary world process', remained convinced that they had no direct relation to the developing proletarian revolution. The possibility of establishing a dictatorship of the proletariat in . . . India and Ireland, he reasoned, was much reduced by the absence of strong working classes in those countries.[1]

So spoke one of the most prominent thinkers of the Bolshevik movement, Nickolai Bukharin, addressing the First World Congress of the Comintern in 1919. While communism did entice many Irish and Indian activists during the period in question, it would never come close to revolutionising either country. There existed a more pressing concern in either case: national liberation. The Comintern made earnest efforts to incorporate this concern into its policies at the Second World Congress of the Comintern in the summer of 1920 with its *Theses on the National and Colonial Question*, the result of a protracted debate between Lenin and Manabendra Nath Roy, a leading Indian communist.[2] This new departure allowed for collaboration between communists and nationalists in colonial regions. The precise form which such alliances might take was not spelled out, but it was assumed that the independent character of the proletarian movement would be preserved.[3] Problems arising out of the ambiguous nature of the policy became apparent in the late 1920s with the formation of the LAI, detailed below. This chapter does not attempt to relate the history of communism in Ireland and India,[4] but instead deals with instances where Indian and Irish left-wing radicals interacted, resulting in increased cause for concern on the part of the British authorities.

It is important to note that during the 1920s certain British Conservative politicians were consumed by anti-Bolshevik intentions. Other than Churchill, whose anti-Bolshevik leanings at this time are well documented,[5] the Home Secretary, Sir William Joynson-Hicks, was fervently anti-communist, but, crucially, so too was the Earl of Birkenhead, the Secretary of State for India from 1924 to 1928. He was regularly kept up to date with reports of communist subversion in India from the Director of DIB who at that time was David Petrie, a future head of MI5. Also in February 1922 in London, an Interdepartmental Committee on Eastern Unrest was founded consisting of members from MI5, the Special Branch, the Indian, Colonial, Foreign and War Offices, and usually attended by members of SIS and IPI.[6] The thought of communist intervention in India either directly or in the form of support for internal unrest was a major concern for the British authorities in the 1920s. The War Office calculated that the Russians could 'place some 80 divisions on a war footing' in Central Asia – vastly more than those available to the Raj – and Birkenhead flatly decided that the Soviet aim in India was 'external attack synchronising with, or consequent upon, internal disruption'.[7] Such concerns resulted in thorough tracking by IPI of Indian subversives of a communist persuasion throughout the UK and Europe, their every move and contact closely monitored. It will be seen, however, that on the whole, apart from perhaps Shapurji Saklatvala, those concerned were initially motivated by an anti-imperialist, nationalist perspective, with communism, given its contemporary popularity, proving a suitable means to an essentially nationalist end. Viewed in this light, it is easy to understand why many of them established contacts with Irish nationalists.

M. N. Roy and Roddy Connolly

M. N. Roy was the sole spokesperson for Indian communism in Moscow. He was a Bengali Indian with no tertiary education who rose to great heights within Comintern structures. He was a staunch communist during the period in question, a stance which culminated in his support of the allied war effort during the Second World War.[8] The Communist Party of India (CPI) also eventually quit the broadly anti-war Indian Congress in 1945, with the majority of Indian nationalists labelling its members 'anti-national', creating a rift from which the CPI would never quite recover. Speaking about this CPI stance in 1945, Jawaharlal Nehru said that

> he was not against communism or Russia. He had himself popularised socialistic and communist views in the past. But the role of the communist Party of India, he said, has made all nationalist India its cent per cent opponents. Opposition to the Indian communists was not merely political. The whole nation was angry with them . . . the communists were in the opposite camp, which cannot be forgotten.[9]

This was a situation not unfamiliar to the Irish Left, with the existence of a predominant ideology in the shape of the national question perennially troubling both the mindsets of communists themselves and the public's perception of them. A look into the background of Roy, and later, some of his Irish counterparts, should help explain the trying position that some found themselves in, where two dogmas, the nationalist and the communist, existed not side by side but interwoven, creating a confusing mesh of ideology. It should also throw some light on the British authorities' growing concern in relation to such individuals. Being purely nationalist or purely communist was one thing, but the two together was a cocktail with which the authorities would rather not have to deal.

Roy's early career was that of a nationalist activist. He was born Narendra Nath Bhattacharya in the late 1890s of Brahmin parentage in the Bengali village of Arbalia.[10] In his early teenage years he was involved in anti-British activity as a member of a terrorist patriotic society and was first arrested in connection with the Howrah conspiracy case, but was acquitted in 1911.[11] On the outbreak of the First World War, Roy joined a newly merged group of activists under the leadership of Jatindranath Mukherjee. These activists were ambitious in their attempts to hamper British rule and sought German help in their efforts, and in 1915 Roy went to Batavia to rendezvous with Germans in an attempt to land arms in India. These schemes, however, failed, and he fled to America in 1916, where he adopted the name Mohendra, or Manabendra, Nath Roy.[12] He stayed for short periods in both San Francisco and New York, but by June 1917 he was indicted for illegal entry and a warrant was issued for his arrest. He was already under investigation as a result of his association with known Indian revolutionaries and their German contacts. Roy absconded to Mexico with his new wife, Evelyn Trent, a left-wing radical and graduate of Stanford University.[13] It was in Mexico that Roy met the Soviet emissary Michael (Mikhail) Borodin, whom he credited with changing his life by breaking down his resistance to Marxist thought.[14] By 1920 he had been invited to Russia and from there was sent on various anti-British propaganda missions to Central Asia and Afghanistan. By 1921 he had finally settled in Berlin, where the British authorities were firmly convinced that he and his wife were keeping themselves busy inventing 'schemes for spreading the communist revolution in India' and recruiting other radicals to their cause.[15] The reports sent to IPI at this time in relation to Roy were all headed with a 'Top Secret' warning:

The information given in this series of notes is derived from a very confidential source. It is requested that it be handled with great care. It comes from a correspondent who is on very intimate terms with M. N. Roy and the latter would have no difficulty in discovering the source of the leakage if he ascertained that the authorities were aware of the facts set out in these notes.[16]

Clearly the authorities had infiltrated Roy's group to great effect. This is not surprising, as Christopher Andrew has noted that agent penetration of the CPI seems to have been extensive and British intelligence reporting on Indian communism prolific. IPI reports on communism, which frequently quoted intercepted Comintern and Communist Party of Great Britain (CPGB) communications, have since become a major source for both Marxist and non-Marxist historians of Indian communism.[17]

Meanwhile IPI agents in the field were discovering that Berlin was rapidly becoming the most important revolutionary centre for communists in Europe. This was further evidenced by the arrival there of well-known Indian conspirators who began working with Roy. It also appears from intelligence reports that Roy was taking an interest in the Irish situation and that Irish radicals were reciprocating. A report of 23 August 1922 noted that an issue of the *Vanguard* urged a general strike to secure the release of political prisoners, and had 'an article on the "Irish Tragedy"', conveying a lesson for India from the Free State fiasco and the tragic betrayal of the principle of Republicanism by its sponsors Collins and Griffiths'.[18] That same month, in what were becoming regular IPI reports entitled 'Indian Communist Party Reports', the following was noted:

> Another recent arrival in Berlin is an Irishman named Mr Read. He reached Berlin on August 15th. He is described as a member of the Irish Communist Party. His father was one of the leaders of the Rebellion of 1916. Since his arrival in Berlin he has been working with M. N. Roy.[19]

The following week's report reveals more:

> Another influential recruit to Roy's cause is an Irishman whose name is given by my informant as Cornell, described as a son of one of the Irish leaders of 1916, and himself one of the leading members of the Irish Communist Party. This man's name is given in another report from Switzerland as O'Connell a son of James O'Connell, who was executed in Ireland for the 1916 Rebellion. The latter report said that this man passes in Berlin under the name of Hawthorne. M. N. Roy described him as editor of a Communist paper in Ireland.[20]

This is clearly a description of Roddy Connolly, whose father, James Connolly, had indeed been executed after the 1916 Rising. Connolly was part of the left wing of the Socialist Party of Ireland (SPI). In September 1921, with Comintern backing, he would transform the SPI into the Communist Party of Ireland, purging it of its more moderate members. Before doing so, however, he had made several trips to Russia. Along with Eamon MacAlpine, a left-wing Irish-American who had arrived in Ireland in 1919, he attended the Second World Congress of the Comintern in Moscow in 1920. The most vital matter on the agenda as far as these Irish delegates were concerned was the discussion of the national and colonial question, which was presided over by Lenin. It was there that Connolly and M. N. Roy first met. Connolly's past, like Roy's, was rooted in the national liberation movement, and no doubt the two men soon realised that they had much in common ideologically.

In June of that year Connolly had been involved in the outbreak of the Irish Civil War on the anti-Treaty side. British authorities were up to speed with his activities, noting, in a nonchalant fashion, his participation in 'the recent fighting in Sackville Street', and going on to say that 'he is a communist but sides for the time being with the Republicans: he appears to be well off . . . Hawthorne is very optimistic regarding the ultimate success of the Republicans, and is constantly travelling backwards and forwards to Ireland.'[21] In June 1922, for example, Connolly was in London. The Metropolitan Police reported, correctly, that this trip was probably made in order to distribute issues of the *Workers' Republic* from the CPGB's London offices to avoid the Irish censor.[22] However, Connolly had travelled to London in the company of George McLay, the Communist Party of Ireland's treasurer, to liaise with Roy's old mentor, Borodin, in the drawing up of a new social programme to which they hoped the Irish republican leaders would sign up. Borodin had been in Britain since the previous March, working for the Comintern under the pseudonym George Brown.[23]

Emmet O'Connor has noted that Connolly had been buoyed by positive reports, sent to the Comintern by the CPGB member (and Borodin's secretary) J. T. Murphy, about how the Communist Party of Ireland programme had received an 'excellent' reception in republican quarters. It was on the back of these soundings that Connolly, as we now know, ended up in Berlin, more than likely on Borodins's advice as he is thought to have funded the trip.[24] The precise nature of Connolly's trip to Germany has thus far remained unclear, other than that he was apparently making attempts to purchase arms and that 'Borodin (had suggested) that the Executive Comintern contribute half the expenses'.[25] It is now clear that arrangements had been made for him to meet up with the Comintern's Indian representative, M. N. Roy, whom he had met in Moscow. IPI reported that Connolly was 'endeavouring to get certain Irish communists to join Roy', and provided a description of him as 'fair haired, rather tall and thin, speaks very quickly, aged about 24'.[26] In a note on M. N. Roy's established connections with Britain and other countries, IPI stated that he had

> established relations with several extremist British and Irish communists who assist his intrigues for the despatch of communist literature and agents to India. Those most directly implicated are . . . Charles Ashleigh, C. P. Dutt, Mr Saklatvala, J. T. Murphy, Connolly and Bridger [sic] Harte.[27]

But more importantly a somewhat sinister note was made on M. N. Roy's IPI file at the time of Connolly's visit, which stated:

> Though not exactly bearing on this point, information has been received from another source that Irish republicans are buying arms and ammunitions in large quantities from a firm in Hamburg. The name and address of this firm are not at present available. The firm have expressed their willingness to sell arms to Indians, provided satisfactory arrangements can be made for their safe delivery to India.[28]

It is not clear whether by 'Irish Republicans' IPI in fact meant that (or even knew if) it was Connolly making these purchases. However, IPI must have considered it a possibility, as it appears in a paragraph directly after references to Connolly. What is clear, though, is that the possibility of Irish and Indian communists purchasing arms with the financial aid of Moscow would have greatly alarmed the British authorities. It is also important to note the distinct possibility that the Hamburg firm in question thought to be selling the arms to Irish republicans could have been run by an Indian, Henry Obed. Obed was to become a name only too familiar with the British authorities in the years to come, as he was an industrious drugs and arms trafficker. Although it is not possible to confirm, the timing fits, as Obed had just arrived in Hamburg from London in June 1922 and had established an export and import business in association with the German firm Rud Schonheit & Co. Two years later he had to leave the city as the Hamburg police suspected him of smuggling.[29] However, prior to that move, IPI was aware that M. N. Roy and Obed had been conspiring and that Obed was, at the very least, smuggling communist literature into India for him, so Roy may have put Connolly in touch with him.[30] The successful smuggling of literature from Europe to India, using various routes, was often used as a 'dry run' for the eventual trafficking of arms, as IPI surmised in relation to Roy when they noted that 'if he succeeds in building up an effective organisation for the smuggling of literature this will doubtless be used later for the smuggling of arms.'[31] Several attempts were made by the British authorities to curtail Obed's increasingly successful endeavours at arms-smuggling throughout the 1920s and 1930s, but to no effect.[32] This 'Mohomedan, Hindoo, born in Lucknow', as Irish military intelligence described him, was eventually arrested in Cork in July 1940 as one of a party of three Axis agents who had landed with sabotage equipment and were imprisoned in Ireland during the war.[33] He later claimed that his intention was to establish contact with the IRA. All of this is looked at in more detail in chapter four.

While Connolly was in Germany, fellow anti-Treatyite Liam Mellows was imprisoned in Mountjoy Jail. He was one of those thought to have been analysing the possibility of adopting the Connolly–Borodin communist programme. His written notes on the topic were famously seized by the Free State's Government and released to the *Irish Independent* in September 1922 in an attempt to blacken his name with the general public by claiming that he had adopted communist politics.[34] The Irish communists were, however, elated and in the *Workers' Republic* claims were made that the republican leaders had adopted their programme.[35] Such news even warranted an appearance in M. N. Roy's *Vanguard* as early as the following week. An IPI report demonstrates how perplexed the British were as a result of some 'questionable entries' in the publication, especially one which detailed 'a document found on the person of Liam Mellows, "Communist General of the Irish Republican Army, captured at the fall of the Four Courts" (which was) set out in extenso, as a model to be copied'.[36] It is probable that Connolly was the source of such material as he was still in Roy's company.

It is also worth noting that Mellows himself had taken a keen interest in India. While on a lecture tour in America in 1918, where he was collecting money for the IRA, he met with Lala Lajpat Rai, the Indian nationalist agitator who had established the Indian Home Rule League of America in 1917. Mellows spoke on Friends of Indian Freedom platforms with him.[37]

Also contained in Mellows prison notes was the remark: 'India. Isn't the time approaching when we should be in closest touch?'[38] The exact date of Connolly's departure from Germany is not certain but in a report dated 15 November 1922 it is noted that 'Connolly, the Irish Communist . . . is not now in Berlin. In all probability he has gone to Moscow.'[39] A 1925 Metropolitan Police report confirmed that Connolly had indeed reached Moscow and had attended a conference where he attempted, in vain, to acquire further financial support.[40] This is a significant British report about Irish radicalism. Entitled 'Communism in Ireland', it is an accurate narrative of the various phases and rifts that occurred within communist circles in Ireland, including the problems that were unleashed with the return from America of the 1913 Lock-Out leader Jim Larkin.[41] It noted that 'Ireland is not a fruitful soil for communism and Larkin will find he is in for a very uphill fight . . . but as a permanent leader he is almost certain to fail'. The report concluded with a somewhat demeaning account of Roddy Connolly in 1925: 'Roderick J. Connolly has dropped out altogether and is now reported to be keeping a shop in Dublin for the sale of Catholic books and emblems.'[42]

Brajesh Singh Lal and the British 'stop list'

One of Roy's close colleagues, Brajesh Singh, was to have more direct contact with Ireland. By 1928 Roy had enlisted the help of several Indian students in Berlin who had been lured there by the high standards of Germany's universities and the low cost of living. Singh was among them. He was the brother of the Raja of Kalakankar, a village near to Lucknow. Singh was a much-needed contributor to Roy's finances.[43] Roy had been expelled from the Comintern in 1928, as he had opposed aspects of its colonial policy in a series of articles which appeared in the *International Press Correspondent*. Roy decided to return to India in an attempt to gain control of the CPI, as he felt that Indian communists were isolating themselves from the nationalist movement, just when the time seemed ripe for increased collaboration.[44]

Singh had been Roy's right-hand man during the course of this campaign, but in 1932 he had chosen to renounce Roy's doctrines and to return to the orthodox communist fold and to Europe.[45] It was on his return that IPI picked up on him, clearly aware of his political tendencies on account of his recent activities in India. In September 1932 he arrived in London and met up with his brother, Raja Audesh Singh, who had been regularly commuting between London and Dublin. The two promptly crossed over to Ireland. Three weeks later Singh returned on his own to arrange for the transport of his brother's motorcar to Dublin. On the very night of his return he realised that police enquiries were being made in relation to his activities. He caught the Irish mail train from Rugby to Holyhead, to avoid the possible attentions of the police at the London terminus, and returned to Dublin without the car.[46] In fact IPI was well up to date with his activities:

> It will be seen from independent information that Brajesh Singh Lal and his brother are actively supporting the Indian–Irish Independence League in Dublin, which is under the control of the group composed of V. J. Patel, R. B. Lotwalla and I. K. Yajnik.[47]

However, it appears that police enquiries were in fact instigated not because of his political activities but on the back of a rumour emanating from DIB that Singh 'had left India surreptitiously in order to murder his erstwhile co-worker in M. N. Roy's interest, Sunder Kabadi, who was strongly suspected of having betrayed M. N. Roy to the Police in India'.[48] It was not long before this somewhat imaginative story was scotched, as Singh and Kabadi were seen to have been the best of friends in London. Yet, from IPI's perspective it was just as well that the monitoring of Singh's activities continued, as they were soon to cause further alarm.

While in Britain Singh made an application for a passport, a request which was under consideration. However, unknown to the officials in London, his previous passport had been confiscated in India, and he had travelled to Europe using his brother's. In the meantime, by October 1932, it had come to the attention of Philip Vickery at IPI that Singh had managed to make his way to Berlin. In a letter to the India Office Vickery noted:

> It is not known how he reached there from Dublin, where we last heard of him – without a passport. It is, however, just possible, although there is no evidence whatever on the point, that he secured some kind of passport in Dublin.[49]

This correspondence, it seems, was treated very seriously indeed and passed through many hands. R. T. Peel of the India Office made a marginal note stating how this was 'a possibility that requires to be verified. It might be serious if Indian suspects took to going to Dublin for their passports.' Sir Malcolm Seton, Deputy Under-Secretary of State at the India Office agreed: 'Yes. I imagine they would have no difficulty in getting passports from the present Irish Free State Govt.' The India Office was rattled. Vickery did not help matters with a follow up note that read:

> Brajesh Singh Lal's name figures on our Stop List, a copy which is (unfortunately) in the possession of the IFS government. I do not imagine that the presence of his name in this list would be regarded by the present IFS government as constituting a bar (more likely indeed an inducement) to the grant to him of passport facilities.[50]

The pointed references to 'the present' Free State Government reflected British concerns at the recent accession to power of Eamon de Valera, which had created a wave of panic in Whitehall. In 1932 IPI were even taking pains to note Indian activists who were reading library books on Irish history and who were also overheard in the British Museum discussing with fellow Indians the lesson to be learnt from de Valera's recent achievements.[51] The British authorities assumed that the de Valera Government would embrace any opportunity to aggravate London, and in this they were correct. Because they shared a common travel area, the Irish and British Governments had a clear understanding over passport and visa controls. They shared 'blacklists' of undesirables and cooperated closely in supervising the movements of foreigners into and out of the British Isles. However, when these arrangements had been hurriedly agreed in 1924, at India Office insistence the names of 'British Indians' had been excluded from lists supplied to the Irish authorities. 'The India Office preferred that all applications from British Indians should be referred to them by the Free State government before passports were issued.'[52] This was apparently not done in Singh's case, and on applying for passport facilities in Dublin he was reportedly given an emergency passport that would remain valid for five years.[53] It is also worth pointing out how both IPI and the India Office were in 1932 seemingly unaware of these arrangements that had been made nine years previously.

Correspondence went back and forth at a swift rate between IPI and the India Office in relation to Singh. They pondered how best to curtail his movements and whether they should provide him with a temporary, three-month passport provided he returned to India. The Government of India had to be consulted first, however, as the possibility remained that his return to India would be more damaging to political circumstances than his remaining in Europe. The more pressing problem remained the straightening out of this passport predicament. By February 1933 Singh had come clean and admitted to using his brother's passport in an attempt to ingratiate himself with the authorities in yet a further application for a passport of his own. The authorities wanted to make sure that the Irish Free State passport was surrendered first. In a note to the India Office Vickery's irritation at the unresolved situation is tangible:

> It was highly reprehensible of the Irish Free State government to issue a Free State passport to Brajesh Singh, seeing that his name was on our passport Black List. It would be little use, however, administering a rebuke because we should merely receive the answer that there had been an oversight. I am much more alarmed at the idea that the passport stop list should be in their possession at all.[54]

He finished with a caustic quip: 'Incidentally, one would like to know what kind of an emergency it was that the Free State considered would last five years!'[55]

The issuing of this emergency passport to Singh allowed him a lot of time in Europe. It infuriated Vickery for one, who attempted to get him to surrender it to His Majesty's Consul in Berlin. He dismissed questions regarding the legalities of impounding an Irish Free State passport and thought that there was no need to anticipate any difficulties in explaining matters to the Irish Free State, saying:

> We could inform them that the passport had been impounded at the request of the Government of India because it was found that Brajesh

Singh Lal had left India by making fraudulent use of his brother's passport which he is believed to have destroyed.[56]

None of this could be proven. The authorities could not pin him down or arrest him 'unless and until we can catch (him) using his brother's passport entering or leaving this country'. This was something that had to be acknowledged over a year later as Singh was still using an Irish Free State passport and freely travelling throughout Europe. It seems that by this stage the authorities were happy enough to acknowledge that it was simply preferable not to have him in India, where his financial assets could do much more damage to the government by way of support to the CPI. His file closes in the mid-1930s, with Vickery's irritation culminating in mordant comments: 'His personal inclinations, which are definitely in the direction of "Wine and Women" – are not such as to make him much of a consequence while in Europe . . . He has sufficient means to support himself in idleness and dissipation generally.'[57]

It is perhaps noteworthy that his 'personal inclination in the direction of women' brought him world-wide attention many years later in the 1960s, shortly after his death. In 1963 Singh had met Svetlana Alliluyeva, Stalin's daughter, while he was working for the Foreign Languages Publishing House in Moscow. The two fell in love and wished to marry, but were denied permission by the Soviet authorities. They arranged a Hindu wedding ceremony instead. Singh died in 1966 and Svetlana was allowed to travel to India to take his ashes to his family, to be scattered in the Ganges. On 6 March 1967 her situation and marriage to Singh achieved international notoriety when she went to the American Embassy in Delhi and petitioned the ambassador for political asylum.[58] It is difficult to know just how Singh, most of his life a steadfast communist, would have reacted to this, his most famous appearance on the world stage.

Shapurji Saklatvala and Ireland

Monitoring the activities of Indians like Singh and Roy in Europe was only a part of the substantial task to which IPI was committed during the 1920s and 1930s in relation to Indian communist subversives. Surveillance was maintained closer to home. One person who warranted quite a lot of attention in England was Shapurji Dorabji Saklatvala, who would become a leading member of the CPGB. Saklatvala was born into a wealthy Parsi family in Bombay in 1874. The family had established the famous firm of Tata Industries, which was originally based on textiles but later expanded to include iron and steel, now probably best known as an automobile manufacturers. Saklatvala travelled to England in 1905 where he joined Tata's London office. It did not take long, however, for him to become involved in left-wing politics, and in 1910 he became an active member of the Independent Labour Party (ILP).[59] In 1917 he was one of the founders of the Workers' Welfare League, and in 1918 he joined the People's Russian Information Bureau. He became a CPGB member after the ILP, at its 1921 conference, rejected the proposed affiliation with the Third International.[60] He later became MP for North Battersea from 1922 to 1923 (as a Labour candidate, when communists were still allowed to be members of the Labour Party) and again from 1924 to 1929, when he stood openly as a communist. However, it was primarily his activities outside the House of Commons that were of concern, as Saklatvala was a tireless political activist in a seemingly endless number of organisations. In her biography of her father, Sehri Saklatvala states:

> For much of his life in England, Shapurji came under Scotland Yard surveillance but unfortunately I cannot have sight of his dossier until 70 years after his death – by which time I shall be beyond reading it. I am therefore unable to state precisely when this surveillance began. But [I am told that] detectives were at his heels within a very short time of his arrival in England; though there is no evidence of any activities in India or in the very early months in England that would warrant such suspicion by the authorities.[61]

Due to the early release of Saklatvala's MI5 file we are now able to decipher the exact nature of that monitoring. As early as 1920 MI5 described him as follows:

> Since 1916 up to the present time he has been one of the most prominent of Indian agitators in England, and he has been connected with all the principal Socialist, Bolshevik and anti-British societies . . . he [is] considered one of the most violent anti-British agitators in England.[62]

Saklatvala was different from other Indian communists during this period in that he had no apparent history of involvement in the Indian nationalist movement prior to his arrival in England; his socialist leanings coupled with his nationality were apparently what induced the authorities to have a closer look at him. Yet what sorts of activities justified such an extreme statement? And could connections that he began to cultivate on his arrival in England, like those with the Irish nationalist community, have brought him under closer scrutiny by Scotland Yard?

It seems that the answer is a resounding 'yes'. His daughter tells us that 'Saklatvala was sympathetic to [the Irish] cause for he was an ardent upholder of the right of the Irish to freedom and independence'.[63]

This is evidenced by his many contacts with Irish activists, in both England and Ireland, throughout his career. In December 1918 the *Labour Leader* reported how, at a meeting organised by Saklatvala in Motherwell,

Tom Johnson, Cathal O'Shannon and [Tom] Farren of the Irish Transport Workers came over from Dublin and . . . convey[ed] the real message of Liberty Hall and Sinn Féin [and] Saklatvala . . .[exposed] the perils of Indian cheap labour and heavy industries.[64]

He also had Jim Larkin Jr over to talk on platforms in the 1920s and 1930s. However, Saklatvala had other Irish colleagues in London, as was revealed in late 1920 when the authorities raided his house and seized his papers. In the wake of this raid MI5 noted that 'altogether he is in a highly nervous state . . . He appears to be a little frightened and is afraid of visiting Art O'Brien (the English Sinn Féin leader).' This report also notes how at that time he had attempted to form an 'English League for an Irish Republic . . . but the idea absolutely failed'.[65] Saklatvala regularly spoke out about Ireland at various public meetings and in published articles, and he often attended meetings of Sinn Féin in Britain, as a result of his friendship with O'Brien. It was noted with much interest in his MI5 file that he had addressed a meeting of the Roger Casement Sinn Féin Club on Blackfriars Road on 5 October 1921.[66] The topic of his speech was 'The Fall of the British Empire'. There were, it seems, several important matters to note from the meeting other than the contents of Saklatvala's speech:

Some of the Sinn Féiners in this club are anxious that the Indians should follow in the footsteps of Sinn Féin and do all they can to make British rule impossible in India. Mr George Mortimer suggested that the ambushing of Crown Forces in Ireland was not murder but a fight to prevent murder. Art O'Brien who is President of this club was present at the meeting.[67]

In the previous July Saklatvala was reported to have 'intend[ed] going to Ireland in August to address the Irish Trade Union Congress. He was however keeping his proposed visit very quiet.'[68] MI5 noted his friendship also with P. J. Kelly, who was president of the Irish Self-Determination League: 'They have a common ground in working for the independence of both countries from the domination of England.'[69] Saklatvala was in contact, too, with one P. J. Keating of the Irish Self-Determination League, and a Home Office Warrant (for interception of post to a named address or individual) in relation to the latter somehow found its way into Saklatvala's MI5 file. Keating, using the alias 'J. W. Hey', was one of the partners of a trading firm with an address in London. He was evidently acting as an intermediary for the sale of large quantities of arms to a British man named John Arnall who was allegedly 'organising and abetting the revolt against the Spaniards by the Rifflis in Morocco'.[70] Thousands of pounds were changing hands and the deal was apparently being financed in England. Saklatvala was guilty by association here, and more than likely little else, as all that was said of the Indian was that Keating was a known supporter of him.[71] Clearly Saklatvala did not want the authorities to become aware of his Irish contacts, especially if he was *au fait* with the activities of Keating. His support of the Irish movement was, however, to be useful in the run up to his first successful election campaign in 1922. He had the support of Battersea's previous candidate, the eccentric Anglo-Irish suffragette and enthusiast for Irish republicanism Charlotte Despard.[72] She lobbied on his behalf, and his election leaflet quoted her as follows:

> I appeal to my Irish fellow countrymen and women in North Battersea – support the Party and support the man, Saklatvala – that will be on your side in the great struggle which is bound to come. Saklatvala spoke for us, as a fraternal delegate, in the last Irish Labour Congress, and his courage, wisdom and determination impressed us all.[73]

On 20 November 1922 Saklatvala took his seat as a Member of the UK Parliament, and a few days later he made his maiden speech to the House of Commons. Irish affairs dominated the speech. Saklatvala addressed the Commons in quite a menacing tone: 'In reference to Ireland, I am afraid that I shall strike a jarring note in the hitherto harmonious music of this house.' He went on to speak at length about the Treaty of the previous year:

> As a House we may say that we are giving this Irish Treaty with a view of bringing peace to Ireland, but we know that it is not bringing peace. Either we are actuated by the motive of restoring thorough peace in Ireland or we are doing it as partial conquerors of Ireland. Everyone knows that the Treaty has unfortunately gone forth as the only alternative to a new invasion of Ireland by British troops . . . the people of Ireland have a right to say that the very narrow majority which in Ireland accepted the Treaty at the time, accepted it also on this understanding – that if they did not accept it the alternative was an invasion by the Black-and-Tans of this country . . . As in 1801 England gave them a forced Union, so in 1922 England is giving them a forced freedom.[74]

Such an outspoken view on Ireland was significant for many reasons. There were few other members of the House of Commons who would have held such a vigorously anti-Treaty outlook, and he was going against the Labour Party line by voicing such views. In addition, it was particularly mischievous, as the House was trying earnestly to go ahead with the Second Reading of the Irish Free State Constitution Bill, he therefore had a captive audience. Saklatvala, however, felt that he owed it to his constituents, and to his Irish fellow activists, to take the bull by the horns:

> I put forward . . . the views of 90 per cent of those Irishmen who are my electors. They have pointed out to me that . . . Irishmen who are living in Great Britain have, by a tremendous majority, voted against it . . . the Irish Treaty is not going to be what we – in a sort of silent conspiracy – have decided to name it. The reality will not be there. The reality is not there.[75]

Four days later the debate on the Irish Free State Constitution Bill began. Approval of the Bill was considered a *fait accompli* with the Labour leader of the Opposition, Ramsay MacDonald, setting the tone: 'the less said about the Bill the better. Criticism is useless, sympathy is dangerous.'[76] Then, much to everyone's astonishment, the neophyte Saklatvala rose to his feet and struck a blow against the Bill's effortless amble though the House in the form of an Amendment: 'I realise the unpopularity I am courting in taking this step, but it was distinctly understood between my electors and myself that they did not wish me to back up a Treaty which was based upon coercion, and was signed under duress.' He went on to describe the distinct differences between the situation in Ireland and the rest of the Empire:

> We have heard today quotations and illustrations of similar enactments for colonies and dominions of the Empire. Is there any real parallel? Was Australia not rejoicing and waiting almost to a man and woman for the day when her Constitution would be confirmed by the House? Was not South Africa, after a great war and defeat, gratefully awaiting the day when the Treaty would be passed . . . The people of Canada, too, were determined to have their Constitution and to work it. The case of Ireland is different. It is no use our pretending that it is not so. We cannot adopt the policy that by driving deeper into the soil the roots of a cactus, and by carefully covering it with soil, roses will grow later on.[77]

He did not refer to India in this portion of his speech, more than likely because he thought that, like Ireland, it was not a natural dominion and he clearly grouped Ireland and India together with other countries in splendid isolation from the likes of Canada and Australia. A few days earlier he told the House:

> No Britisher would for a moment tolerate a Constitution for Great Britain if it were written outside of Great Britain by people who are not British. In a similar way the Constitutions for Ireland and India and Egypt and Mesopotamia should be Constitutions written by the men of those countries, in those countries, without interference from outside . . . Either these governments are independent or they are part of this Empire.[78]

[27]

He went on to describe the bleak conditions he thought would prevail in Ireland on the passing of the Bill:

> We are assured by the Prime Minister that, according to Mr Cosgrave, Ireland is only waiting for the Constitution to be carried through this House, and that they are going to work it out. Mr Cosgrave knows that . . . Ireland is to be prepared to receive this Constitution, not with joy and flags and illuminations, but with martial law, penalties and threats, imprisonment and ships waiting to depopulate the country.[79]

And he concluded in a dramatic manner:

> For 120 years that Act of Union has only produced distress to Ireland and disgrace to this country. I, as your friend – not as your critic or as your opponent – feel that I am conscious bound not to be a party to a bigger and greater mockery . . . Instead of merely expressing a pious opinion, I take my courage in my hands and, true to my convictions, I move this Amendment in order to create an opportunity for myself to vote against this Bill.[80]

Saklatvala's stance was courageous: he spoke out clearly, voicing not only his own concerns but also those of his Irish constituents, after barely a week in the House of Commons. It was, however, to no avail. His attempt to introduce the Amendment, described as 'irresponsible' in the press, was decisively beaten and the Irish Free State Constitution Bill received its Second Reading without challenge.[81]

A few months later, in March 1923, Saklatvala again spoke out in the House in relation to the Irish in Britain. As a result of pressure from the newly instated Irish Free State Government and after information had reached the British authorities that increased attempts were being made to revive the IRA there, Scotland Yard arrested and deported over 100 suspects from cities throughout England and Scotland. They were transported to Dublin on the British cruiser *Castor*, and interned in Mountjoy Prison.[82] However the British Government found itself in something of a legal quandary as many of those deported, although of Irish parentage, were in fact British citizens. Saklatvala and some left-wing cohorts, most notably George Lansbury, vigorously tackled the issue in the House of Commons.[83] Amongst those arrested was Saklatvala's Irish associate, Art O'Brien. The Home Secretary William Bridgeman defended the arrests: 'there has lately been a progressive increase in Irish Republican activity here. We are in possession of material clearly indicating the existence of a quasi-military organisation controlled by a person calling himself "Officer Commanding Britain" '.[84] O'Brien wasted no time in making the most of his friendship with the communist MP and letters of protest addressed to Bridgeman and signed by many of the internees were soon being sent to Saklatvala from the 'C' wing of Mountjoy Prison. Saklatvala succeeded in having the letters publicised in the *Daily Herald* under the heading: 'Deportees Challenge Home Secretary. Imprisoned Men Say Statements Are Deliberate And Contemptible Falsehoods.'[85] It was not long before the action was deemed illegal by the British courts, and the British Government had to ask for the return of the internees 'with the exception of [those] . . . against whom criminal proceedings are contemplated'.[86] Years later, in 1937, after Saklatvala's death, his son Beram in a letter to the *Daily Herald* requested anyone with relevant recollections of his father and his career to contact him. Among the hundreds of responses he received was one from a Delia McDermott, of Bloomsbury, London, which read:

> I noticed your letter recently in the *Daily Herald* . . . I wish to say [your father] took the first step to offer help in the case of the Irish deportees who were wrongfully arrested and sent to Ireland . . . My sister was amongst them and in attending to her affairs when she was imprisoned, I received your father's circular letter sent to her address. To me it was the first ray of hope in a very difficult situation.[87]

The help that had come from a somewhat unexpected source, an Indian communist MP, was greatly appreciated by those affected, and Saklatvala's continued interest in Irish affairs is documented later on in this chapter.

The LAI

The LAI was an organisation of particular interest to Irish and Indian radicals. From the late 1920s it became a vehicle through which connections were clearly established between the two nationalist movements. The benefit that this relationship afforded both sets of activists reached its height in the early 1930s. The LAI was originally a loosely socialist coterie called the 'League Against Oppression in the Colonies'. Its appeal proved widespread and left-wing notables throughout Europe were eager to utilise its full potential. In December 1926 the Government of India reported that the League 'continues to despatch literature dealing with "The Congress of the Oppressed Nations", which is to be held in Brussels . . . reference has already been made in previous reports to the fact that the League is almost certainly financed from Moscow'.[88] This international conference was held in Brussels in February 1927 and was the catalyst that led to the organisation's reformation. It was given a snappier name – 'The League Against Imperialism' – and according to Fenner Brockway, a leading member of the ILP, a precise objective:

To create a two-fold unity: first, between the organisations representing the subject races of the world; second, between such organisations and sympathetic movements in the imperialist countries. The object was to bring about world solidarity in the struggle against imperialism.[89]

Brockway also said of the LAI that there are very few cases in history where a movement has made such rapid international links, and crucially observed that

the whisperings of Labour officials suffering from the communist complex have been supplemented by reports that Scotland Yard is keeping an eye upon the organisation and that one should consequently be careful before associating with it. Of course Scotland Yard has its eyes upon it. A movement which sets out to unite and strengthen the subject peoples of the world in their struggle against imperialism is not likely to be overlooked by the Secret Service of the most powerful Empire in the world![90]

Judging by the volume of information about the LAI in IPI files, Brockway's was a discerning observation.

The suggestion of staging a Congress in Europe at which colonial nationalists could meet with Western sympathisers was first suggested by the CPGB. No doubt this was an idea mooted by influential Indian members of its ranks, including the brothers Clemens and Rajani Palme Dutt. It may also have been instigated after the Comintern had commented unfavourably on the CPGB's progress, or lack thereof, in 1924. It highlighted its neglect of colonial work and instructed it to establish 'very close contact' with the nationalist forces in the British Empire. The CPGB established a Colonial Committee in 1925 under Clemens Dutt's leadership and began to probe for contacts in India, Palestine, China, Egypt and Ireland.[91] The setting up of an international Congress, however, was actually carried through by Willi Munzenburg, General Secretary of the Workers' International Relief and chief propagandist for the Comintern.[92]

From the outset there was evidence of widespread suspicion in relation to this newly formed group. Before securing Brussels as the venue for the first International Congress the intention was for it to be held in Berlin. That would have been a suitable and convenient location as it was Munzenburg's base, but the Weimar Republic refused permission. Paris was then suggested, but needless to say the French authorities refused, fearful of reaction in their own colonies.[93] This gives rise to the question of whether these concerns were legitimate or, more to the point, to what extent Moscow had control over the formation and development of the LAI. Jean Jones has stated that Soviet Russia's initial reaction to the LAI was one of scepticism, as the Russians did not take kindly to Munzenburg's methods of recruiting broad-based support for communist causes.[94] Such doubts began to wane, however, as leading intellectuals and political figures were seen to affiliate themselves with the organisation, most importantly Jawaharlal Nehru, but also Albert Einstein, French writer Henri Barbusse and the American novelist Upton Sinclair. The appointment of a British delegation to the Brussels Congress was organised by Reginald Bridgeman, a Labour Party member and ex-diplomat with aristocratic roots. It is perhaps because such a diverse range of participants, many with no communist affiliations, accompanied the LAI's initial introduction to the world stage, that its communist origins were to remain, at least publicly, in doubt.[95] In fact the LAI was established essentially by two prominent communists who were in regular contact with Moscow, Munzenburg, already mentioned, and the LAI General Secretary, Virendra Chattopadhyaya, who had established himself in Berlin as a spokesperson for Indian communists. The British authorities were baffled as to how Munzenburg had managed to enlist 'the sympathies of some prominent pacifist writers and men of learning'.[96] What they failed to realise was that this organisation provided a much-needed service, namely a forum in which anti-imperialists of a variety of political backgrounds and from around the world could meet and exchange ideas. The potency that this attraction proved to have, at the expense of communist conversions, it might be argued, was an unintended by-product, unforeseen by either the LAI's creators or its detractors.

Irish contacts with the LAI

The Irish representatives at the Congress were well-known, left-wing republicans, Frank Ryan and Donal O'Donoghue. On their return to Ireland they played some part in the formation of an Irish section. One of the first references to an anti-imperialist meeting in Ireland can be found in a Garda report of 20 August 1928.[97] There had been a meeting at Foster Place, with around 600 in attendance, the only figure of note being Frank Ryan. It does not appear to have been very well organised, the main activity having centred on the burning of several Union Jack flags. There is no reference to other speakers or to the speeches' contents, perhaps because of some violence which followed the meeting on Westmoreland Street. The windows of premises flying the Union Jack had been broken and several arrests were made. In contemporary press reports emphasis was laid on the disturbances as opposed to the meeting beforehand.

At this stage it seems, from both police reports and press coverage, that this group which appeared on the streets of Dublin was perceived as nothing more than an offshoot of radical republicans whose concerns were related to primarily Irish affairs. The possibility of it developing significant international connections, communist or otherwise, in the fight against imperialism was not a concern. By October, with the help of Seán MacBride, further events, of a more peaceful nature, were organised. A meeting was held in the Mansion House on 5 October and a Garda report estimates the attendance at around 2,000. Numbers swelled again the following month when Foster Place catered for nearly 3,000 people at a meeting addressed by John Mitchell, Mrs Cathal Brugha and Alec Lynn. The LAI had a ready-made anti-imperialist audience in Ireland.

The India Office and the LAI

Meanwhile, in England, one of IPI's main concerns in the late 1920s and throughout the 1930s was the LAI. Its members, meetings, activities and contacts were all monitored closely. Unlike the Irish authorities, which were concerned with the immediate danger of anti-imperialist meetings and their potential to incite public clashes and street violence (frequent occurrences in Dublin at this time), IPI, infinitely more adept at deducing potential threat, implemented a more thorough approach. Its officers concerned themselves with the LAI's communist affiliations, and probing that element of the organisation became a priority. As far as IPI was concerned,

> the main objects of the League are to foment trouble and discord in the foreign possessions of the Colonial powers and to exploit unrest in the interests of Moscow. The League has addressed itself persistently to the exacerbation of feeling in India.[98]

Reading through IPI's LAI files, it becomes apparent also that many established Irish connections were discernible to the authorities. Considering the Irish personalities involved, however, it is unclear if those contacts were perceived as a matter of concern from a radical left standpoint as opposed to – I would argue – a more obvious revolutionary nationalist perspective. Either way, at one stage Irish involvement in the LAI threw up more problems than the British authorities had bargained for.

Within a year of the formation of the organisation the India Office realised that pragmatic action of some sort was needed to counteract the success that the LAI had had in gaining international support. As a result of liaising with Scotland Yard and other departments, it was decided that measures were to be taken to prevent, if possible, the grant of Empire-wide endorsements on the passports of LAI members. That was by no means an easy task to carry out, as IPI explained to R. T. Peel of the India Office in December 1927:

> There are considerable objections to attempting to put on the black list all those who are known to be connected with the League. In the first place, the membership of the League is rather nebulous. Except perhaps in certain countries, members of the League do not appear to pay subscriptions, but likely persons are 'roped in' on occasions when they are of use, and in this way become members of the League . . . it is therefore difficult to compile a complete and accurate list . . . We do, however, know the names of the various office-bearers of the League, but this again presents a difficulty, because a number of them are Socialist MPs.[99]

It was finally decided that instead of blacklisting the entire known membership of the LAI, a 'special list' would be drawn up of persons (other than Indians) who were consistently active in its endeavours. The list was comprised of what the authorities considered the names

> of the more dangerous persons in the League . . . IPI suggest[ed] that the Home Office should be asked to ensure that no visa for India [be] granted to any of [these people] without previous reference to [IPI].[100]

A follow-up letter in April 1928 supplied the Home Office with a revised version of this list. After consultation with Scotland Yard, IPI was in a position to submit further names of both 'Britishers and Aliens who appear to constitute the main figures other than Indians connected with the League's activities'. The revised list featured some intriguing additions. Three of the newly named were identified as nationals of the Irish Free State, about whom Scotland Yard wrote:

> As regards Landon, McBennett and O'Donoghue, these people are subjects of the Irish Free State. Landon and McBennett are believed to be aliases, since it is known that in addition to O'Donoghue one Peadar O'Donnell and a certain Frank Ryan attended the conference of the League Against Imperialism which was held in Brussels in December last. O'Donnell is a member of the IRA executive council and is editor of the republican weekly newspaper An Phoblacht. Ryan, who is a student, is also attached to the IRA GHQ as Inspector Officer [sic]. O'Donoghue is assistant to O'Donnell on the staff of An Phoblacht and is 'Vice O/C Dublin Brigade', IRA.[101]

Previously attention had been drawn only briefly to IRA attendance at the LAI World Congresses in February 1927 and July 1929 in the shape of those mentioned above as well as Seán MacBride.[102] The meeting referred to by Scotland Yard in the last extract, however, was an executive council meeting of the LAI held in Brussels in December 1927. That O'Donnell, Ryan and O'Donoghue were in attendance also at a gathering of this calibre, and possibly other executive council meetings, implies that they contributed more to the LAI than was previously realised. It is also important to note that in recently released Moscow archive files O'Donnell's name in particular appears quite regularly in relation to the LAI's activities in Europe.[103] Yet the three men's inclusion on the list is of interest for another reason, one that demonstrates how the LAI was providing the British authorities with far-reaching and unforeseen problems. The Scotland Yard report's primary focus, as already mentioned, was on attempts at controlling the movements of LAI members; in relation to the passports of those Irish men referred to, it says:

> As I expect you know, the Free State have their own passports on which they describe themselves as 'citizens of the Irish Free State and members of the British Commonwealth of Nations'. Their passports are accordingly made available for 'the British Commonwealth' an expression which is not officially recognised and could therefore be disregarded if these people turned up in India.[104]

At this point there appears a note in the margin handwritten by Malcolm Seton, asking: 'Did not his Majesty's government adopt it in the Treaty?' Clearly prior to the Irish External Relations Act of 1937, and even among the higher echelons of the British administration, misunderstandings prevailed about the exact legalities of Irish citizenship in relation to Britain and the Empire. The Scotland Yard report continued:

> The alternative would be to ask the Free State government to cancel their British Commonwealth endorsement. This is a matter of some delicacy and one which we feel should, if possible be avoided . . . It frequently happens that Free State subjects turn up abroad with a Free State passport and ask to have it made available for certain countries. The Consul invariably replies that he cannot make an entry on a Free State passport, but that if the subjects care to have a British passport he would be quite ready to issue one with the necessary endorsement.[105]

So an assumption existed that an Irish citizen would readily change his or her nationality in return for a travel endorsement for Bombay or Burma!

The impact of the LAI on British colonial policy was still rippling through Whitehall a year later. A memorandum in relation to the LAI and the possibility of refusing passports to its members was sent to various departments including the India Office, the Home Office and the Foreign Office. Some of the responses were unexpected. The Home Secretary, Sir William Joynson-Hicks, said curtly that he was not concerned and that the matter of refusing passports was one to be arranged with the Foreign Office. Peel responded:

This is rather surprising as our experience in the past has been that it is the Home Office that puts the strongest obstacles in the way of our attempts to tighten up the passport system. However, this leaves the way clear for us to negotiate with the Foreign Office.[106]

Or so he thought, as it was the Foreign Office's response or, more specifically, the Foreign Secretary Austen Chamberlain's that was to prove more serious. Chamberlain was opposed to the idea of treating all members of the LAI as communists, yet was prepared to agree to the refusal of endorsements for India to all persons whom the Home Office considered dangerous. He did not consider this to be any different from arrangements that had already been suggested in official correspondence, and went on to take issue with having been consulted in the first place.

Unfortunately Sir Austen Chamberlain goes on to complain that he is being used to 'pull Indian chestnuts out of the fire', and is being asked to do what is really the business of the Indian government to do in India. He considers that India should refuse admittance, as all other countries do, to those whom she objects to receive.[107]

India, in many ways like Ireland, is seen here as the ever-present thorn in the British Government's side and policy-making in relation to it was a continual strain. Attitudes differed and emotions ran high. Chamberlain's complaints, and the Home Office's suggested response to them, are a prime example of this:

The activities of the LAI are directed against the British Empire as a whole and not just against India. It is not therefore unreasonable to ask His Majesty's government to co-operate in action taken against its members. The Secretary of State has all along agreed to accept full responsibility in Parliament, and the Foreign Secretary is not therefore being called upon to defend his extraction of Indian chestnuts from the fire.[108]

The second World Congress

The second World Congress of the LAI opened in Frankfurt-on-Main on 21 July 1929. The British authorities were still keeping close tabs on the development of the organisation. The LAI's aspiration to establish an international networking system was succeeding and was a cause of some concern. A good example of the LAI's growth in popularity as well as the enthusiasm of its organisers was the proposal to hold a youth congress to coincide with the second World Congress. An 'international preparatory committee' met in Berlin on 10 April 1929 to formulate an agenda and discuss measures necessary for such a conference.[109] The move was a success and an anti-imperialist youth bulletin, published by the youth section of the British LAI, soon appeared. Appearing along-side other articles, such as 'Divide and Rule in Palestine', 'Building Socialism in China', and 'Release the Meerut Prisoners', was one in which Britain's relationship with Ireland was addressed.[110] Similar treatments of colonial histories no doubt had the desired effect of mobilising young workers and socialists in many countries to affiliate themselves with the LAI. Other publications were produced and dis-tributed by the LAI's British section. Two such magazines found their way to the Department of Justice, Dublin, possibly intercepted and passed on by the Customs Service: they were titled *Indian Front* and *Irish Front* and were produced by the same hand, Ben Bradley, then secretary of the LAI's British section.[111] *Irish Front* contained contribu-tions from members, like Tommy Paton, of the Republican Congress based in London and those affiliated with The *Irish Workers' Voice*. Produced later, in the mid-1930s, these publications were purely communist in outlook and demonstrate how the CPGB continued to use anti-imperialist organisations as conduits for the party's own propaganda.

By 1929 LAI branches, or 'sections' as they were referred to, had been established in many non-European countries including Mexico, Nicaragua, Argentina, Brazil, Cuba and South Africa, and the tracing of any form of Indo-Irish collaboration within the LAI structures had increased. Correspondence between the LAI's branches in London and Berlin was being intercepted. In de Valera's MI5 file there is a letter from Bridgeman to Munzenburg, requesting further invitations to the Frankfurt gathering. However, it is the concluding paragraph that con-cerned the British authorities.

> I was recently in touch with one of our Irish friends who asked me whether a communication which he had addressed to Jawaharlal Nehru through you, had duly reached you and been forwarded by you to its des-tination.[112]

There is no mention of the identity of this 'Irish friend'. However in the accompanying letter the interceptor jumps to his own conclusions: 'The last paragraph of this letter would seem to have a certain interest. De Valera is known to be associated with the Irish section of the League.'[113] De Valera's activities were being closely watched by MI5 at this time, as evidenced by his recently released and quite extensive MI5 file. It was particularly important that he was monitored as he had recently founded the new political party Fianna Fáil. De Valera and Fianna Fáil had sup-ported the LAI by sending money to the Frankfurt Congress and occa-sionally endorsed its policies in Ireland.[114] However, this was at a time when the LAI's communist credentials remained unclear, and people like

Nehru happily supported its basic anti-imperialists principles. De Valera and his party, for example, were understandably present at LAI platforms in Dublin which were organised to coincide with republican anti-Poppy Day protests. However, as already noted, the Irish section of the LAI was comprised mainly of those associated with the republican Left. It appears more likely that this 'Irish friend' was either O'Donnell or Ryan, or possibly MacBride who, as a Garda report tells us, attended the Frankfurt Congress as an 'Irish Communist Delegate'.[115]

The Irish questions were dealt with at a morning sitting in which O'Donnell presented the general outline of the Irish freedom movement. MacBride, who made attacks on the British Labour Party, is noted as having remarked that no British delegate had been present during the discussion of the Irish questions. However preoccupied the British delegates were with their own troubles, the Irish had avid listeners in the Indians present.[116] After O'Donnell's talk, Hassan Mirza, an Indian activist in Europe who was suspected by IPI of arms-smuggling, added: 'The defeat of the Irish freedom movement would be a lesson to the Indians not to place their trust in the "bourgeois leaders".'[117]

The second World Congress saw more involvement from the Russian delegates, and it became apparent that a new Comintern policy was in effect, to reverse the previous practice of tolerance towards the non-communist Left and colonial nationalist movements.[118] It was at this conference also that a few new appointees were unveiled, most notably Shapurji Saklatvala. This new direction however was not exactly welcomed with open arms. There is evidence that Munzenburg made some attempts at preventing it and thought it necessary to solicit the help of figures no longer in favour. In a letter to Jawaharlal Nehru, intercepted by the British authorities, the American LAI member Roger Baldwin stated his belief that

> Munzenburg's stand for a real united League (Against Imperialism), rather than the agent of Moscow which the League pretty nearly became as a result of the Frankfurt congress, would be greatly helped by letters from influential persons such as yourself . . . Munzenburg understands very well that it is a stupid thing to make the League simply the tool of Moscow, but Moscow will not give in.[119]

By 1931, however, many of the prominent figures whose support had been warmly welcomed, and whose presence in Brussels had substantiated the LAI's claim to be open to all individuals and organisations supporting the anti-imperialist struggle, had either resigned or been expelled. Among them was Nehru, who in April 1930, in his capacity as President of the Indian National Congress, had directed it to cease all correspondence with the LAI.[120]

Indo-Irish collaboration as the LAI develops in Ireland

By late 1929, after the second World Congress, the LAI Dublin meet-ings had acquired a more international tone. On 10 November 1929 at a gathering in Findlater Place, organised by Frank Ryan and Maud Gonne MacBride, two resolutions were put to the people:

> To pledge themselves to resist by every means possible in their power any display of imperialism and to agitate for the release of the political pris-oners and secondly to have the imperial troops withdrawn from India, Egypt and other oppressed colonies.[121]

The radical press covered the growth of the LAI in Ireland with great zeal. Articles began to emerge containing detailed histories of other countries under imperialist rule, most notably India. In one of *An Phoblacht*'s many reports covering these meetings it was said that there was reason to believe that the British authorities in India were for-bidding the import of Terence MacSwiney's book *Principles of Freedom* as well as Dan Breen's *My Fight For Irish Freedom*.[122]

September 1930 was a busy month in Ireland for those affiliated with the anti-imperialist movement. 'Thousands of republicans', we are told in *An Phoblacht*, 'attended a monster *aeridheacht mór* on the slopes of Lough Leane, near Collinstown West Meath last Sunday to meet the Indian nationalist, Rainzi.'[123] He brought greetings 'from 350 million of his countrymen who were engaged in a life or death struggle to free, not only India, but . . . to help liberate the other down-trodden nations of the world'. This was a prelude of sorts to the main event about two weeks later.

On 24 September a LAI meeting was held in the Mansion House, the focal point of which was events in India. There were several Indian rep-resentatives and over 1,200 people attended. The Garda reported that 'members of the Irregular organisation acted as stewards inside the house and included Michael Price, J. J. McConnell, Joseph Burke, Michael Kelly and Thomas O'Brien'.[124] There were nine speakers in total and on the platform were four men and one woman of Indian nationality, who accompanied Krishna Deonarini,[125] the representative of LAI's Indian section and the main guest speaker. Seán MacBride chaired the meeting and the Irish speakers included Peadar O'Donnell, Peadar O'Maille, Mrs Sheehy Skeffington, Alec Lynn, Helena Maloney and Jim Larkin Jr.

First, a long and aggressive resolution was proposed:

> That this mass meeting of Dublin citizens declares the solidarity of republican Ireland with the Indian masses in their struggle against British imperialism and its Indian allies. We would urge on our Indian comrades

[38]

the lesson of the betrayed Irish revolution and would appeal to them to guard against the dangers that halted our struggle. We greet the Indian masses in revolt and hail the Indian Republican Army. We salute the memory of those valiant men and women who have gone down before the savagery of British troops in India, and we greet the heroic revolutionary fighters now languishing in Meerut and other jails in India. We call on the labouring masses of the Irish race to recognise that imperial Britain and revolutionary India are at war, and that the loyalty of revolutionary Ireland is to the enemy of imperial Britain. [126]

An Phoblacht attempted to instil in its readership a sense of great historical significance to this Indo-Irish collaboration when it stated:

Not since before the 'Treaty' was signed has that historic venue [the Mansion House] seen so large or fervent a gathering . . . the Round Room was packed until not even standing room was available, while an enthusiastic overflow meeting took place on the street outside.[127]

The meeting was concluded by Frank Ryan who read over the motion that was passed, with three cheers for India and then three more for the Workers' Revolutionary Party of Ireland. The Red Flag was sung as the crowd stood to attention.[128]

Rienzi attended another rally the following week, in Cork, and his visit appears to have been a great success. The Garda report informs us that Rienzi, who according to IPI the following year was trying to gain admission to TCD, was accompanied by Madame Charlotte Despard.[129] She played a major part in arranging his visit. Although by this time quite elderly and not an active member of the LAI in London, she was affiliated to another group there that was under the watchful eyes of IPI – the Independence of India League. Despard was involved in the Release the Prisoners Campaign with Maud Gonne MacBride, Helena Maloney and Hanna Sheehy Skeffington, who all became involved in the LAI Irish section. Through her membership of the Independence of India League and her friendship with V. J. Patel she had many Indian contacts in London and was actively involved in Indian nationalist campaigns there.[130]

Around this time IPI became aware of another intriguing Indo-Irish connection in London while tracing the steps of one Philip Rupasangha Gunawardena, who had arrived in England from America around 1929. Born in Ceylon (Sri Lanka), he was a member of the Cosmopolitan Crew, an anti-government political association there.[131] After his arrival in England it did not take long for him to meet with other Indian activists. He joined the Indian Freedom League (IFL) and made regular speeches at its meetings in Hyde Park, and through it soon joined the LAI. He made regular trips to Berlin to carry out work connected with the LAI and was considered by IPI to be an active communist agent of the organisation and was therefore regarded as quite dangerous. It was noted with particular attention that on 16 November 1931 Gunawardena met with Captain J. White 'who has recently been in London associating with known extremists, having come from Ireland by appointment at . . . the office of the LAI'.[132] Captain Jack White, co-founder, with James Connolly, of the Citizen Army and a leading figure in the 1913 Dublin Lock-Out, was by the 1930s liaising with left-wing notables in Dublin. IPI apparently had reason for concern here, noting that,

> according to expressed intention, White was afterwards due to leave for Liverpool, to engage in revolutionary activity among Irishmen. Gunawardena himself later stated that he would be leaving for Ireland about the end of the month, to study the Irish situation. In view of his expected visit to Germany he will apparently only remain in Ireland for a few days.[133]

The following year IPI suggested that Gunawardena's passport should not be renewed so that his movement around the Continent would be hindered. They held out hope that he would return to Ceylon and, denied passport renewal, would be unable to go back to Europe. However, this became doubtful after they were informed that he had been given a letter of introduction to Dan Breen, the celebrated gunman and Fianna Fáil member of Dáil Éireann, to use in connection with another visit which he contemplated paying to Ireland. It appears that Gunawardena took great interest in Irish affairs. IPI was particular enough to note in a 1932 report (just after Fianna Fáil had first come to power) that Gunawardena was overheard in the British Museum discussing with fellow Indians the lesson to be learnt from de Valera's recent achievements.[134]

The decline of the LAI

The 1930s saw the LAI's decline and, in 1937, eventual demise. The consolidation of Nazi power in 1933 forced Munzenburg's LAI International Secretariat to flee to Paris, where it remained for a few months until it finally moved to London in November.[135] Reginald Bridgeman took control of the organisation, which by this stage had a severely reduced membership, encompassing mainly communists and far-left ideologues. The Comintern's change of policy was a success in that the LAI no longer had the affiliation of influential non-communist, anti-imperialist thinkers from around the world. Individuals like Nehru could have helped the group become a legitimate international lobby for those who were genuinely suffering under imperialist rule in the colonies. Throughout 1934 Bridgeman, with increased help from Indians like Saklatvala, was vigorous in his attempts to keep the organisation going and the Secretariat met eleven times.[136] There was increased Irish involvement from the usual suspects, coincident with the Republican Congress in Dublin, which is looked at in more detail below.

Peadar O'Donnell was again present at a conference held in 1934 on Blackfriars Road in London. The invitation to the conference contained a provisional agenda. The speakers were to include 'Conrad Noel, Alex Gossip, Harry Pollitt, S. Saklatvala, Ben Bradley [one of the Meerut prisoners], R. Bridgeman, and fraternal delegates from Ireland, India, China, Palestine and Cyprus'.[137] The two countries that featured most heavily on the agenda were Ireland and India, with the Sunday sitting devoted to 'The struggle of the Indian Workers and Peasants', followed by 'Ireland and the National Fight for Liberation'. A Scotland Yard report details the event and O'Donnell's speech:

> Next came . . . O'Donnell. He said that the Irish Republican Congress came into being, not only to combat British imperialism, but to fight against local imperialists and autocrats. Ireland was now governed more or less on fascist lines. O'Donnell, who criticised Mr de Valera and his government at some length, suggested that an anti-imperialist congress should be held in Dublin next year. This resolution was seconded by the chairman of the Dublin District Committee of the Congress, and was supported by a woman.[138]

As was seen earlier, Irish radicals had their regular trips to London and the Continent reciprocated by the LAI. However it was primarily Indians based in London as opposed to the British themselves, who were keen to advance relations with the Irish.

Saklatvala and Irish radical politics

Saklatvala continued to support the Irish nationalist community through the many political organisations with which he was involved. In November 1924, along with the eccentric English socialist Arthur Field, he revived a moribund society called the East–West Circle, which had been active during the First World War. Its aims were to 'bring East and West together, and use efforts to thwart the imperialist spirit . . . so flagrantly apparent in England'.[139] It was revived primarily to serve as a centre for communist and Bolshevik activity 'because MacDonald and his gang were trying to pose as too respectable'.[140] A Scotland Yard report noted that at a meeting of this new group it was said that 'if Labour was to succeed it was by adopting, not a weak and peaceful policy, but a red-hot communist attitude', and not by 'waving a tiny red flag and going about in a motor-car'.[141] Such rhetoric meant that the authorities would soon be hot on the 'red' heels of the East–West Circle. It was not long before Field was appointed secretary of the group and Saklatvala its president. Field began to issue circulars in relation to the East–West Circle meetings, and a pamphlet appealed 'for subscriptions to a "Special November Collection of the Irish Language Fund" and a "Connemara Relief Fund" '.[142] It is not made clear how much money was collected and where it went, but among the club's membership was Art O'Brien, so it is more than likely that any money from those collections ended up with Sinn Féin.[143]

It appears that Saklatvala had acquired something of a name for himself as a supporter of Ireland, because during a 'mysterious two days' visit to London under an assumed name' in 1926, Eamon de Valera was to attend a secret meeting held at Saklatvala's home.[144] This was brought to the attention of Scotland Yard by Major Phillips of MI5. The meeting was to be at 10.30 p.m., and it was understood that 'de Valera, one Duval from France, and Herr Tills from Germany were to be present'. Observation was kept with no result. At the time of the meeting 'de Valera was known to [Scotland Yard] to be touring Scotland';[145] this was shortly after the formation by de Valera of Fianna Fáil in Ireland, and he had been making increased efforts to travel and fundraise. A tantalising snippet of information emerges from a Scotland Yard communication to MI5, in which the officer expressed himself 'a little worried about this case as it might be awkward both for yourselves and for us if the informant were denounced as a Police spy'. Someone close to Saklatvala, it appears, had tipped off the authorities.[146] One wonders, moreover, what exactly it was that de Valera had to talk to the Communist MP about?

Throughout the following years Saklatvala maintained close contact with Irish circles and, as far as the authorities were concerned, those connections became more radical. This was perhaps considered par for the course, as in 1927 IPI remarked: 'It is interesting to note that Mr Saklatvala is now working directly under the orders of the Comintern.'[147] During 1928 numerous letters from Krishna Deonarine to Saklatvala were intercepted by IPI: 'these letters dealt with the writers' efforts to spread communist propaganda in Trinidad'. The two also collaborated in relation to a visit to Ireland in the wake of the formation of the LAI. Saklatvala was also in regular contact with the Revolutionary Workers' Group, a party founded in Dublin in 1930 and which was under Comintern control.[148] His old friend and ex-Battersea representative Charlotte Despard was affiliated to the organisation, and she allowed the establishment of a Workers' College at her house in

Eccles Street, which also doubled as the headquarters of the Irish section of the Friends of Soviet Russia.

In May 1930 Scotland Yard noted how the communist press was devoting a lot of space to articles dealing with the situation in India. This was shortly after Gandhi had been arrested in the wake of his Salt March; he was detained without trial until January 1931. It was noted that several issues of the *Daily Worker* carried articles inciting British troops to mutiny and advising dockers and other transport workers to prevent shipment and transport of troops, arms and munitions; 'leaflets and speeches from communist platforms have followed these lines and the London District Party has instructed its members in addition to fraternise with Indian seamen'.[149]

In the same month Saklatvala was summoned to Berlin, the communist revolutionary centre. Clearly, concerted attempts were being made by the communist movement to take advantage of the political developments in India. Other leading British communists were asked to attend meetings in Berlin, where they would 'consider plans for immediate action in support of the Indian movement in view of the rapid development of the revolutionary situation'.[150] Saklatvala's increased revolutionary activities, which had become all the more proficient with the formation of the LAI, were of great concern to the British authorities, especially as they had recently received information from a reliable source at the Soviet Embassy in Berlin that, with others, Saklatvala was giving advice on the 'reorganisation of revolutionary cells among coloured troops'.[151]

Saklatvala also made regular trips over to Ireland in the early 1930s to help with the promotion of the newly founded Saor Éire group. As Emmet O'Connor has elaborated elsewhere, the short-lived Saor Éire was a salient example of the widening appeal of communism.[152] The organisation was arguably a more tailored version of the LAI, designed to encompass the IRA and cater for Ireland's more specifically nationalist radical needs. At the helm was Peadar O'Donnell, who had clearly learned much from his involvement in the LAI in the years preceding the formation of Saor Éire. A perceptive observation was made by the head of the Dublin Special Branch about the emergence of Saor Éire and its like: 'The Communist International may be prompting these activities but one gets the impression that they are simply the manifestations of the professional agitator without whom the Communist International would be powerless.'[153] The constitution adopted pledged Saor Éire to the overthrow of British imperialism and Irish capitalism, to bring wealth under the control of the workers and working farmers, and to restore the Gaelic culture. Fraternal greetings were sent to Soviet Russia and in the autumn of 1931 Saklatvala joined Peadar O'Donnell

[43]

and Seán Murray in a series of meetings to organise local branches.[154] The following February he was over again for the general election of 1932 when he accompanied Jim Larkin Sr, who was contesting the election in the North Dublin constituency as a communist, on a tour of the polling stations on election day.[155]

Later on, and as a result of his work with the LAI, Saklatvala's visits to Ireland increased. One such trip to Dublin in 1934 is noteworthy. Early that year a new Indian political group, the Indian Independence League (IIL), was formed in London with Saklatvala and Deonarine at the helm. It was comprised of Indian activists, most of whom were already LAI members, the distinction offered by the IIL being the opportunities it afforded them to concentrate more specifically on all things relating to India and any other political affairs that took their fancy. At an IIL meeting on 27 September 1934 one item discussed was the sending of delegates to the Irish Republican Congress, which was to take place in Dublin later that week. Saklatvala was elected as a delegate by the London branch of the Indian National Congress. He informed the meeting that 'a man named Connolly and his sister, were influential members of the [Republican] Congress and were interested in India and the group should get into communication with them'. Here we find the name of Roddy Connolly cropping up again, and the 'interest in India' spoken of was no doubt as a result of his friendship with Roy in the early 1920s. It appears that an Indian by the name of Yajnik was to accompany Saklatvala on his trip to Dublin.[156] Scotland Yard was being kept up to date on the Republican Congress movement and provided a brief explanation of it:

> The Irish Republican Congress is being called by a group of men and women who broke away from the IRA in April 1934. The 'Connolly and sister' reference made by Saklatvala are Roderick and Nora Connolly O'Brien, son and daughter of James Connolly who was executed because of his activities in the Easter week 1916 rebellion.[157]

At the 1934 IRA convention there was a split involving the secession of the left-wing. Among the latter was Peadar O'Donnell, who proposed the resolution that the IRA should mobilise a united front, called the Republican Congress, that would campaign with the aim of wresting the leadership of the national struggle from Irish capitalism. The fate of the Republican Congress was determined largely by one of the characteristics that it had adopted inadvertently from the IRA: the propensity towards schism.[158] A devastatingly balanced split occurred at its very first meeting. Saklatvala and Deonarine did in fact attend this celebrated Republican Congress meeting in Rathmines Town Hall. Saklatvala received some publicity in the *Irish Press* during this trip, not as a result of his associations with the Republican Congress but because he was still making public declarations against the Treaty, something for which the Fianna Fáil party organ readily found space. He is reported as having claimed to be

> the only member in the British Parliament who had foreseen the result of granting a Free State to the Irish people. He had strongly opposed the Bill for that purpose, holding that those responsible for giving the concession were only a band of thieves. The Treaty was merely subterfuge on the part of British capitalists who wanted to stifle the clamour of the Irish people for freedom.[159]

Interestingly, considering that this split had such a negative outcome for the Republican Congress itself, Saklatvala was most enthusiastic on his return to London. He met with Reginald Bridgeman and Ben Bradley to discuss the proceedings and the resolutions passed at the meeting. He informed them that the leading members of the Irish republican movement were very sympathetically inclined towards the ideal of an India completely free from British rule and influence and that six Irish republicans had promised to attend an upcoming Indian political conference.[160] He apparently considered his trip most worthwhile.

It was a useful excursion for another – unexpected – reason. A few months later, in December 1934, Saklatvala was considering an alternative venue for the IIL meetings, his motive being to discard certain undesirable members from the IIL's wings. IPI reported him as having said that

> Yajnik, he had heard on good authority, [was] either an India Office or Police agent. He added that Yajnik was practically driven out of the Irish Republican Congress and that but for him delegates from the Congress Party would have attended the last Indian political conference. He would not however bar Yajnik from attending any meetings as such action might give rise to a 'spy scare' and keep other Indians away.[161]

It seems that Irish members of the Congress were wary of Yajnik, on what grounds it is not clear. Nor is it apparent from IPI files whether Saklatvala's concerns in relation to Yajnik in particular were accurate, but it seems unlikely. Such alarmist utterances may have had more to do with internal Indian rifts in London than anything else. The one certain thing, however, was that Saklatvala had been under surveillance by the British authorities from as early as 1910. Here we see how, some twenty-four years later, accurate and up-to-date material regarding his activities, involving Irish as well as Indian and wider communist affairs, was still being accumulated by the British authorities on a regular basis.

By 1936 relations among Indian activists in London had become strained, as a result primarily of many non-communist Indian nationalists becoming increasingly uneasy with Saklatvala's extreme left leanings; and it was also accentuated by the November 1935 visit to London of Gandhi's apparent heir and protégé, Jawaharlal Nehru. There ensued a clamour for his approval from various competing Indian factions. Despite Nehru's visit, Saklatvala remained an active and adamant communist campaigner until the last, and indeed attended and organised meetings in the last days of his life. On 15 January 1936 he died of a heart attack.[162] Philip Vickery of IPI recounted the circumstances surrounding his death in somewhat respectful tones:

> At the height of the fray, Saklatvala who had fanned the flames, if he had not actually kindled the spark, succumbed, tragically enough, to a heart attack brought on by his excessive exertions, and the warring factions coalesced, at any rate temporarily, to do him honour in his obsequies. It may be remarked en passant, that the irony of Saklatvala's death lies in the fact that his removal from the political arena may easily do more to further Indian unity than anything that intrepid and undoubtedly sincere warrior was able to achieve in his lifetime.[163]

Saklatvala's death left a void in left-wing Indian factions that was soon filled by V. K. Krishna Menon. Menon was a late arrival to London Indian circles and first came to notice in 1932 as secretary of the India League, which IPI described as 'an instrument for the expression in this country of the policy of Gandhi'.[164] The monitoring of Menon demonstrates the apparent difficulty the British authorities had in distinguishing between left-wing Indian nationalists and communists. Indians of all political persuasions in Britain naturally interacted with each other and it is fair to say that with the exception of Saklatvala, who was undoubtedly motivated first and foremost by communist doctrine, most other Indians were nationalist agitators who would have had only incidental contact with Moscow. Yet Menon's IPI file is littered with observations and suspicions as to his possible communist leanings:

> During 1936 Menon's co-operation with the Communist Party . . . became progressively closer, and from the end of that year onwards there is irrefutable evidence that he took no important action of any kind in regard to the Indian situation without prior consultation with the higher Communist Party leaders.[165]

IPI went on to note that Menon 'availed himself of Communist support to boost meetings which would otherwise have been badly attended and . . . he relied constantly on the *Daily Worker* to ventilate such material as he received from India'.[166] Menon was in fact something of a travelling envoy for the Indian National Congress in Europe, a position that he secured as a result of his close links with Nehru.[167] The attempt to gain publicity and support for the situation in India from any quarter, communist or otherwise, was quite compatible with this agenda. What IPI and the British Government clearly feared was the possibility that Menon would lure the powerful Nehru even further down the Leftist road. Menon, like Saklatvala, saw the potential in building links with the Irish community. This was not simply the cynical exploitation of a political situation: Menon, like many other politically active Indians, had long-established Irish contacts and expressed a genuinely held viewpoint. Menon, and his time in the UK, are discussed in more detail in chapters four and five.

Conclusion

British intelligence files dating from the 1920s and 1930s disclose considerable unease over the activities of left-wing Indian activists in Britain, Ireland and the Continent. Apprehensions existed about their exact relations with established communist parties and their possible contacts with Moscow. The records show also that, to some extent prompted by the Comintern, left-wing collaboration was established between Indian and Irish subversives, and it undoubtedly increased as the years went on, with even the Irish authorities on occasion accommodating Indian radicals, like Brajesh Singh. However, even though many of those concerned were indeed communists, like Saklatvala, Roy and Connolly, it is not possible to conclude that it was this particular common ideology that brought them together. Although the Comintern made increased efforts to incorporate strong aspects of anti-imperialism into its doctrines in an effort to win over nationalist revolutionaries in the colonies, in the case of Indian and Irish activists national liberation was too strong an inherent principle simply to be left by the wayside. The British authorities may have been aware of this predominant ideology and given it due consideration. IPI files from this period indicate that during the interwar years the authorities had an understandable though unfortunate preoccupation with communism. It seems that the strong whiff of communist manipulation pervading organisations like the LAI, and evident among a handful of Indian communists resident in Europe at the time, overwhelmed the subtler fragrances of nationalism and anti-colonialism which characterised the Indo-Irish radical nexus of the 1920s and 1930s and culminated in the formation of the IIIL, as we will see in chapter two.

Notes

1   Kevin McDermott and Jeremy Agnew, *The Comintern: A History of International Communism from Lenin to Stalin* (London, 1996), pp. 159–60. Nikolai Bukharin was a leading Bolshevik activist and theoretician. He played a prominent role in the Comintern from its foundation and was its *de facto* chief in 1926–28. He was executed in March 1938 during the Great Terror: *ibid.*, p. 267.

2   More usually referred to as just M. N. Roy.

3   McDermott and Agnew, *The Comintern*, p. 161.

4   For further reading see Mike Milotte, *Communism in Modern Ireland: The Pursuit of the Workers' Republic since 1916* (Dublin, 1984); Emmet O'Connor, *Reds*; and John Patrick Haithcox, *Communism and Nationalism in India: M. N. Roy and Comintern Policy 1920–39* (New Jersey, 1971).

5   See for example David Carlton, *Churchill and the Soviet Union* (Manchester, 2000).

6   Christopher Andrew, *Secret Service: The Making of the British Intelligence Community* (London, 1985), p. 324.

7   *Ibid.*, p. 327.

8   In 1930, however, as a result of a falling out with the Stalin group, he was thrown out of the Communist Party. He remained a communist until later in life when, in the 1950s, he started to write critical analyses of communism, fascism and liberalism and began the humanist movement in India.

9   'Jawaharlal Nehru on the anti-national role of the Communist Party, 23 October 1945', in B. N. Pandey (ed.), *The Indian Nationalist Movement, 1885–1947: Selected Documents* (London, 1979), p. 165.

10   The year of his birth is not known, but is thought to be somewhere between 1886 and 1893: Haithcox, *Communism and Nationalism*, p. 4.

11   *Ibid.*, pp. 4–5.

12   IPI fact sheet on Roy, no date (?1922), BL, OIOC, IOR, L/P&J/12/46.

13   Haithcox, *Communism and Nationalism*, pp. 7–8.

14   *Ibid.*, p. 9. He founded the Mexican Communist Party and attended the 1920 Comintern Congress as an official representative.

15   Unsigned IPI report, 23 Aug. 1922, BL, OIOC, IOR L/P&J/12/46.

16   *Ibid.*, report on CPI, 23 Aug. 1922.

17   Andrew, *Secret Service*, pp. 324–38.

18   Report on CPI, 23 Aug. 1922, BL, OIOC, IOR, L/P&J/12/46.

19   Report on CPI, 28 Aug. 1922, *ibid.* It is possible that 'Read' is a reference to Paddy Read, one time Wobblie and a communist associate of Connolly; or, more likely, that Connolly chose to use 'Read' as an alias while travelling.

20   Report on CPI, 13 Sept. 1922, BL, OIOC, IOR, L/P&J/12/46.

21   *Ibid.*

22   National Archives of the United Kingdom (hereafter NAUK), Metropolitan Police (hereafter MEPO), 38/19; see also O'Connor, *Reds*, p. 66.

23   O'Connor, *Reds*, p. 66.

24   *Ibid.*, p. 78.

25   *Ibid.*

26   Report on CPI, 1922, BL, OIOC, IOR, L/P&J/12/46.

27   Report on CPI, 1923, BL, OIOC, IOR, L/P&J/12/161.

28   Report on CPI, 13 Sept. 1922, BL, OIOC, IOR, L/P&J/12/46.

29   Various reports on Obed's activities contained in his file, BL, OIOC, IOR, L/P&J/12/477.

30   Reports on Obed's activities dating from 1922 to 1934, BL, OIOC, IOR, L/P&J/12/477.

31   Report on CPI, 1923, BL, OIOC, IOR, L/P&J/12/161.

32   See BL, OIOC, IOR, L/P&J/12/477 and L/P&J/12/94. The latter is a file titled 'Arms Traffic from Europe' which deals primarily with Obed's activities.

33   Eunan O'Halpin, *Defending Ireland* (Oxford, 1999), pp. 240–2.

34 Milotte, *Communism*, p. 62.
35 *Workers' Republic*, 30 Sept. 1922.
36 Report on CPI, 11 Nov. 1922, BL, OIOC, IOR, L/P&J/12/46.
37 Desmond Greaves, *Liam Mellows and the Irish Revolution* (London, 1971), p. 205.
38 *Ibid.*, p. 368.
39 Report on CPI, 15 Nov. 1922, BL, OIOC, IOR L/P&J/12/46.
40 Unsigned London Metropolitan Police report, handwritten date on cover sheet given as 27 April 1925, NAUK, MEPO, 38/19.
41 For further reading on James Larkin see Emmet O'Connor, *James Larkin* (Cork, 2002).
42 Unsigned London Metropolitan Police report, handwritten date on cover sheet given as 27 April 1925, NAUK, MEPO, 38/19. This is a somewhat inaccurate account of Connolly: a Department of Justice file dating from the 1920s indicates that at the time he was working for Russian Oil Products: NAI, Department of Justice (hereafter JUS), 5074A.
43 Haithcox, *Communism and Nationalism*, pp. 164–5.
44 *Ibid.*, pp. 167–70.
45 Report on Brajesh Singh Lal, dated 1934, BL, OIOC, IOR, L/P&J/12/462.
46 Vickery to Williamson, 2 Oct. 1932, *ibid.*
47 *Ibid.*; see chapter two for further information on the Indian–Irish Independence League and these figures.
48 Vickery to Clauson, 14 Oct. 1932, BL, OIOC, IOR, L/P&J/12/462.
49 Vickery to Clauson, 17 Nov. 1932, *ibid.*
50 Vickery to Clauson, 24 Nov. 1932, *ibid.*
51 Extract from a Scotland Yard report on Don Philip Rupasangha Gunawardena, 25 May 1932, BL, OIOC, IOR, L/P&J/12/409.
52 Minutes of meeting held at the Passport Office, 11 Feb. 1924, NAUK, Records of the Foreign Office (hereafter FO), 372/2091; see also O'Halpin, *Defending*, pp. 75–6.
53 Vickery to Clauson, 3 Feb. 1933, BL, OIOC, IOR, L/P&J/12/462.
54 *Ibid.*
55 *Ibid.*
56 Vickery to Clauson, 12 April 1933, *ibid.*
57 Report on Brajesh Singh Lal, dated 1934, *ibid.*; Brajesh's younger brother, Dinesh Singh, became Nehru's private secretary before, significantly, becoming India's Minister for External Affairs in the 1960s at the time of Brajesh's death.
58 Taken from a letter from the Ambassador to India (Bowles) to the President's Special Assistant (Rostow), and attached Memorandum for the Record, 15 March 1967, *Foreign Relations of the United States 1964–68*, vol. 14, Soviet Union, online document 208, available at: www.state.gov/r/pa/ho/frus/johnsonlb/xiv.
59 Sehri Saklatvala, *The Fifth Commandment: Biography of Shapurji Saklatvala* (Salford, 1991), pp. 1–34; *Dictionary of Labour Biography*, vol. 6 (London, 1982), pp. 236–7.
60 Saklatvala, *Shapurji*, pp. 82–110.
61 *Ibid.*, p. 52.
62 Extract from MI5 Black List, vol. 21 (Indian Volume), no date, but possibly 1921, NAUK, Records of the Security Service (hereafter KV), 2/611.
63 Saklatvala, *Shapurji*, p. 89.
64 Extract from the *Labour Leader*, 18 Dec. 1918, in NAUK, KV, 2/611.
65 Report of the search of Saklatvala's rooms, 1 Dec. 1920, NAUK, KV, 2/613.
66 Extract from Scotland Yard report on Sinn Féin in Great Britain, 27 Oct. 1921, NAUK, KV, 2/614.
67 *Ibid.*
68 Report on Saklatvala, July 1920, NAUK, KV, 2/613. This is a reference to the Irish Labour Party and Trades Union Congress (ILPTUC) which he did attend.
69 Extract from Scotland Yard report on the Irish Self-Determination League, 16 March 1922, NAUK, KV, 2/614.

70 Home Office Warrant 'taken out by Scotland Yard on J. W. Hey or P. Keating', 24 June 1922, NAUK, KV, 2/614. Between 1919 and 1923 the Spanish army suffered unexpected defeats by the Moors in their last remaining colony, Spanish Morocco. Approximately 12,000 Spanish soldiers died. Reaction at home resulted in a *coup d'etat* by General Primo de Rivera: Stanley G. Payne, *Politics and the Military in Modern Spain* (London, 1967), pp. 187–207.

71 *Ibid.*

72 Despard is looked at in more detail in chapter two.

73 Saklatvala, *Shapurji*, pp. 144–5.

74 *Hansard*, vol. 159, 23 Nov. 1922, cols 115–16.

75 *Ibid.*

76 *Hansard*, vol. 159, 27 Nov. 1922, cols 359–63.

77 *Ibid.*

78 *Hansard*, vol. 159, 23 Nov. 1922, col. 113.

79 *Hansard*, vol. 159, 27 Nov. 1922, cols 359–63.

80 *Ibid.*

81 *Ibid.*

82 O'Halpin, *Defending*, p. 22; Saklatvala, *Shapurji*, pp. 201–2.

83 *Hansard*, vol. 161, 12 March 1923, cols 1043–8.

84 *Ibid.*, col. 1044.

85 Saklatvala, *Shapurji*, pp. 219–20.

86 O'Halpin, *Defending*, p. 22.

87 McDermott to Beram Saklatvala, 20 Feb. 1937, Saklatvala papers, BL, IOR, Manuscripts (hereafter MSS), EUR D 1173.

88 BL, OIOC, IOR, L/P&J/12/226; see also L/P&J/12/277; according to Reginald Bridgeman, the secretary of the British section of the LAI, by 1931 there were 17,000 members in India, with representatives in every province.

89 *New Leader*, 26 Aug. 1927.

90 *Ibid.*

91 John Callaghan, 'The heart of darkness: Rajani Palme Dutt and the British Empire – a profile', *Contemporary Record*, vol. 5, no. 2 (1991), p. 262.

92 Jean Jones, 'The League Against Imperialism', *Socialist History Society Occasional Paper Series*, no. 4 (London, 1996), p. 4.

93 Babette Gross, *Willie Munzenburg: A Political Biography* (Michigan, 1974), p. 185.

94 Jones, 'The League Against Imperialism', p. 6.

95 Many Labour Party members were to reach a crisis of conflict with regard to LAI membership. The Labour and Socialist International (LSI) opposed membership to the LAI, correctly believing it to be a communist front body. Matters came to a head in 1927 when British Labour Party members George Lansbury and Fenner Brockway had to choose between the LAI and their party. They both chose the latter. Brockway had earnestly maintained that the LSI's suspicions in relation to the LAI were unjustified. See *New Leader*, various articles throughout 1927.

96 Unsigned secret report on Munzenburg, 29 Sept. 1930, NAUK, KV, 2/772.

97 Garda report, 20 Aug. 1928, NAI, JUS, 8/682.

98 Note on Reginald Francis Orlando Bridgeman, 1935, BL, OIOC, IOR, L/P&J/12/277.

99 India Office Minute, 21 Dec. 1927, BL, OIOC, IOR, L/P&J/12/268. The MPs who were declared LAI members and were finally named on the revised list submitted to the India Office by IPI in 1928 were James Maxton, John Beckett, Ellen Wilkinson and Col. C. E. Malone. However, Wilkinson and Malone, like Brockway and Lansbury before them, had already resigned their membership of the LAI in late 1927, after the LSI had rejected any form of affiliation with it.

100 *Ibid.*

101 *Ibid.*; extract from Scotland Yard report contained in Vickery to Peel, 12 April 1928, BL, OIOC, IOR, L/P&J/12/268.

102 For some examples see Seán Cronin, *Frank Ryan: The Search for the Republic* (Dublin, 1980); Donal O'Drisceoil, *Peadar O'Donnell* (Cork, 2001); Milotte *Communism*; O'Connor, *Reds*, deals with the LAI in more detail than the others.

103 My thanks to Barry McLouglin for this information.
104 Extract of Scotland Yard report contained in Vickery to Peel, 12 April 1928, BL, OIOC, IOR, L/P&J/12/268.
105 *Ibid.* In theory Irish Free State citizens remained British subjects until 1935 with the passing of the Irish Nationality Act. In practice, however, the change came much earlier, when in April 1924 the Irish Government rejected British demands to put the term 'British subject' on passports: Mary Daly, 'Irish nationality and citizenship since 1922', *Irish Historical Studies* (May 2001).
106 Peel to Seton, 28 March 1929, BL, OIOC, IOR, L/P&J/12/280.
107 *Ibid.*
108 *Ibid.*
109 Vickery to Peel, 11 April 1929, BL, OIOC, IOR, L/P&J/12/385.
110 *Ibid.*; the article in question is reproduced in Appendix 1.
111 Bradley had extensive experience in India having been contracted by the Government of India as a civilian worker in the early 1920s. He joined the CPGB in 1923. In 1927 under Comintern orders he returned to India as part of a select group entrusted with the task of organising Indian labour and co-ordinating the activities of the Indian Left. He was one of three British subjects among the thirty-one trade unionists subsequently arrested and famously labelled the 'Meerut prisoners': Jean Jones, 'Ben Bradley: fighter for India's freedom', *Socialist History Society Occasional Paper Series*, no. 1 (London, 1994).
112 Bridgeman to Munzenburg, 19 March 1929, NAUK, KV, 2/515.
113 *Ibid.*; MI5 to Home Office, Foreign Office, IPI etc, 22 March 1929.
114 O'Connor, *Reds*, p. 142.
115 Garda report, 24 July 1929, NAI, JUS, 8/682.
116 Speeches at the congress consisted primarily of assaults on the British Labour Party, or more specifically James Maxton, by CPGB and Russian delegates furious with the British Labour Government's colonial policy.
117 Garda report, 24 July 1929, NAI, JUS, 8/682.
118 Jones, 'The League Against Imperialism', p. 13.
119 MI5 report on Munzenburg, 23 Jan. 1930, NAUK, KV, 2/772.
120 Jones, 'The League Against Imperialism', p. 16.
121 Garda report, 10 Nov. 1929, NAI, JUS, 8/682.
122 *An Phoblacht*, 30 Nov. 1929.
123 *An Phoblacht*, 13 Sept. 1930. The correct spelling of this name is 'Rienzi' and his full name was Adrian Kola Rienzi, a native of Trinidad, of Indian parentage. He was also known as Krishna Deonarine. He was affiliated to the LAI British section in the early 1930s. An article in *An Phoblacht*, 27 Jan. 1934, tells us how he became an appointed trustee of the Vithalbhai Patel fund for foreign propaganda on behalf of the Indian nationalist movement. He attempted to establish Indian newspapers in London, Dublin and New York. See also BL, OIOC, IOR, L/P&J/12/372.
124 Garda report, 25 Sept. 1930, NAI, JUS, 8/682.
125 Actual spelling 'Deonarine'; as already mentioned, Deonarine and Rienzi were one and the same person.
126 *An Phoblacht*, 4 Oct. 1930. This entire issue of *An Phoblacht* was devoted to Indian affairs. The front page is covered with illustrations depicting the 'imperialist terror in India', and throughout its pages are articles detailing the lives of prominent Indian nationalists and their fight against British rule.
127 *Ibid.*
128 Garda report, 25 Sept. 1930, NAI, JUS, 8/682.
129 BL, OIOC, IOR, L/P&J/12/270.
130 Patel and Despard were co-founders of the Indian–Irish Independence League and are discussed in chapter two.
131 History sheet of Don Philip Rupasanha Gunawardena, 7 July 1931, BL, OIOC, IOR, L/P&J/12/409.
132 *Ibid.*, extract from Scotland Yard report, 25 Nov. 1932.
133 *Ibid.*

134 *Ibid.*
135 Jones, 'The League Against Imperialism', p. 31.
136 *Ibid.*
137 Extract from Scotland Yard report, 8 Nov. 1934, BL, OIOC, IOR, L/P&J/12/274.
138 The man was Ryan and the woman was possibly Despard. I have not come across any references to this proposed Irish Congress other than a file contained in NAI, Department of External Affairs (hereafter DFA) titled 'World Congress of the LAI in Dublin, June 1935' which is unfortunately restricted.
139 Extract from Scotland Yard report, 19 Nov. 1924, BL, OIOC, IOR L/P&J/12/226.
140 *Ibid.*
141 *Ibid.*
142 *Ibid.*
143 *Ibid.*
144 Scotland Yard to Vernon Kell of MI5, 14 Dec. 1926, NAUK, KV, 2/614 and NAUK, KV, 2/515.
145 *Ibid.*
146 *Ibid.*
147 Extract taken from DIB 'Summary of Intelligence for the week', 22 Feb. 1927, NAUK, KV, 2/614.
148 Report on the LAI (British section), 15 Sept. 1931, BL, OIOC, IOR, L/P&J/12/271.
149 Scotland Yard report, 22 May 1930, NAUK, KV, 2/614.
150 *Ibid.*
151 *Ibid.*, SIS report, 22 Aug. 1929, contained in Saklatvala's MI5 file.
152 O'Connor, *Reds*, p. 171; see Richard English, *Radicals*, chapter 2, for more detailed reading on Saor Éire.
153 O'Connor, *Reds*, p. 171, and Neligan to Department of Justice, 5 May 1930, NAI, DT, S 5074B.
154 O'Connor, *Reds*, p. 173.
155 *Ibid.*, p. 175.
156 This is Indulal Kanayalal Yajnik, one of the founder members of the IIIL, who is discussed in more detail in chapter two.
157 Report, 'New Indian political group', 27 Sept. 1934, BL, OIOC, IOR, L/P&J/12/372.
158 For further reading on 'Republican Congress' see for example English, *Radicals*, chapters 3 and 4.
159 *Irish Press*, 5 Oct. 1934.
160 Extract from Scotland Yard report, 11 Oct. 1934, BL, OIOC, IOR, L/P&J/12/372.
161 Extract of Scotland Yard report, 20 Sept. 1934, *ibid.* Apparently the six Irish republicans who had committed themselves to attending the meeting did not show up.
162 Saklatvala, *Shapurji*, pp. 476–82.
163 Report on Nehru's visit to London, 12 Feb. 1936, BL, OIOC, IOR, L/P&J/12/293.
164 History sheet of V. K. Krishna Menon, 10 June 1940, BL, OIOC, IOR, L/P&J/12/323.
165 *Ibid.*
166 *Ibid.*
167 Patrick French, *Liberty or Death: India's Journey to Independence and Division* (London, 1998), p. 99.

CHAPTER TWO

V. J. Patel and the Indian–Irish Independence League

> Mr V. J. Patel, ex-President of the Indian Legislative Assembly, arrived in Dublin on Sunday morning. His first public act was to go to St. Stephen's Green, to the unveiling of the Madame Markieviecz Memorial by Mr de Valera. A white-clad, grey-haired figure, in a square white Gandhi cap, Mr Patel looked quite at home in this Dublin crowd, who pressed round to shake hands and wish India God-speed.[1]

Ireland and India in the late 1920s were tempestuous imperial appendages, both still in the Empire, while aggressively pulling on their reins. The newly established Irish Free State took the lead in Commonwealth affairs at the Imperial Conferences throughout the 1920s and played a significant role in the cooperation that ensued between the dominions to secure freedom of action on the world stage. Ireland had undoubtedly paved the way for the Statute of Westminster in 1931, and a mere ten years after the Treaty the Irish Free State had established diplomatic relations with the United States, France, Germany and the Holy See. Ireland had also been elected to a seat on the Council of the League of Nations and was concluding its own political and commercial treaties.[2] All of this was not realised without British concern and, inevitably, resistance; for example the registration of the Anglo-Irish Treaty with the Secretariat of the League of Nations in 1924 was achieved in the face of stiff British opposition.[3]

Those developments attracted attention, not only in Britain and Ireland but throughout the Commonwealth. In the wake of the Statute of Westminster a concerned Australian citizen, having noted how a New Zealand newspaper suggested that the legislation might have been more aptly called 'the Statute of Dublin', wrote to the Editor of *The Times* to give his perception of Ireland's recent track record:

> At previous Imperial Conferences every effort to bring about closer and more effective cooperation has been impeded by the presence of a Southern

Irish delegation only concerned to emphasise its independent status and to score points against the government of Great Britain.[4]

He was not to know that what he had described as 'the nagging separatist spirit of Southern Ireland [that had] been allowed to dominate the proceedings' was merely the lacklustre sibling of a more vibrant and vocal nationalist entity that would soon come to the fore. As the Cumann na nGaedheal Government was making constitutional advances in the imperial sphere, Eamon de Valera's concern grew. In 1926 he had formed Fianna Fáil and had re-entered parliamentary politics. The alarm that paralysed both the Irish Free State and British Governments at the prospect of a successful election campaign in the new party's favour was palpable. In fact, a blatant inability to accept such an outcome was epitomised by the British Government's initial plan of action after Fianna Fáil came to power in 1932; one of simply facing down de Valera until Cosgrave was returned to office.[5]

It was an ill-conceived plan, implemented in the hope of an outcome that would never happen, as de Valera remained in government for a further sixteen years. But in doing so he would gradually marginalise a section of his supporters – the more radical republicans who had been reduced to covert activities on the sidelines and kept under some restraint by the Cosgrave administration. Although some were disillusioned by what they saw as de Valera's 'selling out' in 1927 and entering Dáil Éireann, there is no denying that many believed his coming to power would bring to an end Ireland's membership of the British Empire.

In any event, many occupied themselves with their own revolutionary activities in the shape of the formation of various anti-imperialist and communist/left-wing organisations locally as well as collaboration with those in Britain and on the Continent.[6] During this period of increased activity things looked more encouraging to them. Indeed, de Valera had initially courted their favour by releasing political prisoners who had been rounded up by the previous regime. On the horizon there seemed to be a sea-change in favour of those who, only a few years previously, had bitterly lost a civil war fuelled by their dogmatic anti-imperialist principles. On 13 March 1932, soon after the successful Fianna Fáil election campaign, Charlotte Despard wrote from Roebuck House to a British communist friend, Charles Wilson. The more radical faction's hopes and expectations are evident in her words:

> You may have read about the desperate struggle through which we have been passing here. The people have triumphed, our brave prisoners were released, and tumultuously welcomed. After ten years of terrorism we have entered, we hope, upon a better era.[7]

In India in the late 1920s one thing dominated all else: the widespread anger and resentment at the all-white Simon Commission, which was duly boycotted by Congress. It was a reaction that surprised everyone by its ferocity.[8] David Petrie of DIB said in 1929 that the situation confronting the Government of India was the gravest he had known in the course of some twenty years' contact with revolutionary movements. He added, grimly:

> There has never been a time when speeches by supposedly responsible politicians can have afforded so much direct support and encouragement to the revolutionaries as since the appointment of the Simon Commission in November 1927 . . . it is enough to state that the Commission has been continuously and vehemently denounced as the final proof of England's perfidy and of her unalterable determination to exploit and to enslave Indians in perpetuity.[9]

Most significantly, however, it was under those intense circumstances that Jawaharlal Nehru was pushed to the fore of domestic politics, having returned from a two-year sojourn in Europe where he had liaised and learnt from many of those Indian revolutionaries in exile there. He passed a last-minute resolution in Congress calling not for dominion status but for complete independence. Things were heating up.

Back in Dublin, less than five years after entering parliamentary politics, de Valera had won an election and the revolutionary was to become President. The many similarities between both Ireland and India's nationalist struggles were acknowledged formally in 1932 with the formation of the IIIL by V. J. Patel, I. K. Yajnik, Mary (Mollie) Woods, Maud Gonne MacBride and Charlotte Despard.

Vithalbhai Javerbhai Patel

Vithalbhai Javerbhai Patel, like Mohandas Gandhi and Mohammad Ali Jinnah, came from the province of Gujarat. His younger brother, Vallabhbhai or Sardar Patel, was to become the better known of the two sibling agitators in India.[10] He returned from England in 1913 after passing his Bar exams, and became the main influence behind most of the civil disobedience campaigns of the 1920s. Sardar soon became known as Gandhi's 'deputy commander' and was one of his closest associates. The brothers were born in a village south of Ahmedabad into a family of *patidars*, or small landowners, with significant influence in the local community.[11] During the first three years of Indian independence, Sardar served as Deputy Prime Minister, Minister of Home Affairs, Minister of Information and Minister of State. He died in 1950, and it is generally believed that his death was hastened by the anxiety he experienced in coming to terms with Gandhi's death, two years earlier. Vithalbhai, on the other hand, had spent much time in the 1920s and early 1930s travelling throughout Europe and America in the combined role of publicist–speaker promoting Indian independence. As a result of his time abroad during these crucial years in Indian history he is a lesser-known figure in the Indian independence movement, this despite serving as the President of the Indian Legislative Assembly from 1925 to 1930. Vithalbhai died in 1933, long before India achieved its independence, and other Indian activists have since eclipsed the memory of the important role that he played in the nationalist struggle.

Patel visited Ireland on four occasions, the first of them in 1920. He had been in London since 1919 as secretary to the Indian National Congress deputation that travelled over for discussions in the wake of the Montagu–Chelmsford reforms.[12] Being in England at that time meant that he was able to hear and read at first hand about the founding of Dáil Éireann and the ensuing War of Independence. He travelled over to Dublin the following year, though his trip was not well documented and, other than a 1932 IPI report, where it is noted that 'when in Dublin in 1920 he was friendly [with] Michael Hayes TD and ex-Speaker of the Dáil', there is scant information about that visit.[13]

Patel's political profile was increased considerably after being narrowly voted in as President of the Indian Legislative Assembly in August 1925. Contesting that election had formed part of a new initiative by Congress to try to win control over the legislative bodies. It was considered a great success for the Bombay Swarajists and a menacing augury for the Government of India, as only two months previously Patel was advising his followers to 'prepare for an eventual battle, non-payment of taxes, and the conduct of an extensive propaganda campaign against British imports'.[14] He was unanimously re-elected in January 1927. By that stage Patel, in the eyes of the British, had re-emerged as a key Indian subversive and major source of aggravation. It was apparent that he was becoming more extreme in his outlook and he was considered part of the gradual rise of a radical left-wing element in India. He was associated with one of the few effective *satyagraha* (non-violent) campaigns in the 1920s, the Bardoli campaign.

During 1927–28 his brother Sardar organised a campaign against the payment of increased land levies in their hometown of Bardoli, Gujarat, where the Government had increased taxes following a poor harvest. The activists divided the region into sections, each with a commander overseeing activities. Every day 15,000 copies of a news sheet were circulated by horsemen and drums were beaten whenever bailiffs came to a village with the intention of impounding property. Disruption on such a scale alarmed the authorities greatly.[15] The Bardoli campaign was a success and the authorities finally restored the old revenue assessments. All of this meant that Vithalbhai's second visit to Dublin was duly noted, both by the contemporary press and by the British intelligence services. Also, given this recent experience in his home province of Gujarat, it is hardly surprising that he would soon liaise with figures from the left-wing of the Irish republican movement, people like Peadar O'Donnell and Frank Ryan who, simultaneously, thousands of miles away, were promoting similar radical tactics in the fight against British imperialism.

Patel arrived in London in April 1927 on a three-month visit in order to study the procedures of the House of Commons. During his time in London he is reported as having been a 'regular and unwearying visitor at the sittings of the House in the Distinguished Strangers' Gallery'.[16] It is perhaps surprising that little of note was recorded by IPI in relation to his visit to Ireland in July. This was most likely due to the apparently official purpose of his stay in Britain, to study democratic procedures. He was accompanied by the prominent left-winger Jamnadas Mehta, President of the All-India Railway Federation.

The main purpose of Mehta and Patel's visit to Ireland was to extend the latter's analysis of legislative bodies by encompassing trips to the country's two governments. We are told that the two Indians paid brief visits to the Irish Parliaments in Dublin and Belfast. Patel met W. T. Cosgrave and members of his ministry and then saw Lord Craigavon and other members of the Northern Irish Government. He did manage to grab some headlines while in Belfast. One report of his visit stands out: at a public function, he took it upon himself to tell those in attendance that Ireland was simply too small to afford the upkeep of two governments.[17]

The Times, commenting on Patel's 1927 research trip to the House of Commons (which was carried out 'largely at the public expense'), noted:

> Some of his actions on this visit to London seemed deliberately offensive, and there was a distinct change of tone and attitude when he returned to his duties in the Assembly . . . Indeed, the President showed a mischievous pleasure in giving rulings which had the effect of wrecking or retarding government legislation, and in manufacturing occasions for sharp disagreement with the leader of the House.[18]

This ostensibly increased agitation on the part of Patel was not an isolated occurrence. In April 1930 the situation in India had reached boiling-point. Gandhi had just finished his Salt March and this particular phase of civil disobedience was spreading rapidly, with other marches being staged throughout the country and the boycott on foreign cloth virtually complete. Anti-tax campaigns also flared up and many political leaders were arrested. Indian officials nationwide began to resign in protest, and Patel was one of 300 to do so in Gujarat alone.[19] He handed in his resignation as President of the Indian Legislative Assembly on 24 April 1930. In his letter to the Viceroy he stated:

> My people are engaged in a life-and-death struggle for freedom. The civil disobedience movement initiated by Mr Gandhi is in full swing. At such a juncture my proper place is with my countrymen, with whom I have decided to stand shoulder to shoulder, and not in the chair of the Assembly. Recent events have disillusioned my hope of a change of heart on the part of the British Government and a change of spirit in the day-to-day administration of India . . . In such a situation the only honourable, patriotic course is to sever my connexion with the Government of India and take my legitimate place in the fight for freedom.[20]

He was arrested and imprisoned in Coimbatore later that year for his involvement in the civil disobedience campaign, and was released in January 1931 due to ill-health, with fifty-one days of his six-month term left to serve.[21] He was arrested again the following year, but was again released early, in March 1932. From then on, the place that Patel was to occupy in India's fight for freedom would be abroad, publicising India's situation and soliciting favours as best he could. His position was to an extent forced on him, however, his failing health requiring him to attend a specialist health clinic in Europe. Nevertheless, his extensive experience travelling throughout the Continent, as well as his high profile, meant that he was able and determined enough not to let his health impinge on the task in hand.

Margaret Cousins

Patel encountered an Irish woman in India who, while campaigning for Indian independence, often drew attention to her experiences in Ireland by way of comparison. She was the one-time Irish suffragette Margaret Cousins, who had moved to India with her husband in 1915, though she had stayed in touch with her erstwhile Irish campaigners, with whom Patel would soon establish contact, Hanna Sheehy Skeffington and Charlotte Despard. Cousins became the first non-Indian member of the Indian Women's University at Poona. She was primarily a Theosophist and not initially involved in the campaign for Indian Home Rule, but as the domestic movement gained momentum she realised that she had a part to play.

By the late 1920s DIB became aware of her gradual politicisation and opened a file on her. It noted that 'her earlier history shows that she was an active militant suffragette and was sentenced to one month's imprisonment at Dublin in 1910 for breaking windows in the State Apartments and Prison Board offices, Dublin Castle'.[22] DIB was also aware that she appeared 'at first to have confined her activities to the cause of education and culture in India, and, it was not till 1929 that there was any open manifestation of her leaning towards politics'.[23] Crucially it was also noted that it was a trip to Ireland in 1929 that re-ignited her interest in campaigning. She 'lectured in Dublin and Belfast on "India Today" stating that Home Rule should be granted to India'.[24] On her return to India in 1930 she appears to have entered 'wholeheartedly into Gandhi's movement', beginning a *swadeshi* tour of India, dressed in *khaddar* (traditional Indian homespun cloth), during which she advocated the boycott of foreign goods. On the back of such activities DIB saw fit to begin intercepting her mail and it was noted that she attempted to get Irish activists like Hanna Sheehy Skeffington, 'a lady of known extremist tendencies', over to India to participate in an All-Asian Conference that she was organising. DIB noted that Cousins told Sheehy Skeffington that they could 'easily get into the country as visitors . . . and later disclose their credentials as Irish representatives for the Independence movement'.[25] Similarly, DIB picked up on Cousins' articulation of what she saw as a blatant connection between Ireland's and India's recent histories in her letter to the Tamil Nadu Congress Working Committee in November 1930. Offering her services to the body, she wrote:

> No woman who had worked for Home Rule in Ireland could logically do otherwise than proudly stand shoulder to shoulder with the Indian people in their similar great cause, especially in the days of repression and the worst of all ironies, repression by the Labour Government.[26]

In 1932 it came to the attention of IPI that Cousins was involved in the organisation of an Indian conference in Geneva at the beginning of that October. The impromptu group formed in order to bring the case for India's freedom to the attention of delegates to the Assembly of the League of Nations. Although the conference 'took place in a very orderly and unobjectionable manner', it did concern IPI that Cousins organised a 'deputation to wait upon de Valera on September 29th'. IPI's report, which was duly sent on to DIB in advance of Cousins's return to India, went on to note that even though 'de Valera apparently did not appreciate beforehand that this unofficial deputation was interviewing him in his capacity as President of the Council of the League of Nations', nonetheless this did 'not prevent his giving his views in his private capacity and at considerable length. He gave the deputation to understand that at one stage or another force would have to be employed in India.'[27]

The following December Cousins was back in India, and as a result of her increased involvement in the civil disobedience movement, and in particular an 'inflammatory' speech she gave at Madras in protest against the emergency ordinances that were introduced into the penal code, she was arrested and imprisoned for a year. In this famous speech she told her audience:

> While I was away, I read of the terrible sacrifices that you were called upon to suffer. I can only be ashamed to stand here before you as a member of the Western race – only I am one with you (*applause*) and that I belong to the Irish race (*applause*) which is heart and soul with you in this struggle. I had many talks with Mr de Valera in Geneva. I know that his heart beats with you every moment (*applause*).[28]

As I have pointed out, however, while her Irish heritage may have inclined her to empathise with those Indians she encountered while working for the swadeshi movement, Cousins was a Theosophist first and foremost, and she believed in the Gandhian doctrine of non-violence in the attainment of Indian independence. She reinforced that belief at a meeting in Nellore, in March 1931, when, addressing nearly 3,000 people, she stated that although

> she was proud of her Irish nationality [and] that her sympathies were with Indian national aspirations, India was using methods different from those used by Ireland in her fight against "John Bully" . . . and [she] concluded with an appeal to carry on the fight on economical lines.[29]

Meanwhile, some of her erstwhile suffragette co-campaigners in Dublin were awaiting the arrival of the Indian politician V. J. Patel.

The women of Roebuck House

Patel had cultivated some Irish contacts during his initial two short trips. However, it was his third trip in 1932 that culminated in the formation of the IIIL. The idea of setting up an Indo-Irish association clearly originated with Despard and Patel when they had met in London that spring.[30]

Despard was a long-suffering political activist and social reformer, a path she followed despite her aristocratic background, although without her family's support she would not have had sufficient income to provide for her comfortable way of life. She was involved in the campaign for the abolition of the workhouse, in the fight for women's suffrage, in the resistance to conscription and the crusade for a negotiated peace after the First World War, in the battles for Irish and Indian independence and finally, towards the end of her life, she became an ardent left-wing socialist and, eventually, a communist.[31] Despard was born and raised in Kent, the daughter of a Royal Naval Officer, although the family was of Irish descent. In particular, her involvement in the Irish campaign and her relocation to Dublin in order to become more active were to be a cause of much embarrassment to her family – her brother, Field Marshal Lord French, had been sworn in at Dublin Castle in May 1918 as Lord-Lieutenant, Viceroy of Ireland. Despard commuted regularly to London, and was in contact with various Indian activists there. In Dublin her main associate was fellow activist Maud Gonne MacBride. The two were close friends and lived together for some years in Roebuck House before Despard purchased a home in Eccles Street in the 1930s.

MacBride more than likely played a large part in fuelling the idea of the IIIL, as she too was a founding member, and she had already written much (and as early as 1900) on the plight of India.[32] She had established herself as a popular political writer and speech-maker long before her marriage in 1903 to (and well-publicised divorce from) Major John MacBride, a nationalist hero in 1916. She had spent some of her childhood at school in France, whenever her father, a widowed captain in the British Army, was not stationed in England or Ireland. She returned to France in 1887, soon after her father's death, and began a thirteen-year affair with the married French journalist Lucien Millevoye. During that time she founded the Paris Young Ireland Society, wrote for Millevoye's *La Patrie* and established her own journal, *L'Irlande libre*.[33] Her increased travelling and campaigning in Ireland and abroad (especially a number of successful tours of America) contributed to the demise of her relationship with Millevoye in 1900, and by spring 1904 she had married, borne the child of and initiated divorce proceedings from John MacBride. In the wake of the extensive publicity that followed her filing for divorce and with her popularity waning, she began to spend much of her time in France.

Her divorce appeal failed in 1908, and as her marriage separation verdict was deemed valid only in France she moved there on a more permanent basis in order to retain custody of her son Seán. In Uinseann MacEoin's *Survivors*, Seán MacBride recalls this time on the Continent and, in so doing, revives some early memories of his own burgeoning nationalism, when he relates that 'it was natural that I should be in touch with what was going on because while we lived in France, we had a lot of Irish and Indian revolutionary leaders of one sort or another passing through or staying with us'.[34] It is likely that the Indian nationalists he refers to were Sarat Chandra Bose, Madam Vikaji Rustomiji Cama, Sardar Singh Rana and Shyamji Krishnaverma. We know MacBride had dealings with Sarat Bose, brother of Subhas Chandra, from later correspondence between Irish and Indian nationalists.[35]

[61]

Cama was a woman who had a lot in common with Maud Gonne MacBride, a tireless political activist who set up and edited nationalist journals in Paris and Berlin. She had arrived in London in 1901 and, just as MacBride's time working with evicted families in Donegal and Irish political prisoners in the 1890s was a turning point in her life, Cama's experiences in Bombay during the plague epidemic of 1897 had made her bitterly anti-British.[36] Owing to increased surveillance by the British authorities, Krishnaverma, the famed founder of India House in London, relocated to Paris in 1907, Cama following suit in 1909.[37] While in Paris Cama, along with Rana, was smuggling revolutionary literature and explosives into India. It is likely that MacBride had already made contact with these heavyweight activists while in London, as Despard had been at the opening of India House in July 1905.[38] At any rate, in Paris in the early 1900s a loose network of anti-British Indian and Irish agitators was emerging, and this would form the backdrop for the formation of the IIIL some twenty years later.

The Woods family

By the late 1920s, MacBride was working in Dublin with another political activist who had Indian contacts, Mary (Mollie) Woods, who came from Monasteraden in County Sligo. In the early 1900s she went to work for Major General O'Farrell, Surgeon-General of the Royal Army Military Corps. She travelled with the family to Malta when he was appointed Governor there. It was probably as a result of her interaction with General O'Farrell that she became interested in Indian affairs, as during his service in the British Army he had spent much time on the subcontinent.[39] As with MacBride's son Seán, Woods' son Tony (who later served as staff captain in the IRA, was on the anti-Treaty side in the Civil War and in the Four Courts in June 1922) threw some light on this period of his mother's life:

> Altogether you could say she had quite a cosmopolitan existence for those days. Coming back to Ireland at the turn of the century, she married my father and from 1917 onwards, she was very involved with Maud Gonne MacBride, Mrs Despard and the ladies of Roebuck House.[40]

She married Andrew Woods, who although a strong Ancient Order of Hibernian man and a friend of Arthur Griffith, is described by his son as having been 'politically minded in a bookish way . . . while my mother was a political extrovert and a strong nationalist'.[41] The family settled at 131 Morehampton Road, around the corner from the O'Rahillys. Woods was a great friend of many IRA members at the time, and she was therefore privy to much that was going on in the revolutionary movement. At one stage during the War of Independence she was actively working for Michael Collins and purchased on his behalf a number of HQ houses, one at St Mary's Road, Ballsbridge, while the Woods' home on Morehampton Road was a well-known safe house.[42] Peadar O'Donnell recounted how, upon his escape from jail in 1923, he lay concealed between the rafters and slates in a dark corner of the Woods' attic as a raiding party searching for mutineers passed through the skylight.[43] Much later on and nearing his death, Ernie O'Malley stayed with the family also and was well regarded and admired by them all.[44]

The Woods family, with their staunch nationalist and anti-Treaty background, became involved in the left-wing republican movement in the years after the Civil War, especially Mollie who was a prominent member of the Women's Prisoners' Defence League. But she was also drawn to the anti-imperialist debate that raged throughout Europe in the aftermath of the First World War and in the wake of the Russian Revolution. This was an interest that no doubt flourished as a result of the many Indian connections she made during these years. Indeed her daughter Eileen married an Indian medical student, Tripura Charan Dey.

Dey was born in Calcutta in August 1900. His family owned a large retail store and so could send him to St Xavier's Jesuit College in Calcutta, and afterwards to Calcutta University where he became involved in politics. During that time he came to know many of the nationalist leaders, including Gandhi and Subhas Chandra Bose. Apparently as a result of his political activities his family was given a warning by the authorities and he decided that it would be in his and their best interests to leave India.[45] He arrived in London and travelled from there to Dublin where he enlisted as a postgraduate student at the Rotunda Hospital and TCD. While Eileen Woods was studying at the Royal Irish Academy of Music in 1930 she met Tripura and they fell in love. They married six years later in London and had their reception in the Indian restaurant Veeraswany's, off Piccadilly Circus. It was probably as a result of her daughter's relationship with an Indian activist that Mollie's interest in all things Indian increased, and her close friend Charlotte Despard had already made many Indian connections in London. Indeed it is possible (but not ascertainable) that Dey's decision to undertake postgraduate studies in Dublin as opposed to London was due to his having already met and been influenced by Despard, as she was actively promoting Irish colleges to Indian nationals in London as a less costly and more accommodating alternative.[46] Dey also was under surveillance on arrival in London because of his activities in India, something he no doubt realised himself; moving to Dublin, then, was perhaps the preferred option.[47]

[63]

Mollie Woods had achieved some kudos among nationalist activists in the early 1930s, as she travelled over to London in 1931 and met Gandhi during the second Indian Round Table Conference. Despard was more than likely the only other Irish activist to have met him, but much earlier, in 1914, and in her capacity as a suffragette. Gandhi had been impressed with her and is reported as having said: 'Mrs Despard herself is a wonderful person. I had long talks with her in London, and admire her greatly, and much appreciate her advocacy of "spiritual resistance".'[48] Gandhi would have had less time, for her, by now, quite blatant communist espousals.

During Woods's meeting with him, many years later, she invited him to stay with her in Ireland. Gandhi contemplated a visit to Dublin, where he would be put up in Tony Woods's family home in Blackrock. His reaction to the invitation was such as to solicit a small letter-writing campaign by Woods on her return. She wrote to 'all members of political and cultural life in Ireland', her expressed purpose being 'to ask you to be good enough to permit your name to be added to those who are extending an invitation to Mr Gandhi'.[49] She attempted to address all aspects of Irish opinion and to address the political divisions of the time when she stated in the final paragraph of her letter that

> arrangements are being made to take care of his few personal wants while here, but the friends here who are anxious to extend the invitation to him are very anxious that all sections of the community, representing all classes, will join in making his reception a national, rather than a section, reception.[50]

She enjoyed the help of the Jewish Fianna Fáil member and TD Robert Briscoe, who was at that time also in London. Briscoe continued attempts to persuade the Mahatma and his colleagues to travel over by writing to Gandhi's son, Devadas. The tone of Briscoe's correspondence would lead one to believe that very little inducing was necessary. Writing from London he had this to say to Woods:

> I was more than pleased at the fruitful result of your visit to London, not only of the pleasant visit to Gandhi, but also the fact of his accepting your invitation to be our guest in Ireland, which I felt sure would be the result after the preliminaries here had been gone through . . . I will, of course, expect you to be back again soon, as your help and assistance will be necessary for the completion of whatever arrangements are necessary. [51]

With the plans in progress the impending visit of Gandhi was announced exclusively by the *Irish Press*.[52] The paper told its readers that Gandhi 'thought it would be a tragedy not to visit the country now that he was so near' and that 'his love for Ireland is bound up with the admiration he has for the Irish, who had been an inspiration to India throughout their long struggle'. Gandhi is reported to have expressed the wish to meet people of various shades of political thought, and also to see the principal industries; and 'he intend[ed] to pay a visit to the different cities, including Belfast, and also to visit the Gaeltacht'.[53] However, the much-anticipated visit was not made and although the failure of the Round Table Conference possibly contributed to the cancellation of his Irish trip, there may have been other factors at play. As evidenced in the Woods letter soliciting support for the visit, Gandhi apparently harboured concerns about the political situation in Ireland, and the possible conclusions that would be drawn from his visit; whether by the Irish Government, the more radical republicans or, indeed, the British Government. According to the *Irish Press*, Gandhi wanted it

> to be made quite clear that his visit [was] for the purpose of seeing Ireland and the people of Ireland, and, he said, that if he thought that his visit might in any way be misunderstood or misinterpreted, he would hesitate before coming.[54]

This was perhaps not as surprising as it might seem. Unlike more radical Indian nationalists such as Patel, Bose and Nehru, from the outset Gandhi had not been a supporter of the Sinn Féin movement due to its violent methods, even though he understood the significance for India of Ireland's struggle. Although, in the end, Gandhi never made it to Ireland, barely a year later Woods again played a major role in the visit of a prominent Indian to Ireland and the formation of a new and dynamic Indo-Irish organisation.

Patel's 'dash to Dublin'

Throughout the spring of 1932 Charlotte Despard and her Indian associates in London were making preparations for Patel's third visit to Ireland that summer. No doubt de Valera's recent success in the Irish elections contributed to a renewed fervour and clamour on the part of radical nationalists in both London and Dublin to have Patel visit Ireland. Despard herself had played an active and somewhat novel part in the Fianna Fáil election campaign. Throughout February 1932 she was active in the constituencies of Cosgrave's ministers, where she could be found perched on a stepladder right beside their platforms with a speaking trumpet, urging the crowds to vote for de Valera. Out of respect for her age she was never moved.[55] In late spring she travelled over to London. Patel would soon disembark and she needed to prepare for the various meetings that would be held on his arrival.

[65]

IPI was busy tracking Patel's activities on mainland Europe and some of his utterances the previous April in Austria caused one particular agent to report in unusually alarmist tones:

> The lecture was an outrage on truth and fair-mindedness. The language used by Patel against the British Government and the whole British nation was often nothing short of scandalous. The audience was incapable of judging the real facts of the case or of the unprincipled scurrilousness of the attack.[56]

Clearly, Patel's manner and the tone of his speeches in Austria were being reported more meticulously as his planned itinerary became apparent. The reporter quite pointedly noted that Patel's next ports of call were said to be Ireland and the United States. Also, he was particularly concerned at how the lecture was delivered 'in a clever way' with a 'good deal of subtle innuendo . . . the whole thing clearly made a great impression on the audience'. He was also at pains to stress how he was seemingly unable to express just how worrying a subject he considered Patel to be, as 'a mere perusal of these notes (taken during the lecture) cannot convey a full impression of the lecturer's whole manner and attitude'.[57]

By June Patel had reached London where the Friends of India were organising a conference to coincide with his arrival. IPI estimated that attendance at the conference was around 250, most of whom were easily identified as belonging to one of a number of 'usual suspect' groups for a gathering of this calibre: 'half were Indians, and of the other half white women predominated, a small section of Englishmen at the back were very obviously communists'.[58] Charlotte Despard was in attendance and was considered one of the more distinguished guests. She was a staggering 87 years old and her indomitable reputation and punishing schedule had not abated in her old age. Having returned from a tour of Russia with other left-wing republicans, including Hanna Sheehy Skeffington in 1930, she was now a committed communist. Her presence on the platform was noted by the chairman (the novelist and playwright Lawrence Housman, a committed socialist and pacifist) as 'a happy augury, since she had been many times associated in championing "lost causes" . . . which had ultimately turned out to be victorious'. Despard spoke in strong terms in relation to India, saying that she was entirely opposed to co-operation with the British. Alluding to the recent Fianna Fáil victory in Ireland she stated that 'she had stood for no co-operation in the case of Ireland, and for no compromise and it looked there as if another cause many times considered as lost was going to prove victorious'.[59] She thought that India could take heart from recent happenings in Ireland and hoped for a closer relationship between the two countries. She then took the opportunity to announce to the crowd the possibility of the formation of an Indo-Irish organisation and IPI took great care to note the declared objectives:

It was hoped before long to found a Friends of India headquarters there [Ireland] from which uncensored literature could be distributed to the European Press. It would prove very helpful as England had always shown herself extremely sensitive to adverse criticism in foreign newspapers.[60]

Atma Kamlani, a Friends of India Association member, was in attendance at the conference and shortly afterwards she wrote to Woods:

Mr V. J. Patel will be leaving for Dublin on Saturday . . . he is not addressing meetings but will be seeing people in private. Mrs Despard talked to us here about starting an Indian organisation in Dublin. Mr Patel wants to explore the possibilities of this proposal. He has not yet decided where he is staying, but I have given him your address, as he will write to you to get some introductions if necessary. I hope you will give him any help that he will need.[61]

Patel arrived in Dublin for the third time late in the evening of 2 July 1932. He was accompanied by R. B. Lotwalla, who, the *Irish Independent* tell us, was 'the well known Indian diplomatic correspondent of the *Irish Independent*'.[62] IPI described Lotwalla, a merchant and newspaper director, as having been in 1923 a 'leading patron of communism in Bombay'. By 1927 it noted that he had

frequently come to notice on account of his socialist and communist activities . . . [He] is an intimate friend of Shapurji Saklatvala [and] recently visited Europe where he is said to have met C. P. Dutt and other undesirables, and it is furthermore reported that he was being used to bring back money to India for communists.[63]

Significantly IPI went on to say that even Lotwalla's daughter was involved in subversive activities:

Lotwalla's daughter is said to be a person of extreme views. Writing in the *Kranthi*, the Marathi organ of the Workers' and Peasants' Party, Bombay, this lady describes her recent visit to Ireland, where she 'interviewed several patriots who were fighting for national freedom'. She has come to the conclusion that in order to attain Swaraj, India must work on the lines of the Irish revolutionary movement.[64]

Five years later her father, along with Patel, would be in Ireland where they would meet revolutionaries and examine the situation for themselves. Their first public venture was on 3 July 1932, when they attended the unveiling of the Madame Markievicz Memorial by de Valera in St Stephen's Green. Also present were Minister Frank Aiken and Seán T. O'Kelly, and Maud Gonne MacBride. Senator Laurence

O'Neill, while introducing the Indian activist said that Patel, 'like themselves, was fighting for the independence of his country'.[65] Patel is described in the press as 'a striking and picturesque figure in white' who 'on being introduced to the gathering received a rousing welcome'.[66] IPI noted that when asked to comment on the Irish situation Patel said that 'England was now showing her intentions in a way that would lead India to see that little benefit would be obtained by negotiations'.[67] This was presumably an off-the-cuff comment referring to the ongoing Anglo-Irish correspondence in relation to the land annuity repayments due to the British Exchequer which de Valera decided to retain on coming to power. This particular story was receiving extensive coverage in the media for the duration of Patel's visit.

The British Government was concerned about the Patel–de Valera meetings during these trips to Ireland. It was something that William Peters, the British Trade Commissioner in Dublin and the only British representative in Ireland, had reported on. Although doing so was outside of his remit, Peters tried earnestly to keep the British Government's sparsely populated in-tray on de Valera's intentions up to date. Commenting on the Patel–de Valera friendship he had this to say in July 1932:

> It rather emphasises the fact that many of us have urged, that the Congress Party are largely founding themselves on the methods by which the Irish Free State secured practical independence of Great Britain.[68]

Enclosed with this report, was a clipping from the Irish *Daily Telegraph* which noted that 'Patel, former Speaker of the Indian Legislative Assembly, who has been in England for the last two weeks, left London suddenly for Dublin on Saturday'. Unaware that the visit had in fact been planned well in advance, it went on to say: 'it is understood that he went in response to an urgent invitation from Mr de Valera'. Patel's 'dash to Dublin' was also considered something of a revelation by the *Irish Independent* which devoted an entire page to the report, saying that 'his departure caused a minor sensation in Indian circles in London'. The various possibilities as to the actual purpose of his visit were considered:

> Mr Patel was accompanied by Mr Lotwalla, the well-known Indian merchant . . . rumours and stories are current that his mission is to establish an Indo-Irish trade relationship. Mr Lotwalla has a great influence among the Bombay merchants who have totally boycotted British goods in India.[69]

So the possibilities of establishing a more formal and pragmatic relationship between the two countries was brought to the public's attention.

Something along the lines of an IIIL was possibly being suggested here, if not yet expressly publicised. The article goes on to offer another possible reason for the trip, one which corresponds with what Despard had been promoting to Indian students in England:

> It is a problem that in England there are 2,000 Indian students trying to obtain higher degrees in different subjects. They spend something like £50,000 annually. They can obtain the same higher degrees in medicine and engineering etc from the Dublin University, while at the same time spending a less amount, as the cost of living is cheaper than in England. Will Mr Patel discuss this problem . . . ?[70]

However, the final possibility put forward in this, quite extensive, coverage of Patel's visit to Dublin, is perhaps the most intriguing:

> But the most interesting story is that President de Valera may suggest the name of Mr Patel to be included in the proposed tribunal to settle the Irish question. There may or may not be any truth in these stories. Only Mr Patel or Mr de Valera can clear the whole situation.[71]

As Lotwalla, Patel's travelling companion and colleague, was apparently the source for this piece, in his capacity as Indian diplomatic correspondent of the *Irish Independent*, we can take it for granted that this is a reliable account of the Indian activist's expressed intentions while in Dublin. And if that was the case, further investigation is warranted into whether Patel was either asked or considered by de Valera to sit on a Commonwealth Tribunal to settle the escalating Anglo-Irish difficulties. And there is evidence to suggest that Patel, apart from facilitating the establishment of the IIIL, did indeed have another, less evident, purpose in visiting Dublin at this time.

Patel's biographer Ray Chowdhury tells us in his 1934 book that de Valera 'recognised in Vithalbhai an astute, subtle, far-seeing and diplomatic politician'.[72] He stated that de Valera asked Patel at this 'urgent meeting' if he would agree to be his appointee if arbitration before a Commonwealth Tribunal on the question of the retention of the land annuities was to go ahead on the insistence of the British Cabinet. If this was so, and the timing fits in neatly with de Valera's correspondence on the issue with J. H. Thomas, the Secretary of State for the Dominions, de Valera was clearly trying to avoid problems like those encountered during the work of the 1924 Boundary Commission and the appointment of Justice Feetham as chairman.[73] (At the time it was generally believed that Feetham, because of behind-the-scenes pressure from the British, did not have the Irish Free State's best interests at heart.) Thomas had insisted that in the case of the non-payment of the land annuities, any arbitrator put forward should again, as with the Boundary Commission, be from the Commonwealth. In suggesting

Patel, de Valera would be doing just that, as well as proposing someone who was blatantly biased in his favour, something that would not have escaped the Cabinet's attention. The minutes of a meeting held between de Valera and the Prime Minister Ramsay MacDonald on 15 July 1932 show de Valera playing his cards close to his chest in relation to the appointment of particular arbitrators. Yet, in the light of this new information about the talks with Patel the previous week, one cannot help but read more into de Valera's protestations:

> He added that even if there was a name within the Empire which would be acceptable to him he could not now possibly propose or accept such a name, as it would be said that he was going back upon his demand for freedom of choice. As a matter of fact, he had no such name in mind.[74]

Information in the National Archives may suggest, rather than confirm, that de Valera did, at some stage, have Patel in mind. A long list of questions concerning Patel's career were sent from the Department of the President to the Department of External Affairs for verification. It was duly forwarded to John Dulanty, the High Commissioner in London, who promptly responded in great detail.[75] It also seems quite probable that de Valera at the very least had discussed with Patel the issue of the land annuities. Patel had experienced a similar set of circumstances in his own province of Gujarat. As already mentioned, in 1927–28 Patel's brother Sardar, a lawyer, organised a campaign against the payment of increased land taxes in their home town of Bardoli. That campaign had been successful, with the authorities finally restoring the old revenue assessments. Patel's biographer maintains that his name was suggested and was not acceptable to MacDonald who 'knew Vithalbhai would be far too independent . . . and the least likely to be pliable to the subtle influences of his wily diplomacy'.[76] De Valera is said to have then asked Patel to recommend other suitable Indian candidates, and

> Vithalbhai unhesitatingly advised the Irish President to propose Jawaharlal Nehru and Subhas Chandra Bose together in his place [but that] the names proposed could hardly be expected to receive more favourable consideration at the hands of MacDonald who had no illusions about their general suitability for this purpose and about their political inclinations.[77]

Chowdhury can be considered a reliable source as he was working closely with Patel and other prominent Indian activists. He had arrived in England in 1929 and began working as a Reuters correspondent. He took advantage of his position to gain extensive coverage for the cause of Indian independence and 'appears to have used Reuters to give publicity in India to the doings in this country of Saklatvala, G. S. Dara's

Gandhi Society and I. K. Yajniks' Indo-Irish League (Dublin)'.[78] By 1933 IPI had opened a file on him and was considering an attempt to curtail his activities by hinting to certain publishers that his intentions were questionable and suggesting that he be watched, even though Clauson, Assistant Private Secretary at the India Office, noted: 'presumably Fleet Street has its own Secret Service'.[79]

In any event, the deterioration of Anglo-Irish relations meant that Commonwealth arbitration did not take place. Crucially, Patel's visit and talks with de Valera coincided with the British Government's decision to consider financial resolutions to counteract the non-payment of the land annuities, culminating in the Special Duties Bill, passed the following week. The Bill provided for the possibility of imposing duties of up to 100 per cent on Irish imports, and was followed by a prolonged Anglo-Irish trade war which had long-term effects on the Irish economy. However, in the immediate aftermath of this decision, a somewhat vexed de Valera would not be seen to compromise on arbitration by putting forward a name from within the Commonwealth, Patel's or otherwise.

Patel had a few other important engagements while in Dublin. As already noted, he met privately with de Valera twice in Leinster House, once on 5 July, when the meeting was said to have lasted four hours, and again the next day when it lasted for two. It was stated that the two men had discussed 'the question of the future relations of India and the Saorstát . . . and . . . the possibility of trade development between the two countries was under consideration'.[80] His hotel room at the Shelbourne became a meeting place for political figures of the day. Other than those obviously involved in organising his visit, like Maud Gonne MacBride, Despard and Woods, he entertained a selection of other prominent left-wingers such as Seán MacBride, Frank Ryan and Peadar O'Donnell.

He also had an unplanned but nonetheless pleasant encounter with an old friend, Commander Kenworthy (later Lord Strabolgi), who also happened to be in Dublin. The First World War naval commander was elected a Labour MP in 1926 and held office as the opposition Chief Whip in the House of Lords from 1938 to 1942. On his death in 1953 he was described in *The Hindu* as 'a particular friend of Indian freedom. Nobody in the Labour Party was more passionately devoted to that cause.'[81] Kenworthy was also a writer, and in 1931 had published a book titled *India: A Warning*.[82] He and Patel bumped into each other in the foyer of the Shelbourne. The *Irish Press* reported the meeting:

A happy reunion took place . . . yesterday when Commander Kenworthy and Mr V. J. Patel . . . met by chance. They are both old friends. They met before the Round Table Conference in London last year and also at the meeting of the Indian Legislature Assembly some years ago. 'We are both in a struggling country,' said Commander Kenworthy as he shook the hand of Mr Patel, who returned with a nod. 'Yes, and India is struggling too.'[83]

In an interview with the socialist journalist and writer R. M. Fox (husband of the children's author Patricia Lynch) for the *Irish Press*, Patel explained to the Irish public what he meant by his rejoinder to Kenworthy.[84] Referring to the overcrowded conditions in the jails, he claimed that criminals were set free in order to accommodate political prisoners: 'Everything is suppressed in India', he said, 'but everything goes on – meetings, picketing, Congress organisation and papers. The police attack men, women and children with their laities – metal ringed bamboo canes.' He considered the tactics adopted by the British to be born simply of irritation: '[W]e are too many', he said, 'the British cannot cope with us. They have one to every million of our people. It plays on their nerves and [they] resort to brute force, but they cannot crush out India's population.' Significantly, he was asked about the religious divisions reportedly emerging, to which he responded in tones reminiscent of de Valera in pre-partition Ireland:

[I]t is no problem . . . it would disappear with the attainment of our freedom. In the big towns antagonisms are skilfully engineered, but there is nothing real in it. India will gain freedom through suffering. Ireland had to suffer during their centuries of struggle.[85]

Finally he took pains to note the success of the campaign in India to boycott British goods, and the impact it was having in the struggle against British rule:

In the meantime they have lost the Indian market. It is rapidly becoming more expensive for Britain to hold India than to lose her. I am inclined to believe that within ten years Britain will have left India and we shall be free.[86]

Throughout his time in Dublin Patel was encouraging the Irish population to take up the boycotting of British goods that was proving so successful in India. Again, as with the land campaign, mirror-image tactics had been adopted in Ireland with the beginning of the economic war. Aspects of the Irish equivalent, specifically those adopted by the left-wing IRA, were more aggressive, such as the campaign against Bass beer.[87] Indeed, a few months after Patel's visit *An Phoblacht* carried advertisements for a new shop which could facilitate those wishing to boycott British goods in their entirety, the Indian Stores on Dame Street. An advertisement for the shop stated simply: 'Tea Direct From India. Buy Irish First, Then Buy Indian.'[88] The owner, interviewed by an

An Phoblacht journalist shortly after the shop had opened,[89] said that soon after his advertisements appeared in the paper his stock of tea had sold out, 'there having been a run upon it all last week'. He proudly told the paper that 'his tea pays no British duties, being supplied direct; it is cheap and excellent'. He hoped to stock Irish beet sugar as soon as possible, but in the meantime was stocking Czechoslovakian crystal sugar. He also sold Irish honey and Indian sweet meal. The industrious owner was apparently 'a relative by marriage of Mahatma Gandhi and wears proudly his Gandhi cap'. He hoped 'shortly to have a stock of Indian flags, portraits of Gandhi and other Indian leaders as well as Indian literature, curry, pickles, rice and other products'.[90] The report ends ominously with the information that the manager had run into some trouble with the British authorities as a result of his activities: 'British agents have already made themselves busy, they have called to the shop and asked that Gandhi's picture in the window not be displayed, making veiled threats. But Indians in Dublin are not worrying'.[91] An account of this nature would, no doubt, have aroused the interests of *An Phoblacht*'s readership.

On the evening of 8 July 1932, Patel attended a meeting of the Irish section of the LAI in College Green. The *Irish Press* estimated attendance at around 3,000 and gave great weight to Patel's presence when it reported that 'the Indian Nationalist leader, in his picturesque dress and Gandhi cap, was the central figure . . . loud cheers rang out as soon as [he] was recognised'.[92] As was seen in chapter one the LAI was a communist front organisation and this is a prime example of its ability to woo to the one platform an impressive gathering of non-communist nationalist agitators of international renown. A resolution was proposed by Frank Ryan, and seconded by Maud Gonne MacBride, sending greetings and a pledge of support from the citizens of Dublin to the people of India in their struggle for complete independence and separation from England. Regarding the resolution, MacBride said that she was

> very glad to second it because its carrying into effect was of great national importance. India free was Ireland free . . . Sympathy without support was little use. A way which each individual could help India was by the boycott of British goods. India was carrying out a great boycott of English goods, and hitting English trade very hard. Ireland is said to be England's best customer, it is up to us to make her her worst customer.[93]

Although Patel did not speak at the meeting (probably due to his precarious health at the time), he was prominent on the platform, and Ryan, while proposing the resolution 'asked Mr Patel to take back with him a message to India that the people of the nation should profit from the example of Ireland'. Patel later told an *Irish Press* journalist that he 'was delighted with the enthusiasm of the crowd'.[94] A copy of the resolution passed found its way into Patel's IPI file in London, where agents were diligently recording the movements of any LAI-sponsored activity in Europe.[95] In the weeks following, IPI again noted that 'there is evidence that the LAI is very anxious to develop contacts in Ireland'.[96]

The formation of the IIIL

A crucial behind-the-scenes aspect of Patel's stay in Dublin was making arrangements for the foundation of the Indo-Irish organisation mooted in London a few weeks earlier, and this he did with MacBride, Despard and Woods when he was not on public engagements. Unfortunately there is little record of these meetings, many of which happened late at night in MacBride's St Stephen's Green residence, but it seems clear from the correspondence that continued between Mollie Woods and Patel, after he had left, that a certain amount of ground had been covered and they had indeed laid the foundations for the establishment of an Indo-Irish political association, which was instigated the following month and publicised in *An Phoblacht*:

> In pursuance of the suggestion of Mr V. J. Patel, a prominent leader of the Indian National Congress, and an ex-President of the Indian Legislative Assembly who has recently been in Dublin, a small meeting of some Indian and Irish friends of Indian Independence was held this evening in Republican Offices, 12 St. Andrew St., to consider the steps necessary for organising a permanent committee here.[97]

The 'usual suspects', MacBride, Despard and Woods, were joined by, among others, Tripura Dey, I. K. Yajnik, Moss Twomey and Mrs Peadar O'Donnell. After some preliminary discussion it was resolved to inaugurate a body called the 'Indian-Irish Independence League' which would

> work by every possible means to secure the complete independence of India and Ireland, and to achieve the closest solidarity between the Irish and the Indian masses in their common struggle against British imperialism.[98]

IPI was quick off the mark in noting these activities even before the IIIL was formally established or publicity began in *An Phoblacht*. Vickery thought them significant enough to write a detailed letter on the topic to Horace Williamson, head of DIB. He had already written in relation to Patel's intended trip to Dublin, but now had cause for further elaboration:

In my letter on the subject of V. J. Patel's visit to Dublin, I mentioned the suggestion made by Lotwalla for the setting up of an Indian publicity bureau in Dublin. The scheme, which has gained the approval of de Valera's party, appears to foreshadow the formation of a society some-what on the lines of the Friends of India.[99]

The Friends of India was a successful and popular initiative in London, and Despard, as seen earlier, was quite involved in its activities. Vickery noted how she and Woods were busy disseminating Friends of India literature in Dublin. IPI was aware even at this early stage that Seán MacBride and Peadar O'Donnell were playing a large part in facil-itating the establishment of the IIIL:

Seán MacBride and Peadar O'Donnell, the Editor of *An Phoblacht*, are helping (the former is making one or two changes in the constitution) and it is said that a public meeting will be called as soon as the composition of the committee has been completed.[100]

Crucially, however, IPI was especially concerned about Indian radicals becoming involved and noted that 'while the Indian most in evidence is Dr Tripura Charan Dey, I. K. Yajnik went over to Dublin on July 18th . . . [and] was busying himself with the press, visiting *An Phoblacht* and the *Irish Press* with a view to propaganda'. Vickery was particularly sat-isfied to have located Dey and to be in a position to update Williamson on his activities. Williamson evidently still considered Dey quite objec-tionable due to his activities in India, although he was unable to find any proof of Dey's alleged subversive credentials other than his liaising with Irish radicals:

It is interesting to find Tripura Charan Dey . . . working in this connec-tion: you will remember that I was unable to find any confirmation of your theory that he and Dr Amiya Kumar Bose[101] were concerned in the smuggling of arms to India. This is the first we have heard of any activ-ity at all on Dey's part.[102]

Some domestic partisan politics also came to the fore in this report, Vickery noting that Yajnik had told Lotwalla (who, along with Patel, had been ingratiating himself with de Valera) that 'Peadar O'Donnell, who was their best ally, thought that they should organise on the broad-est possible basis, so as to ensure the co-operation not only of de Valera's party, but of the Trade Unions also'.[103]

It seems that Maud Gonne MacBride in particular was concerned that a lack of resident or prominent Indian members would hinder the progress of the organisation or, at the very least, affect its credibility.[104] In order to prevent such developments Patel decided to send over Indulal Kanayalal Yajnik from London.[105] Yajnik, as we have seen, had already been in Ireland the previous July when he attended the first meeting of those interested in founding the IIIL, and had made a special contribution to *An Phoblacht* about the campaign to boycott British goods.[106] Now he would return on a short reconnaissance mission to document the IIIL's activities but, as Patel told Woods, 'later he will settle down there and devote himself exclusively to the work of the League . . . he is a good organiser and a keen student of politics and most suitable for our work'.[107]

Yajnik, himself a Gujarati socialist, had been involved in the *satyagraha* campaign with the Patel brothers, and earlier, in 1923, had shared a cell with Gandhi in Yerwada Prison. He was a member of the Workers' and Peasants' Party and a close associate of Lotwalla. It is not clear when he had travelled over to Europe but more than likely he had been involved in the Round Table Conferences and stayed on working with the group of Indians who had established an Indian National Congress section based in London. Before Yajnik had left on his Irish assignment he prepared by writing to the Irish Self-Determination League of Great Britain and to the Sinn Féin representative in London, Joseph Fowler.[108]

It was possibly Shapurji Saklatvala who had put Yajnik in touch with him, as Saklatvala had corresponded with Fowler and had spoken at various meetings organised by the Irish Self-Determination League throughout the 1920s.[109] Fowler ran a bookshop in Bedford Row, central London, and was a good friend of both Despard and MacBride, so Yajnik was keen to meet up with him for some advice before he travelled across to Ireland. Yajnik arrived in Dublin in mid-September 1932 and had in his possession a letter of introduction to Mollie Woods from Patel. He had been preceded two weeks earlier by other prominent Indians who became involved in the IIIL, Raja Audesh Singh and his wife, accompanied by a Mr and Mrs Mehta. Patel had also written the Singhs a letter of introduction to Woods:

> I have great pleasure in introducing my friend, Mr Singh who is coming to your town for having [*sic*] a major operation performed on his wife. Mr Singh is a devoted nationalist and a staunch follower of the Indian National Congress . . . I trust that you will treat him with the full confidence he deserves, and introduce him to our circle of friends . . . Two other friends of mine Mr and Mrs Mehta are accompanying Mr and Mrs Singh. You can safely rely on them too and treat them similarly.[110]

As noted in chapter one, Audesh Singh, the Raja of Kalakankar, was well known to the British authorities and although his motives for travelling to Ireland may have been innocent enough, given the poor health of his wife, soon his brother, the well-known communist Brajesh Singh, was commuting to Dublin and they were all helping with the running of the IIIL and staying with the Woods family. Yajnik's intentions in helping with the foundation of the IIIL, however, were more overt.

By October, with Yajnik's involvement, the IIIL's constitution had been amended, finalised and published. The object of the IIIL was 'to help by every means possible to secure the complete national, social and economic independence of the people of India and Ireland', and there followed a list of methods which should be adhered to in order to fulfil that objective. The first two declared methods were: '1. Organising in Ireland and where else possible a complete boycott of British goods and concerns. 2. Establishing an Indian Information Bureau to spread the truth about the Indian struggle, and to counteract imperial lies generally.'[111] It could be said that in the wake of Patel's visit these two initial aims had been somewhat successfully followed through. There was increased coverage of the Indian situation in *An Phoblacht* due to the formation of the IIIL and Yajnik's and O'Donnell's collaboration. Cooperation with Irish republicans involved with the IIIL saw Indian nationalist journalists, such as Pulin Behari Seal and Ray Chowdhury, in addition to Yajnik, find an outlet for their anti-imperialist writings. Campaigns to boycott British goods had been instigated in Ireland at various stages since the War of Independence, and these were revived with gusto after the onset of the economic war. But arguably it was the IIIL's initiative in publicising the immensely successful Indian boycott campaign that provided renewed vigour for the Irish version. It was a ploy that had the added benefit of attracting people of a non-socialist, republican background who would be motivated less by partisan domestic politics and more by altruistic, if essentially anti-imperialist, principles.

The other methods to be adopted were 'taking steps necessary to link up the Indian and Irish movements in order to make effective the fight against the common opponent – the British Empire' and 'exploring all possibilities of [establishing an] effective trade alliance between Ireland and India, in order to defeat British imperialism in its attempts to isolate and attack India in the economic field'.[112] To some extent the former had already been achieved through the activities of the LAI.[113] The final, and more ambitious, aspiration with regard to formally establishing a trade alliance would rear its head again in the years to come. It appeared to be the most obvious and pragmatic development for this bond, the maturation of a nationalist alliance into a soon-to-be post-independence intra-Commonwealth relationship that might cater towards reciprocal preferential trade agreements. However the difficulties in attaining such a goal were many and somewhat obvious, with geographical distance being the major obstruction to such developments.

It is interesting to note that Yajnik had clearly developed a love of all things Irish as a result of his connections with these Irish revolutionaries, and on his return to India in the mid-1930s was producing pamphlets about the Irish movement for distribution there. His papers contain reams of notes and pamphlets depicting various periods of Irish history as far back as the ninth century. He even produced and distributed a booklet about the Gaelic Athletic Association. Yajnik introduced this brochure by giving a detailed breakdown of the other booklets he would soon produce about the Irish independence movement. His pamphlet-writing was somewhat prolific.

> I send out this little Brochure on the Irish Athletic Movement as the first of a series of about a dozen pamphlets on the various phases of Ireland's fight for cultural, economical and political emancipation. The series will give the principles, policies and programmes as proclaimed by the makers of modern Ireland, – Thomas Davis, on the national language and culture; James Finton Lawlor, on the peasants' struggle; Michael Davitt, the founder of the land league; Arthur Griffith, the father of Sinn Féin; Patrick Pearse, on national independence and education and James Connolly on the freedom of the working class. I sincerely trust that the words of the Irish masters will ring in the ears of my fellow countrymen and evoke a response in their hearts.[114]

Patel's last ventures

Hugh MacGregor, the information officer at the India Office, noted that Patel, who returned to England in late July 1932, had been 'holding forth in the smoking-room of the National Liberal Club to all and sundry including very many Indians'.[115] MacGregor was aware that Patel's next stop was to be the US, and he wrote a long and somewhat tetchy letter on the subject to Angus Fletcher, the director of the British Library of Information in New York. MacGregor clearly thought Fletcher needed to be properly forewarned in preparation for Patel's visit. Referring to Patel as 'the evangel' throughout the correspondence, he began sardonically:

> I gather that the views you may have to combat on his lecture tour in the USA will include a description in glowing terms of the character of the Indian people, their love of law and capacity for administration, their high principles, their self-restraint, simplicity and idealism, their courtesy, their benign social life and their industry. Their very virtues, of course, have been traded on by England and this country has always held India for the self-interest of Englishmen, providing a market for English goods and a gigantic establishment for English administrators. The Englishman in India has always been a soldier to crush the people, a law-giver and

administrator merely to suppress native interests and native initiative, a foreign czar to maintain his superiority by insolent contempt of the people he rules. Hence the division created in the vast country to secure this power. Hence his utter disregard of his own treaties . . .[116]

The correspondence continued in this vein for a further two pages. If not quoting directly from Patel's own speeches, MacGregor's tirade was worthy of consideration for inclusion in some of Patel's future talks, had he the opportunity to see the correspondence for himself. MacGregor concluded:

So there you are. You see what you and the USA may be in for. But I think you already have in your lockers sufficient and powerful enough ammunition to scatter this sort of stuff . . . He has it in mind that America might make the cancellation of England's war debt conditional on the recognition by England of the rights of India to independence. There is likely also in present circumstances, to be a bid for Irish-American support.[117]

On 18 September 1932 Patel left Southampton for New York.[118] He was about to commence a propaganda tour of America, something he had been meaning to do for many years but which ill-health had prevented. IPI noted that 'Mrs M. J. Woods, 131, Morehampton Road, Donnybrook near Dublin, who is a member of the Committee of the Indian–Irish Independence League, has sent letters to Irish Republican clubs in the United States of America, to introduce Patel'.[119] It is believed that the final incentive to embark on a trip came from de Valera, who not only assured Vithalbhai that he would assist him with his plans if necessary, but is said to have helped draw up the entire programme of his visit.[120] The interlude was similar to de Valera's American tour: a campaign to place India's cause at the forefront of the American press and to attempt to gain further recognition of India's right to political independence.

Evidence of de Valera's direct involvement in helping with the trip is found in his correspondence with Joseph McGarrity, a leading Clan na Gael figure based in New York. He wrote to McGarrity in August: 'Mr Vithalbhai J. Patel desires to get in touch with you during his stay in the United States. I enclose particulars of his career . . . I should be glad if you would see Mr Patel.'[121] McGarrity replied assuring de Valera that he would be honoured to meet with Patel and considered it his duty 'to be of any service I can to him on his mission here'. Interestingly McGarrity later verified an observation made by MacGregor regarding division among the ranks of Indian revolutionaries resident in the USA, a situation not dissimilar to those found amongst Clan na Gael and Irish activists there at various stages.[122]

MacGregor thought that Patel's reliance on Ghose, 'who seems to have got in first and nobbled the evangel to some extent', would result in his alienating other Indian camps there who 'did not all like our Mr Ghose'.[123] The individual referred to here was the well-known Indian activist Salindranath Ghose, who had been in the USA since 1917, at which time he had met up with a group of Indian revolutionaries, popularly known as the Ghadr movement.[124] As early as 1920 IPI was aware that he was writing articles for the Irish republican press and was 'a firm believer in the Indo-Irish link'.[125] Ghose was an advocator of physical force; as such he was considered very dangerous by the British authorities and his activities in the USA were closely scrutinised. By 1929, when it was thought that he was going to attempt to return to India, it was considered

> perfectly clear from the information which we receive regularly of Ghose's grandiose schemes, which are largely inspired by his Irish-American and communist friends, for a formal declaration of India's independence coupled with the opening of an Indian legation in Washington, that he is not likely to cease revolutionary activity on his return to India.[126]

The note concludes that it would be highly preferable to have Ghose stay in the USA where, 'fortunately, owing to the reputation for dishonesty which he has acquired amongst his country men in the USA, his power for harm is limited'.[127] Bearing this in mind, it is interesting to note McGarrity's follow-up note to de Valera detailing the strange meeting that ensued with Patel in New York. McGarrity, in a rushed, handwritten note, informed de Valera that he had

> called by appointment . . . on Mr Patel at the hotel, we announced our presence on the floor on which Mr Patel had his rooms. Mr Groshe [Ghose] an Indian Hindoo [sic] took message and asked us to wait 5 or 10 moments. We waited for 45 minutes and called again, were admitted, and found Mr Patel did not know we were waiting and seemed suspicious of Mr Ghose for failing to announce us, told us to communicate direct to himself as he was mistrusting everyone . . . even of hotel employees. Said he was for no half way measures and . . . asked for cooperation of our people here with India against the British. I talked of our cause.[128]

Clearly Patel had grown weary of Ghose's overbearing manner and involvement in his US tour, and it was not long before his services were dispensed with.[129]

During the course of his six-month stay in the US Patel sought an audience with the President, presumably to attempt to discuss Britain's Indian policy. Such a solicitation was considered dangerous enough by Ronald Lindsay, British Ambassador in Washington, especially as one of the Assistant Under-Secretaries of State had phoned him making enquiries about Patel. Clearly the possibility of his being granted an audience with the President was under consideration. Lindsay duly informed the Foreign Secretary, Sir John Simon, of the developments, and he enclosed a copy of the letter which was sent in reply, enlightening the US official as to Patel's credentials.[130] The British Embassy in Washington wrote to the Department of State:

> He is an implacable anti-British propagandist and there is reason to believe that his visit to this country was arranged to a great extent under the auspices of a Mr S. N. Ghose, an Indian who has lived for some time in New York and can justly be described as a professional agitator against Great Britain. The object of his visit to the United States is to enlist support for the Indian independence movement . . . there is no limit to the verbal violence which he is prepared to use against the present administration in India. I imagine that you will want to pass on some or all of the above information to a third party and I would ask that it may be treated as confidential.[131]

The British Library of Information in New York was kept busy reporting Patel's movements back to London. Collaboration with Irish-American organisations that would help facilitate his tour had clearly been successful, with or without the aid of Ghose. They noted an increase in Irish 'cooperation with Indian agitators' since Patel's arrival in the US, and how Irish organisations in several centres were cooperating with his Indian agents to arrange meetings and provide publicity for him. On 28 September, for instance, Patel was guest of honour at a luncheon given by the Baltimore Emmet Club, an organisation advocating locally a 'free and independent Ireland'.[132] He also met with Irish Americans at a gathering in Chicago where he spoke about the Irish land annuities question in such detail that again one is forced to conclude that he and de Valera had talked about the matter at great length:

> But in President de Valera [England] has found a new problem, a big one. One that she cannot surmount. As England claims debt from the Irish nation in the shape of the so called land annuities, de Valera says 'Very well. We shall compare debits and credits. We shall do so before an impartial tribunal, not an English one. We shall not only discuss the debts we may owe England, but we shall determine the debts and the certainty of paying them that England owes Ireland.'[133]

Drawing comparisons between the advances of Ireland and India in the imperial sphere for his Irish-American audience, he concluded:

> We are far behind the advanced stage you have reached in Ireland. Within 18 months the oath of allegiance should be gone; the Governor-General

is already gone; with him will go the annuities. Then the Irish Republic will be a fact. The removal of these impediments are not an end in themselves. A united Ireland, free, is the real end.[134]

Ill-health again dictated Patel's movements, and by March 1933 he had to return to Europe for treatment. Ironically, Campbell reported that, before leaving the US, Patel was said to be worried about the state of Gandhi's health and told friends that 'he may be called back to take a lead in India should the expected happen and Mr Gandhi die as a result of the treatment he received from the British Government'. This drew a smile from R. T. Peel of the India Office who wrote a margin note saying 'This is a bit steep!'[135] He was possibly amused that Patel's opinion of himself was rather healthier than his actual physical condition, as he was clearly nearing death's door.

Patel's final trip to Ireland was for a few days at the end of March 1933 on the return leg of his journey, when he again met with de Valera.[136] By this stage he must have already planned to seek help in Switzerland for his deteriorating health, as de Valera handed him a letter of introduction from the Department of External Affairs to Seán Lester in Geneva stating that 'the Minister wishes you to introduce Mr Patel to any people who he desires to meet, and generally, to give him all the assistance you can'.[137] The following month the IIIL sought permission to have a statement by Patel broadcast on Radio Éireann. After consultation with the Department of External Affairs it was decided by the Department of Post and Telegraphs to inform Nora Connolly O'Brien, who had written in her capacity as publicity secretary of the IIIL, that permission could not be granted.[138] In doing so, External Affairs stressed to the Department of Post and Telegraphs 'that in conveying this decision to the League your Department should explain that, through its membership of the International Broadcasting Union, the Irish Free State Government are precluded from granting facilities for a broadcast of this nature'.[139] This is an interesting footnote to the life of the IIIL, yet it is unfair to say that, as a result of the refusal, support for the IIIL 'did not necessarily translate into state policy', for, after all, de Valera had met with Patel on several occasions.[140] It did, however, demonstrate how, given their new found position as government officials, one time revolutionaries who no doubt supported Patel's cause found it necessary to toe the line in relation to international broadcasting conventions. The blatant provision of a vehicle in the form of the state broadcaster for Patel's propaganda would have had impacted even further on the precarious relationship with the British at the time. It is almost analogous to the position de Valera found himself in while looking for recognition of the Irish Republic in the US in 1919: although many sympathised with his cause, the implications of official recognition were many and delicate. Perhaps de Valera was only too aware of this ironic role reversal, as more subtle assistance to Indian revolutionaries, in the shape of aiding and abetting the movements of known Indian radicals throughout Europe via passport controls, seems to have been provided quite readily by his Government. This was seen in chapter one in relation to Brajesh Singh, and will be seen later in relation to Chaman Lal; and crucially, in chapter three it will be seen that the de Valera Government not only let Subhas Chandra Bose land in Ireland when he was banned from doing so in England, but deliberately misled the British authorities as to his activities while there.

In one of his final interviews, with the *Neue Freie Presse*, Patel's spirit of resistance was as determined as ever. He spoke of the Indo-Irish friendship, and, perhaps alluding to the recent formation of the IIIL, expressed himself in what could only be interpreted by the British authorities as very sinister tones:

> My first stop in Europe was Dublin, where I had an opportunity of talking with the leaders of the Irish Independence Movement . . . Freedom and independence from England are the goal of each of these peoples – it can become our common goal. We march separately and strike united – perhaps we shall march together and strike together. I cannot speak of that today, as in the interest of the cause, our discussions were secret. I shall only say that we discussed lines of action which the Irish and the Indian people will shortly follow together.[141]

Patel died in October 1933 in a nursing home in Geneva, where he had been lying ill for some time. His obituary in *The Times* was not complimentary. The readership was told that Patel had played a conspicuous though mostly mischievous part in Indian political developments of the post-First World War period, that he was 'self-indulgent, ease-loving, wily and [had] a sense of sardonic humour'. He took 'every opportunity to denounce the connexion with India. In pursuit of this aim he visited the United States and the Irish Free State, where he cordially supported Mr de Valera's attempts to abrogate the Treaty with this country.' The obituarist credited Patel with being the catalyst for the renewed unrest that developed in India in the 1930s and, perhaps overstating his influence on domestic affairs at that time for dramatic effect, remarked that 'his evil influence on Mr Gandhi when the latter was returning to Bombay from the second Round-Table Conference no doubt contributed to the unhappy decision at the beginning of 1932 to revive civil disobedience'.[142] Somewhat symbolically, at Patel's bedside in Geneva was the man who would take up the radical torch left by his passing in the fight for Indian independence and who would also have significant contacts with Ireland: Subhas Chandra Bose.

Indo-Irish epilogue

Patel had continued correspondence with Mollie Woods in her capacity as the secretary of the IIIL right up until his death. The IIIL's most momentous task came some three years later when it organised Bose's much-publicised visit to Dublin.[143] IPI kept tabs on the organisation and noted its formal demise in 1945. This came about when two students, Subrata Ray Chaudhuri and Dilip Sen, visited Ireland in June 1945 as representatives of the Cambridge University Majlis (or Indian Society).[144] IPI was under the impression that the students were 'particularly anxious to revive the Indian Irish Independence League – which ceased to function soon after the outbreak of war in 1939'. The students' visit was quite a success. They addressed five meetings and were officially received by de Valera, who they thanked for his 'generous donation towards the relief of famine in Bengal – for which', noted IPI, 'the British Government were blamed'.[145] At a press conference in Dublin the Cambridge Majlis representatives told the Irish public that it was the desire of every Indian to come to Ireland as they regarded it as a spiritual home: 'they had watched with great admiration the heroic struggle of the Irish people against British imperialism for seven hundred years. This to every Indian is like a legend.' Their interpretations of Irish opinion with regard to India are indicative of the radical company they were keeping. The students believed that

> Irish public opinion, which was strongly sympathetic to India, regretted that Indians had not taken stronger action to expel the British from their country; and that a large body of Irishmen who supported Subhas Chandra Bose had declared on more than one occasion that history might have been different if the present Indian leaders had shared his extreme views.[146]

The industrious students' desire to revive the IIIL was unsuccessful, but it did reap some rewards. The following September IPI became aware that, because of the winding up of the 'Irish–Indian Independence League of Dublin, the organisation's funds, amounting to £98' were presented to the Cambridge University Majlis by Mrs Maud Gonne MacBride. In a letter to Subrata Ray Chaudhuri, MacBride stated that the object of the donation was to assist the Majlis in its campaign for Indian self-government. She had wound up the IIIL as she was of the opinion that 'it could serve little useful purpose in Éire as an overwhelming majority of the people in the country strongly supported India's demand for freedom'.[147]

[84]

Conclusion

Insufficient attention has been paid to the considerable interest that Indian activists had in Irish politics in the 1920s and 1930s, which naturally heightened in the wake of de Valera's coming to power in 1932. The gradual constitutional developments which came in the wake of the 1932 election made Ireland an exciting and educational destination for Indian activists attempting to learn the radical tricks of the imperial secession trade. It is also important to note that these Indians were of significant standing in their own independence struggle, like the one-time President of the Indian Legislative Assembly Patel, the Raja of Kalakankar, Jamandas Mehta, the President of the All-India Railway Federation and the Gujarati socialist I. K. Yajnik. It was an interest that was reciprocated by Irish nationalists, including de Valera himself, but also other shades of Irish political opinion, from the radical left-wingers MacBride, Ryan and O'Donnell to the Cumann na nGaedheal TD and former Dáil chairman Michael Hayes. These contacts were not merely rhetorical, but at the level of high politics. Nor were these connections transitory, as evidenced by the establishment of the IIIL and the visit to Dublin by the Indian radical Subhas Chandra Bose a few years later (detailed in chapter three). Crucially, even though neither Irish nor Indian historiography has yet documented this nexus, the British intelligence services of that time certainly did. There was much unease at this burgeoning Indo-Irish relationship. Were Indians taking a leaf out of the Irish revolutionary book? If so how would such lessons materialise and aggravate the already troublesome conditions in India? A look into the career of Subhas Chandra Bose should reveal just how.

Notes

1 *Irish Press*, 3 July 1932.
2 Gerald Keown, 'Taking the world stage: creating an Irish foreign policy in the 1920s', in Kennedy and Skelly (eds), *Irish Foreign Policy*, p. 26; see also D. W. Harkness, *The Restless Dominion* (London, 1966).
3 Keown, 'Taking the world stage', p. 28.
4 *The Times*, 28 March 1932.
5 O'Halpin, *Defending*, p. 129.
6 See chapter one.
7 Letter from Despard to Charles Wilson, 13 March 1932, Women's Library, Metropolitan University of London, Charlotte Despard Papers (hereafter WL), 7/CFD.
8 Anthony Read and David Fisher, *The Proudest Day: India's Long Road to Independence* (London, 1998), p. 207.
9 Note by David Petrie on revolutionary crime and terrorism in India, 19 June 1929, BL, OIOC, IOR, L/P&J/12/296.
10 Vallabhbhai Patel was also known as the 'Iron Man' of India and usually referred to as *Sardar*, a title meaning chief. He shares his first two initials, 'V. J.', with his elder

brother and as a result the two can be easily confused; for example, see NAI, DFA, 5/47, where a fact sheet on Vithalbhai incorrectly contains some information about Sardar's career.

11 French, *Liberty*, pp. 50–2.
12 *The Times*, 24 June 1919.
13 Extract from Scotland Yard report, 6 July 1932, BL, OIOC, IOR, L/P&J/12/436.
14 *The Times*, 24 Aug. 1925.
15 French, *Liberty*, pp. 50–1.
16 *The Times*, 16 July 1927.
17 Extract from *Irish Independent*, 4 July 1932, typed out and on file in BL, OIOC, IOR, L/P&J/12/436; and *The Times*, 16 July 1927.
18 *The Times*, 23 Oct. 1933.
19 Read and Fisher, *Proudest*, p. 229.
20 *The Times*, 26 April 1930.
21 *Ibid.*, 8 Jan. 1931.
22 History sheet of Mrs Margaret Cousins, 1932, BL, OIOC, IOR, L/P&J/12/458.
23 *Ibid.*
24 *Ibid.*
25 *Ibid.*
26 *Ibid.*
27 Vickery to Williamson, 4 Nov. 1932, BL, OIOC, IOR, L/P&J/12/458.
28 Extract from report of the Deputy Commissioner of Police, Crime Branch, Madras, 5 Dec. 1932, BL, OIOC, IOR, L/P&J/12/458.
29 History sheet of Mrs Margaret Cousins, 1932, BL, OIOC, IOR, L/P&J/12/458.
30 Kamlani to Woods, 30 June 1932, National Library of Ireland (hereafter NLI), MS 17,832.
31 For further reading on Despard's life see Andro Linklater, *An Unhusbanded Life: Charlotte Despard, Suffragette, Socialist and Sinn Féiner* (London, 1980); and Margaret Mulvihill, *Charlotte Despard: A Biography* (London, 1989).
32 See article titled 'India' in *United Irishman*, 12 May 1900.
33 Karen Steele, *Maud Gonne's Irish Nationalist Writing 1895–1946* (Dublin, 2004).
34 Uinseann MacEoin, *Survivors* (Dublin, 1980), p. 107.
35 Letter from Bose to Woods, 7 Dec. 1933, in Subhas Chandra Bose, *Letters, Articles, Speeches and Statements, 1933–36*, ed. S. K. Bose and S. Bose (Oxford, 1994), p. 41.
36 Arun Coomer Bose, *Indian Revolutionaries Abroad, 1905–22: In the Background of International Developments* (Allahabad, 1971), p. 14.
37 *Ibid.*; see also pp. 19–20. For more information on 'India House' see Introduction.
38 *Ibid.*, p. 17; see also Political and Secret Home Correspondence, vol. 233, BL, IOR, L/PS/3/420; and Visram, *Asians in Britain*, p. 151.
39 See the witness statement (WS) by Mollie Woods, NAI, Bureau of Military History (BMH), WS 642.
40 MacEoin, *Survivors*, pp. 311–19.
41 *Ibid.*
42 Many prominent IRA men had stayed in the Woods' home for long periods while on the run, and one of the final letters that Liam Mellows wrote just before his execution was to Mollie Woods: information provided to the author by Aideen Austin, née Woods, daughter of Tony Woods, granddaughter of Mollie Woods; see also NAI, BMH, WS 642.
43 Information, Aideen Austin. See also C. S. Andrews, *Dublin Made Me* (Dublin, 2002) pp. 280-1.
44 *Ibid.*
45 Correspondence with Lal Wright, née Dey, Tripura Dey's daughter.
46 Report on Friends of India Conference, 18 June 1932, BL, OIOC, IOR, L/P&J/12/436.
47 Vickery to Williamson, 21 July 1932, BL, OIOC, IOR, L/P&J/12/436.
48 Mulvihill, *Charlotte Despard*, p. 86.
49 Letter from Woods addressed 'to all members of political and cultural life in Ireland', 30 Sept. 1931, NLI, MS 17,832.

50 *Ibid.*
51 *Ibid.* Briscoe to Woods, 30 Oct. 1931; there is also a short letter on file from Seán Lemass who said that he would have 'great pleasure if [his] name was added to those extending the invitation to Mr Gandhi to visit Ireland'.
52 *Irish Press*, 14 Sept. 1931.
53 *Ibid.*
54 *Ibid.*
55 Linklater, *Unhusbanded*, pp. 238–9.
56 Report of a lecture given by Patel in Vienna, 29 April 1932, BL, IOR, L/P&J/12/436.
57 *Ibid.*
58 Report of the Friends of India Conference, 18 June 1932, *ibid.*
59 *Ibid.*
60 *Ibid.*
61 Kamlani to Woods, 30 June 1932, NLI, MS 17,832.
62 *Irish Independent*, 4 July 1932. Ranchoddas Bhavan Lotwalla (sometimes spelt Lotvalla) was apparently earning money as an Indian correspondent for the *Irish Independent* while in London. This was not unusual for Indians at the time, who saw a possible market for anti-British journalism in Ireland. Pulin Behari Seal worked as a correspondent for *An Phoblacht* in the 1930s.
63 Weekly report of DIB, Home Department, Government of India, 13 Oct. 1927, BL, OIOC, IOR, L/P&J/12/167; see chapter one for further information on Saklatvala, Dutt and other Indian communists.
64 *Ibid.*
65 Extract from Scotland Yard report, 6 July 1932, BL, OIOC, IOR, L/P&J/12/436.
66 *Irish Independent*, 4 July 1932.
67 Extract from Scotland Yard report, 6 July 1932, BL, OIOC, IOR, L/P&J/12/436.
68 Peters to Secretary of State for India, Samuel Hoare, 6 July 1932, BL, OIOC, IOR, L/PO/6/76.
69 *Irish Independent*, 4 July 1932.
70 *Ibid.*
71 *Ibid.*
72 R. Chowdhury, *Ploughboy to President: Life Story of V. J. Patel* (Calcutta, 1934), p. 1210. IPI's file on the writer and journalist gives his full name as Bhibuti Bhusan Ray Chudhuri: BL, OIOC, IOR, L/P&J/12/465. However, as he published his book on Patel under the name R. Chowdhury, he is here referred to as such.
73 For correspondence between de Valera and J. H. Thomas in relation to the land annuities dispute in June and July of 1932, see Catriona Crowe, Ronan Fanning, Michael Kennedy, Dermot Keogh and Eunan O'Halpin (eds), *Documents in Irish Foreign Policy 1932–1936*, vol. 4 (Dublin, 2004) (hereafter *DIFP* 4), pp. 64, 66–7.
74 *Ibid.*, pp. 88–91.
75 List of questions sent to Department of External Affairs, 2 Aug. 1932, and response from Dulanty, 12 Aug. 1932, NAI, DFA, 5/47.
76 Chowdhury, *Ploughboy to President*, pp. 1209–10.
77 *Ibid.*, p. 1210.
78 Vickery to Clauson, 24 Jan. 1933, BL, OIOC, IOR, L/P&J/12/465.
79 *Ibid.*
80 *Irish Independent*, 6–7 July 1932.
81 *The Hindu*, 10 Oct. 1953.
82 *Ibid.*
83 *Irish Press*, 5 July 1932
84 *Irish Press*, 9 July 1932.
85 *Ibid.*
86 *Ibid.*
87 Adrian Hoar, *In Green and Red: The Lives of Frank Ryan* (Dingle, 2004), pp. 100–1
88 *An Phoblacht*, 17 Sept. 1932.
89 *An Phoblacht*, 1 Oct. 1932.
90 *Ibid.*

91   *Ibid.*
92   *Irish Press*, 9 July 1932.
93   *An Phoblacht*, 16 July 1932.
94   *Ibid.*
95   See Appendix 2.
96   LAI report, 18 July 1932, BL, OIOC, IOR, L/P&J/12/272.
97   *An Phoblacht*, 30 July 1932.
98   *Ibid.*
99   Vickery to Williamson, 21 July 1932, BL, OIOC, IOR, L/P&J/12/436.
100 *Ibid.*
101 This is possibly a reference to Subhas Chandra Bose's nephew, Amiya Nath Bose.
102 Vickery to Williamson, 21 July 1932, BL, OIOC, IOR, L/P&J/12/436.
103 *Ibid.*
104 Patel to Woods, 16 Sept. 1932, NLI, MS 17,832.
105 More usually referred to as I. K. Yajnik.
106 *An Phoblacht*, 29 July 1932.
107 Patel to Woods, 16 Sept. 1932, NLI, MS 17,832.
108 Yajnik to Fowler, 1 Sept. 1932, NLI, MS 27,097 (9).
109 See NLI, MS 27,097 (4–5) for Saklatvala–Fowler correspondence, and chapter one,
     this book, for further information on Saklatvala's Irish contacts.
110 Patel to Woods, 2 Sept. 1932, NLI, Ms. 17,823. It is more than likely that the 'Mr
     Mehta' referred to was Jamandas Mehta, the President of the All-India Railway
     Federation who had accompanied Patel on his trip to Ireland in 1927, a staunch left-
     winger and heavily involved in the independence movement in India. It is signifi-
     cant that he travelled over to Dublin, this time with Audesh Singh.
111 *An Phoblacht*, 1 Oct. 1932; see Appendix 3 for the IIIL constitution in its entirety.
112 *Ibid.*
113 See chapter one.
114 Nehru Memorial Library (hereafter NML), Delhi, Private Papers Collection, Papers
     of Indulal Yajnik; see all of file no. 19 for material relating to Ireland and loose pam-
     phlets no. 2 within file no. 19, for the GAA booklet specifically.
115 MacGregor to Fletcher, 26 July 1932, BL, OIOC, IOR, L/P&J/12/436.
116 *Ibid.*
117 *Ibid.*
118 Extract from Scotland Yard report, 28 Sept. 1932, BL, OIOC, IOR, L/P&J/12/436.
119 *Ibid.*
120 Chowdhury, *Ploughboy to President*, p. 1212.
121 De Valera to McGarrity, 19 Aug. 1932, NLI, MS 33,364.
122 For further reading on the development of tensions within the Irish nationalist
     movement in America, see F. M. Carroll, *American Opinion and the Irish
     Question 1910–23* (Dublin, 1978), pp. 156–62.
123 MacGregor to Fletcher, 26 July 1932, BL, OIOC, IOR, L/P&J/12/436.
124 See Introduction for further information on this group. Prior to travelling to the
     USA, Ghose was a Professor of Science at the University of Calcutta, and a known
     expert in the manufacture of bombs. Fearing arrest, he left India having failed to
     obtain a passport: History sheet of Salindra Nath Ghose, dated 1930, BL, OIOC,
     IOR, L/P&J/12/197.
125 *Ibid.*
126 Vickery to Mr P, 1929, BL, OIOC, IOR, L/P&J/12/197 (I have been unable to ascer-
     tain P's identity). It is also interesting to note here that Gerald Campbell, of the
     British Consulate in New York, reported to Lindsay in Washington that Ghose was
     successfully lobbying for financial assistance among the Irish in New York, and
     that they had also helped him organise meetings against the Governments of India
     and Great Britain: Campbell to Lindsay, 29 Oct. 1931, *ibid.*
127 *Ibid.*
128 McGarrity to de Valera, 29 Aug. 1932, NLI, MS 33,364.
129 Campbell to Lindsay, 28 Dec. 1932, BL, OIOC, IOR, L/P&J/12/437.

130 Lindsay to Simon, 5 Jan. 1933, *ibid.*
131 Shone to Carr, 19 Dec. 1932, *ibid.*
132 Report from British Library of Information, New York, to Foreign Office, 3 Oct. 1932, BL, OIOC, IOR, L/P&J/12/436.
133 Chowdhury, *Ploughboy to President*, p. 177.
134 *Ibid.*
135 Campbell to Lindsay, 28 Dec. 1932, BL, OIOC, IOR, L/P&J/12/437.
136 Vickery to Clauson, 31 March 1933, *ibid.*
137 Murphy to Lester, 28 March 1933, NAI, DFA, 5/47.
138 NAI, DFA, 33/59; see various correspondences with the Department of Posts and Telegraphs throughout April 1933.
139 Murphy to Department of Posts and Telegraphs, 20 April 1933, NAI, DFA, 33/59.
140 Bose and Eilis, 'India's cause is Ireland's cause', p. 63.
141 Translation of interview with Patel, *Neue Frie Presse*, 18 May 1933, BL, OIOC, IOR, L/P&J/12/437.
142 *The Times*, 23 Oct. 1933.
143 See chapter three.
144 Extract from Scotland Yard report, 1 Aug. 1945, BL, OIOC, IOR, L/P&J/12/4.
145 *Ibid.*; see chapter four for further information about the Irish Government's donation to the Bengal famine appeal during the Second World War.
146 *Ibid.*
147 Extract from Metropolitan Police report, 26 Sept. 1945, BL, OIOC, IOR, L/P&J/12/4.

CHAPTER THREE

Subhas Chandra Bose and Ireland

> So many of my countrymen go to London but do not care to go to Dublin where one can see in the flesh and blood some of the men and women who have made and are making history. In my part of India – Bengal – there is hardly an educated family where books about the Irish heroes are not read and, if I may say so, devoured. Nowadays it is becoming more difficult to get books on Ireland because the government think that the Irish revolutionaries will open the eyes of the Indian people.[1]

It is safe to say that popular adulation of Subhas Chandra Bose, or Netaji as he is often referred to, has reached an unprecedented level in Indian society.[2] In recent years Bose iconography, with streets and an airport named after him, has overshadowed even that of his one-time rival Gandhi. Communists and Hindu nationalists claim him equally as their own. He is revered more now than during his lifetime. As Patrick French has wryly pointed out, there are many who insist that Bose did not die in an air crash in 1945, that he is alive and well and, like Elvis Presley and Lord Lucan, will reappear at an appropriate moment.[3]

Bose's story is representative of the lesser-known radical, aggressive and revolutionary road to Indian independence, one that is the antithesis of the world-renowned, Gandhi-inspired, non-violent struggle against the Raj. He died unexpectedly and relatively young. Significantly, he is seen as the one leader of India's freedom movement who dared to fight the British with the sword, yet was not associated with the creation of Pakistan and the partition of his country. In drawing attention to some of these factors one cannot help but acknowledge echoes of the death of Michael Collins, someone who Bose himself admired greatly.[4] In the same way Ireland has suffered the long-standing Collins versus de Valera debacle, Bose left in his wake an Indian people with even more vehement divided loyalties, Gandhiji or Netaji? In 2005 a group petitioned a Calcutta court to postpone the screening of a new film, *Netaji Subhas Chandra Bose: The Forgotten Hero* by the distinguished Indian director

Shyam Benegal, on the grounds that it depicts Bose as being a married man (it is claimed that Bose swore not to wed until India was free), and that Bose was far from 'forgotten'.[5] As recently as August 2005 Bose's legacy excited much attention when it was revealed that the British Government had in fact planned his assassination during the Second World War.[6] So who was this lauded Bengali and what was his connection with Ireland?

Roots of a revolutionary

Bose was born in 1897 in the town of Cuttack, Bengal, to a devout Hindu mother and a lawyer father who was highly respected in his field. Although Bengali was spoken in the family home, Bose acquired an exceptional command of the English language. When he came second in his high-school exams his parents decided that he must continue his studies. He went to read for a degree at Presidency College, Calcutta, one of British India's most prestigious colleges.[7] During his time there the first instances of rebellious behaviour went on record when, in 1916, he was suspended for his part in a corridor fracas with the professor of history who, it was alleged, had called one of Bose's colleagues 'a rascal' and had 'boxed his ears'.[8] Although he was allowed to return to his studies a year later his father decided that it would be best for him to travel to England to sit the Indian Civil Service (ICS) examinations: a job in the ICS promised a lifetime of security and stability.

Having arrived in England in 1919, however, he enrolled as a non-collegiate student at Cambridge. While in England his sense of Indian identity and of nationalism grew. He is quoted as having said at this time: 'nothing makes me happier than to be served by the whites and to watch them clean my shoes'.[9] In order to keep his father happy, Subhas sat the ICS examinations thinking that he would not do well enough to be accepted; in fact he came fourth, but he refused to join. A vigorous writing campaign to persuade him otherwise was initiated by his father, but this served only to convince Subhas that working for the ICS was not what he wanted in life. In 1921 he returned to India with a clear plan in place: he would offer his services to his new political guru, the powerful regional leader 'Deshbandhu' Chittaranjan Das of east Bengal. In response to Gandhi's call for non-cooperation in the aftermath of the Rowlatt Acts, Das had sacrificed his successful law firm and his penchant for Western dress to lead the non-cooperation movement in Bengal. He took Bose on board, impressed by his dedication and enthusiasm. Das was elected Mayor of Calcutta, and during the 1920s Bose worked with him and was put in charge of the city corporation. It was this type of hands-on and productive work at grassroots level that Bose was to thrive on. He was in charge of publicity, and one of his first tasks was to organise a national college in opposition to the Raj's institutions. Bose's love affair with 'the corporation' had begun: whenever he visited a city, he would first go to its municipality and city corporation,[10] as was the case when he subsequently visited Dublin.

It was not long before his work acquired a more urgent tone and he began to organise the picketing of shops selling foreign goods in Calcutta.[11] In 1924 he was arrested on suspicion of supporting violent revolutionaries and deported to Burma, where he was imprisoned; no charges were ever brought and he was held without trial for three years.[12] This was for Bose the first of many arrests, imprisonment and detention being commonplace for most prominent Indian politicians of the time. As with Gandhi, who was often released due to sickness and fasting, prison conditions had a dire effect on Bose's health. He suffered from recurrent abdominal pain and intestinal problems and, as India Office records show, it was because of his apparently deteriorating health that he was released in 1927.[13] He returned to work with renewed energy and soon was recognised as the fresh young face of Indian nationalism. Within Congress circles many of the old guard were beginning to feel threatened by his impatience and vigour and what they perceived as his more radical line. Gandhi was particularly perturbed. IPI summed up Bose's activities at this time with some accuracy, yet as always applied too much weight to what they regarded as communist inclinations:

> By 1928 [Bose] had again plunged into political and terroristic [sic] activities, including the organisation of an 'Independence League for Bengal' which issued a manifesto on Bolshevik lines. [He] also renewed his activities in the Indian National Congress, in which he was a rival of Gandhi and advocate of a more militant policy.[14]

By 'terroristic activities' IPI probably meant Bose's part in setting up the Congress Volunteer Force in Calcutta in 1928. The young men and women recruited by Bose wore khaki uniforms.[15] Activities mainly encompassed drilling in the early mornings on the streets of Calcutta during the annual Congress meeting. Bose spent much of 1928–33 in prison, either interned or arrested for involvement in unlawful demonstrations or other activities. In 1930 he was elected Mayor of Calcutta while in jail. In 1933, Bose's ill-health worked to his advantage again, as the emergence of more serious symptoms resulted in his release from prison. Doctors were convinced, mistakenly, that he had developed tuberculosis and he was allowed to travel to Switzerland for treatment.[16] However Bose foresaw difficulties when he was given a restricted passport: Germany and Great Britain were explicitly excluded from the list of endorsed destinations. This was to be the source of some trouble later.

A right or left winger?

An IPI report of 1935 on Bose stated that he was believed in 1922 to be in touch with communist agents abroad, particularly M. N. Roy, and that from this time on he showed a tendency towards communist ideology.[17] An increasing concern about Bose's activity is understandable, though whether he could with justification be branded a communist at any stage of his career is debatable. Indeed, the ideology he often espoused throughout his life has been sternly criticised as naive and unsophisticated.[18] He was neither communist nor fascist, but apparently both:

> In spite of the antithesis between communism and fascism there are certain traits common to both. Both communism and fascism believe in the supremacy of the state over the individual. Both denounce parliamentarian democracy. Both believe in party rule. Both believe in the dictatorship of the party and in the ruthless suppression of dissenting minorities. Both believe in planned industrial reorganisation of the country. These common traits will form the basis of the new synthesis . . . It will be India's task to work out this synthesis.[19]

This extract is from Bose's *The Indian Struggle*, first published in 1935, and the same passage was quoted subsequently in an IPI file and drew the comment:

> The general views of Bose in relation to communism are given at the end of his book . . . He does not altogether approve of communism because of its non-national and anti-religious character.[20]

This indicates recognition on the part of IPI that Bose's outlook was not entirely straightforward. Bose was asked in 1938, after 'fascism had started on its imperialist expedition', to clarify these and similar statements on his personal ideology. In conversation with Rajani Palme Dutt (an ardent communist), Bose was adamant that he was always more favourable towards communism.[21] This chameleon-like stance is evident throughout his career; it was not born of ignorance but was rather a useful political tactic. Yet throughout the 1930s an emphasis on Bose's alleged communist inclinations is evident, at the expense of consideration of other ideological leanings that could prove more dangerous to the Empire. As noted in chapter one, this is in accordance with a general criticism of inter-war British intelligence surveillance for an excessive focus on the actions of communist or Bolshevik suspects and organisations.[22]

[93]

In 1933 IPI reported that Bose was calling for Gandhi's resignation, saying that he had done much for India but that he stood for a policy which had outlived its use.[23] According to the report, Bose's position was that '[n]o country has ever achieved independence without bloodshed', and records that he had

> recommended India to follow the Irish example, that is to adopt the strongest form of non-cooperation with regard to taxes, combined with militant activities all over the country by scattered organisations which would fight the forces of government, both police and army.[24]

By 1933 Bose's letters were being intercepted. According to one of Vickery's weekly reports, 'these letters showed a tendency on the part of Bose to advocate communist rather than terrorist tactics'.[25] In a report in the same file Vickery reverses that judgement in noting that Bose 'suggests the adoption of the Irish method whereby the entire army was kept engaged by means of guerrilla warfare, while the civil administration was completely wrecked by volunteers'. Not only is this clearly advocating terrorist tactics, but it is a blatant instance of the real and perilous results of Indians using Ireland as an influence. So it appears that, while on the scent of Moscow and the Comintern, no other odours were detectable, even by an Irishman like Vickery.

Blatant imitations of Irish tactics had already occurred and it appears that the imperial Government had not learnt from recent experience. The report quoted above is dated 1933, three years after one of the largest Bengali revolutionary uprisings, the Chittagong Armoury Raid. While the British officials were preoccupied with the first phase of the civil disobedience movement, and believing that they had put terrorism behind them with the Bengal Criminal Law Amendment Acts of 1924–25, Bengali revolutionaries turned to Burma as an alternative site of re-organising. The rising was led by Surja Sen and began on 18 April. It was inspired directly by the Irish struggle. Those involved are said to have 'acquired a pastiche of information on different phases and leaders of the Irish freedom movement',[26] and had read histories of the Fenian James Fintan Lalor as well as Dan Breen's *My Fight for Irish Freedom*, relying on his account of the Easter Rising as a model for the armoury raid in 1930. Also, a biography of de Valera was found at the house of one of the insurgents, Ganesh Ghosh, the day after the raids began. The uprising was even timed to coincide with the anniversary of the Irish 1916 Rising, though Easter itself meant little to the non-Christian revolutionaries.

The Chittagong uprising was an elaborately planned attack in which the insurgents managed to occupy major colonial sites, including the Armoury and the telegraph office in Chittagong, for over four days. The aftermath was even more debilitating for the officials, as for almost three years many of the leaders evaded police detection.[27] Manini Chatterjee has argued that Breen, Pearse, Lalor and de Valera reflected disjointed fragments of a freedom struggle thousands of miles away in Ireland, but taken together they offered an ideology as well as a blue-print for action to Sen and his men.[28] Perhaps more tangible evidence of the impact that the Irish Rising had on those men, however, can be seen in the leaflet which they distributed proclaiming India's freedom; for, as Chatterjee pointed out, its text mirrored almost exactly the Proclamation of Independence made by Pearse on behalf of the provi-sional Government of the Irish Republic.[29]

Roving ambassador for Indian independence

From 1933 to 1936 Bose was a roving ambassador for Indian indepen-dence in Europe, though some of his time was spent in hospitals and health retreats, and he underwent an abdominal operation in Vienna.[30] Although he was allowed to visit Europe to obtain treatment for his condition, his illness clearly does not explain why he had remained there for three years and travelled extensively. The British authorities were more than aware that his sojourns in most of the Continent's main cities were made not on grounds of health but were for solely political purposes. However, the general thought prevailed that his presence in Europe rather than India was the lesser of two evils and IPI ensured that during this time he was closely shadowed. These years are usually referred to as Bose's exile, and during that time his role was not unlike that of de Valera in America from 1919–20. Although Bose was not seeking anything as definite as de Valera's goal of recognition for the Republic, nor had he a status equivalent to that of 'President of the Irish Republic', the interlude was similar in as much as it was a propa-ganda campaign to place India's cause at the forefront of the European press as well as an opportunity to meet with and mobilise influential Indians already resident on the Continent.

Europeans who were favourable to Indian independence were courted with considerable aplomb, including Mussolini himself, as well as de Valera. Bose is said to have presented both men with a copy of his book *The Indian Struggle*, and IPI reported that 'President de Valera is understood to have sent a cordial message of appreciation'.[31] There is evidence that Bose paid regular trips to the Irish Legation during one of his long sojourns in Berlin. The Irish representative, Charles Bewley, thought one such visit he had from Bose, in April 1934, significant enough to report on to Dublin.[32] The purpose of Bose's visits, it seems, was to make preparations for a trip to Ireland. In this chapter

[95]

I focus on Bose's interest in Ireland and his eventual visit there in 1936 rather than analysing his entire European trip. This is a worthwhile process for several reasons, among them the fact that a visit to Ireland was a long held dream, but also because his trip to Dublin in particular was considered the most successful aspect of his European tour.[33]

Mihir Bose sheds light on the general perception of Ireland among Indians at the time and in doing so provides us with Netaji's probable mindset in anticipation of his visit:

> For radical Indians, particularly Bengalis, Ireland was a magic[al] country. It had done the impossible – proved that even the mighty British Empire was vulnerable. Indians had devoured Irish history, and the lives of Irish heroes had through endless re-telling acquired the status of ancient Hindu myths. Bose himself could recall the tremendous enthusiasm when Terence MacSwiney's family sent a message of condolence on Jatin Das' death.[34]

Bose in fact referred to this message from the MacSwiney family in a letter to Mollie Woods.[35] As we saw in chapter two Vithalbhai Patel was also in Europe seeking treatment for his health at the same time as Bose. However his condition was terminal and he died in Geneva in 1933. Bose spent a lot of time with him in hospital and was with him when he died. Mollie Woods corresponded with Patel up until his death. As Patel's condition deteriorated Bose began to reply to her letters on Patel's behalf and soon they were in regular correspondence themselves. It was an important contact to have established, as it was Woods who mainly helped organise Bose's itinerary while in Dublin. In a letter dated 9 January 1936, he wrote:

> No arrangements have been made up till now about my visit to Ireland and I look up to you to help me in this matter . . . Please make the necessary arrangements for my meeting President de Valera, the party leaders, the lord Mayor etc . . . Some time ago there was a statement in the Indian papers that the National University of Dublin wanted to confer an honorary degree on me. I do not know from where this news emanated nor as to whether it is true. Perhaps you can find out.[36]

As it turned out an honorary conferral was not on the cards, but this demonstrates both Bose's eagerness and the enthusiasm for the visit on the part of the Indian press evident in its readiness to report such rumours.

Dublin paves the way

As early as 1933 the Department of External Affairs in Dublin was aware that Bose intended to visit Ireland. Bose's application to land in the Irish Free State is noted on a memorandum of a discussion between de Valera and John Hearne, the legal adviser to the Department of External Affairs, on 18 August 1933 when the President himself directed that Bose be allowed to land provided the Department of Justice had no objection.[37] External Affairs informed the Department of Justice that he had applied to the Berlin legation for an endorsement on his passport entitling him to enter the Irish Free State. As Bose was *persona non grata* to the British authorities the Department of Justice was asked if it was opposed to Bose travelling to Ireland on his undertaking that he would not cross to the UK.[38] The Department of Justice raised no objection, but its reply went on to say that 'the Minister is not clear as to the powers under which Mr Bose who appears to be a British subject is prevented from entering the UK and he would be glad to have any available information at this point'.[39] As a result of this query a letter was later sent to the British Home Office's Aliens' Department:

> One Subhas Bose, who is stated to be an ex-mayor of Calcutta, has applied for permission to visit this country. It appears that Bose has been informed that he will not be permitted to land in Great Britain and we should be glad to have any information which may be readily available concerning him.[40]

This letter was purely of a fact-finding nature, an attempt by the Irish Government to ascertain Bose's current status *vis-à-vis* the British authorities. The letter failed to mention that the Free State would raise no objections to Bose's proposed visit. The Home Office reply stated that Bose was 'previously a State Prisoner in India and was released solely in order to enable him to come to Europe for medical treatment'.[41] It went on to say that Bose had 'managed to secure endorsements for a considerable number of European countries additional to those originally noted on his passport'. While not elaborating on Bose's questionable past and why they had concerns about him making such an extensive journey, the letter ended simply: 'we understand that the Government of India are very anxious that no further endorsements be granted'. This was a somewhat tame way of ending the correspondence and was probably a deliberate effort on the part of the British to conceal the alarm which engulfed the Home Office at the very mention of Bose's movements. With former rebel de Valera now in power, and no doubt still acquainting himself with the nuances of official inter-state correspondence, it was paramount that the British Government did not let its guard down.

This episode is interesting for another reason. The Minister for Justice, P. J. Ruttledge, had been correct to query 'the powers under which Mr Bose who appears to be a British subject is prevented from entering the UK'. No such powers existed; the British were bluffing. In fact a serious blunder had occurred among the imperial administrators in relation to the other endorsements on Bose's passport. When it had been issued at Allahabad, on 13 February 1933, written in red ink under the column 'Observations' was: 'Not valid for entry into Germany or the United Kingdom.'[42] On 25 March Bose approached the British Consul in Vienna who readily endorsed his passport for Hungary and Czechoslovakia. No doubt feeling lucky, Bose approached him the following month and again was obliged when endorsements were added for Yugoslavia, Romania, Bulgaria, Greece, Turkey, Spain, Portugal, Sweden, Norway and Denmark. In June, the British Vice-Consul in Prague added Belgium, Holland and Poland to his passport. However, these eager officials had overlooked the red ink. It was apparently bureaucratic shorthand for saying that, excepting Germany and the UK, no endorsements for other countries should be given without India Office permission. W. J. Clauson of the India Office commented harshly:

> This is amusing. While we ponderously debated here about Germany, the Consul at Vienna endorsed a passport for most other countries in the world. But no doubt it does not matter. The more he travels, the more likely he may die, presumably. [43]

IPI was also kept up to date about Bose's intentions, and in October 1933 was able to report that 'it is now known that while in Berlin, Bose tried to ascertain whether it would be possible for him to go to the Irish Free State'.[44] In 1935 it noted that articles were appearing in the *Irish Press*, 'the Free State government organ, giving a résumé of Bose's career and alluding to a forthcoming visit by him to Dublin'. It went on to state:

> Bose, who will be feted and invited to broadcast (the broadcast being relayed to America), has been granted a Free State visa on the understanding that he does not attempt to visit England from an Irish port. Although there is apparently no immediate idea on Bose's part of travelling to Dublin, he proposes to do so when his health permits.[45]

Clearly movements of this variety were catching the attention of the British intelligence services, and the IPI report concluded by noting that 'significance attaches to the incidents referred to in the last two paragraphs; these contacts with leaders of European states have undoubtedly been achieved with a view to the extensive advertisement both of Bose himself and of the Indian National Congress'.[46]

In the 1920s DIB and IPI reports relating to Bose had been short and concise, and indicated that the British authorities did not take Bose and his Volunteer Force of khaki-clad students very seriously. Gradually, as the years passed, there was a significant change in attitude towards

Bose. As he made his way through Europe and received the attention of many of its leaders, IPI reports on him became longer and more detailed, and acquired a more serious tone. The growing concerns about Bose's activities are revealed in a significant document in his IPI file dating from 1935. Apparently Vickery had been discussing him with Sir Charles Tegart, who in 1923 had been asked to take over the leadership of IPI from Wallinger but instead became Chief Commissioner of the Calcutta Police. He had been in correspondence with a 'Mr J. T. Donovan, CIE (an ICS man who retired very recently from Bengal and is at present in a banking job in Dublin)'.[47] Donovan informed Tegart of a move to give Bose a civic reception in Dublin and an honorary degree from the National University, something Bose himself had already heard on the grapevine. Donovan thought that

> if Subhas Bose was still tarred with the communist brush, it was possible that the Mayor of Dublin would jib at receiving him and that the National University also might be induced to alter their intentions about a degree. He asked Sir Charles whether any evidence of this could be furnished, in which case he would see what could be done through purely private channels.[48]

Tegart suggested to Vickery that they should avail themselves of the offer of assistance 'which would not commit us in anyway' and said that he would pass on 'anything that we cared to give to Mr Donovan'. Vickery agreed and thought that 'if any spoke was to be put in his [Bose's] wheel, it should be done as soon as possible':

> My view would be that we ought to do all we can to prevent this visit and that Sir Charles Tegart's suggestion is a useful one which offers a definitely promising opening and one that we are scarcely likely to get elsewhere.[49]

We can see here how Irish servants of the British intelligence services, such as Tegart and Vickery, were able to liaise with the minority community at home – those Irish loyal to the Crown. Vickery expressed his uncertainty as to exactly how much Donovan knew of Bose and how much of such information should be revealed to his 'Irish Free State friends', but he nevertheless put together a package to be sent to him which contained a sketch of Bose's career and 'a rough appreciation of Bose's Communist connections'. Tellingly, he concluded: 'Mr Donovan may not want to pass this on in toto, but actually there is nothing in it which the Irish Free State authorities need not know.' Evidently, there were reservations about making the Irish authorities aware of either the British authorities' monitoring capabilities or of their wholly negative appreciation of a man who was soon to be the Irish Free State's guest. To what extent Donovan's intervention was successful, if at all, is not known; suffice to say that an honorary degree was not conferred on Bose when he was in Dublin. It is noteworthy also that Vickery and Tegart were happy to take Donovan's advice as they proceeded to overstate Bose's communist connections in their synopses, especially with regard to his relationship with M. N. Roy.[50] Possibly Donovan and others were hoping that, in the wake of Ireland's 'Red Scare' four years earlier, tarring Bose with the same brush would have resulted in a negative reception in Dublin.[51] But Bose's predominantly nationalist ideology would win out; anyway, by this stage Bose was in Germany courting those of an ideology directly opposed to communism, in the form of the Nazi Government. Tegart would rear his head again in an apparently similar set of circumstances where he provided his services in retirement during the Second World War.[52]

Netaji arrives

Bose's intention to visit Ireland finally reached the public domain via a short report in the *Irish Times* on 25 January 1936:

> Information has been received here that the exiled Indian leader Subhas Chandra Bose left Vienna yesterday for Dublin, where he will endeavour to re-organise the Indo-Irish League started by the late Mr V. J. Patel, the first President of the Indian Parliament. A number of London–Indian nationalists are proceeding to Dublin to meet Mr Bose, who is not allowed to visit England.[53]

Bose arrived in Cobh on 31 January 1936. The Immigration Office there informed him that he could not enter the UK, and in reply Bose stated his intention of leaving Cobh for the Continent within two weeks.[54] He made his way to Dublin and arrived there on 2 February. The next day was the busiest one of his crammed schedule. He was received at Government Buildings by de Valera and later in the evening at the Mansion House by the Lord Mayor, Alfred Byrne. Vickery's feel for Irish politics is divulged in the margin of an IPI report on Bose's trip. Where it states that Bose met with the Lord Mayor, he scribbled: 'I gather that Bose didn't get much out of him!'[55] Alfred Byrne was an ex-member of the Irish Parliamentary Party and soon to be a member of Cumann na nGaedheal, but Donovan's earlier-expressed hope that he 'would jib at receiving [Bose]' if he knew him to be a communist clearly did not hold true.[56]

As mentioned earlier, a visit to a city's corporation was a priority for Bose, and he managed to fit in a Dublin Corporation meeting and watched proceedings from the public gallery. Later that night he was guest of the IIIL at a reception in the Broadway Restaurant, where Maud

Gonne MacBride, President of the IIIL welcomed him. On 5 February he listened to proceedings in the Dáil from a seat in the Strangers' Gallery. He had interviews with the Minister for Defence, Frank Aiken, the Minister for Finance, Seán MacEntee, the Minister for Industry and Commerce, Seán Lemass, as well as Labour Party leader William Norton, Fianna Fáil TD P. J. Little and the Secretary of the Department of External Affairs, Joseph Walshe. On the evening of 7 February he was received by the Executive Committee of the Dublin Trades Union Council. He also attended a meeting of the Women Prisoners' Defence League in Cathal Brugha Street, which also was organised by Maud Gonne MacBride. On 10 February he attended a meeting of the Universities Republican Club at Gardiner's Row. His final engagement, a reception held in his honour in the Shelbourne Hotel, was perhaps the most elaborate. Bose addressed the gathering where speakers also included the prominent left-wing activists Peadar O'Donnell, Seán Murray and Frank Ryan;[57] among the guests were Erskine Childers and the IRA's director of intelligence Seán MacBride.[58]

The press embraced Subhas Chandra Bose, and his every movement while in the country was well documented. All of the newspapers took care to note the generally anti-imperialist rhetoric of his pronouncements. He regularly referred to Britain's harsh treatment of the Indian population over the years. The *Irish Times* quoted him as saying that India 'had nothing in common with Britain and [Indians] could never forget that they had been treated for a century and a half like something less than beasts'.[59] The *Irish Independent* reported Bose saying, on his departure, that in

> India he would endeavour to emphasise the great value of political alliance between Indian nationalists and Irish republicans. He added that he found the Irish people very sympathetic to Indian independence. He would also endeavour to send unofficial ambassadors of the Indian National Congress to Dublin.[60]

The *Irish Press* in particular delved into the relevance of Bose's visit, attempting to imbue its readership with a sense of the historical significance of such Indo-Irish connections. Its reports were longer and drew attention to the specifically nationalist parallels found in the two countries' independence movements. It regularly addressed the issue of political prisoners, a theme common to both:

> Mr Bose said that he had been eight times imprisoned in India for nationalist activities and was virtually exiled since 1933 . . . since 1930 there were 2,500 uncharged political prisoners in jail in Bengal, not to speak of those sentenced . . . one man had been on hunger strike for nearly two months.[61]

[101]

Bose would have been aware that his Irish audiences would receive such utterances empathetically, unlike the audiences addressed earlier in his European tour, which, although well disposed, would not have genuinely understood the practicalities of a protracted struggle from within and against the world's greatest Empire.

Although the Irish Special Branch was kept busy during Bose's stay, its reports were less informative than IPI's. The following passage referring to some of Bose's speeches perhaps throws light on the Special Branch's apparent lack of urgency as compared to the diligence of its British counterpart:

> His remarks related chiefly to the questions of freedom in India and to the outlining of circumstances and conditions obtaining in that country. His public utterances could be termed as definitely anti-imperialistic but he did not say anything which would indicate that he was otherwise than friendly towards the present government in An Saorstát.[62]

Given that relatively neutral evaluation of Bose by the Irish authorities, it is most curious to note that although British intelligence kept close tabs on his movements, its Special Branch still saw fit to probe its Irish counterpart for more information. Detective Sergeant Marsden, stationed at Holyhead, wrote to Dublin Castle in anticipation of Bose's sojourn in Ireland:

> My information as to the general character and political affiliations of Bose suggests the probability of his endeavouring to co-operate with one of the extreme political organisations in An Saorstát, viz the IRA or the Congress Party. I do not believe that his political views are such as would lead one to suspect his co-operation with the Communist party.[63]

This synopsis of Bose's politics was in partial contradiction of the views of some of his fellow intelligence officers at IPI. Marsden's communication was duly forwarded by Dublin Castle to the Department of Justice, a Garda officer adding the following:

> From the attached communication you will note that Detective Sergeant Marsden requests that he be informed of Bose's activities while in this country, and I would be glad if arrangements could be made to have this request complied with. I have found that co-operation with Sergeant Marsden has been most helpful to me at times in relation to the departure and arrival of certain persons engaged in political activities.[64]

However helpful the detective had been to this Garda Officer, his superiors had clearly decided not to return the favour. The Special Branch, with the agreement of the Department of Justice, decided 'to direct D/Garda Nolan to send a non-committal reply to the Holyhead Det. Branch as soon as the British Indian Leader leaves the Saorstát'.[65] That reply painted a picture very different from what had actually occurred during Bose's time in Ireland:

> With reference to your communication regarding the visit of the above-named gentleman to the Irish Free State, I beg to inform you that Mr Bose arrived in Ireland, having travelled via Le Havre and Cobh, on 31 January 1936 . . . The party proceeded direct to Dublin and remained in that city until Tuesday 11th, when they travelled to Cork . . . During his visit to Ireland Mr Bose met and conversed with people of all classes of political opinion. He also spoke at some meetings and attended social functions in Dublin, otherwise his visit was uneventful. He did not attract much attention while here.[66]

So, nothing of the extensive press coverage or information on the official government receptions was sent on to the British Special Branch.

IPI, however, managed to fill in many of the blanks in the information provided by the Irish authorities. As well as reporting each engagement, it was able to report that Bose had visited Mary MacSwiney in Cork before travelling on to Dublin by train where

> he was met . . . by Maud Gonne MacBride and other members of the Irish–Indian Independence League, which, it will be remembered, was formed by the late V. J. Patel, when he visited the Irish Free State, some three years ago.[67]

Interestingly it appears that Scotland Yard had informed IPI that Bose had been furnished with strong letters of introduction to various personalities in the Irish Free State by Art O'Brien, the Irish diplomatic representative to France. The two had met shortly before, in Paris, when Bose had called on O'Brien en route to Ireland.[68] IPI described those in attendance at the Indo-Irish reception held in Bose's honour in the Broadway Restaurant as a 'gathering [of] some 30 persons . . . all of whom belonged to the ultra-Republican Group, as for example Mrs Despard and Mrs Sheehy Skeffington'. It noted that Sheehy Skeffington had spoken of 'the heroic service rendered by Bose to India and to all the countries suffering under the yoke of British Imperialism'. It stated also that Bose had met with many officials of the Dublin Government and that in his meeting with the Minister for Industry and Commerce, Seán Lemass, 'he discussed possibilities for increased trade between India and the Free State'. IPI's evaluation of Bose's visit to Ireland, its impact and possible fallout, demonstrates that the Irish attempt to tone down matters had been in vain:

> Much has been made of Bose's visit in the Irish papers, and it is known that arrangements have been made for as much publicity as possible to be obtained for it in the Indian Press – in fact, it may be said that Bose's chief reason for going to the Free State was to secure as much advertisement for himself as was practicable.[69]

The report further illustrates the accuracy of IPI's interpretations of the intentions of the de Valera Government: while the Indian's anti-imperialist whirlwind tour had not been solicited, the Irish were only too happy to accommodate a like-minded rebel:

> It must, however be noted. . . that the interviews granted him were of his own seeking and that a like consideration would have been accorded by Free State Ministers to anyone known to be *persona non grata* with the British Government.[70]

There were also some interesting observations on the status quo in Irish politics at the time and the distancing that had occurred between de Valera and the more hard-line republicans. In a pertinent summing-up, IPI noted:

> It must be remembered that Bose went to Dublin as a friend of the late V. J. Patel, and as such was assured of a warm welcome from the members of the Irish Republican Group, whom Patel had come to know intimately . . . This Group, although it was originally responsible for putting the de Valera faction into power, now constitutes a bloc of irreconcilables and extremists which is rather a thorn in the side of the more moderate, though nevertheless, still anti-British party which is now in the saddle.[71]

Its detailed record of Bose's speeches and talks while in Ireland reveals concern that he had expressed the opinion that India as a whole had been influenced by Ireland's fight for independence and considered it important that the two countries should maintain connections. IPI was also irritated that Bose had made the most of his refusal of entry to the UK. The level of vexation went up a notch when the author of the report strangely observed that 'in alluding to his own imprisonment, [Bose had] omitted to mention that he had been compassionately released before the expiry of his sentence in order to permit him to secure medical treatment in Europe'. IPI did grant, however, that in expressing himself as he had in Ireland, and in his choice of examples, 'Subhas Bose showed great skill in adapting himself to the mentality of his audience'.

There is an ominous report of note in one of Bose's IPI files dating from 1936 and concerning Ireland. IPI had received information pertaining to Bose from a reliable source in Berlin, part of whose brief was to identify anti-British activity among Indians in Europe. The unknown author of the report stated:

> The following information was given to me in strict confidence . . . [b]y a violent and well-informed opponent of the present German Government . . . it was obtained at first hand from an Indian supporter of Bose, and may be accepted as accurate and genuine as far as my informant is concerned.[72]

After detailing Bose's somewhat fruitless meetings with German officials in January 1936 the report went on to describe his more successful encounter with Mussolini. It related specifically that 'assistance is
consequently reaching the instigators of the anti-British movement in
India through the Italian Consul General in Bombay and – as a more
secure channel – through the Riunione Adriatica, where the funds can
be disguised as ordinary insurance transactions.'[73] In conclusion the
Berlin report stated that there was reason to believe that 'arrangements
have also been made for the supply of weapons needed by terrorists
from or via Ireland'. With little else to go on here, the truth of this claim
is difficult to ascertain, although there have been various reports, not
all of them unfounded, of secret shipments of arms from Germany to
Ireland since the early 1920s.[74]

'Impressions of Ireland'

Two important sources give us first-hand accounts of Subhas Chandra
Bose's impression of his Irish visit: a statement that Bose released on
reaching Lausanne, on 30 March 1936, entitled 'Impressions of Ireland';
and the letters Bose wrote to Woods in the wake of his trip, which naturally had became more lengthy and more personal as the two had by then
met.[75] He had travelled to Lausanne en route to India in order to meet up
with Jawaharlal Nehru.[76] In his 'Lausanne statement' he said that he had
'learned much that will be useful and interesting to us in India'. It seems
that his meetings with Irish ministers were most worthwhile. He felt
that these men were somewhat unique and easy to relate to:

> Besides having prolonged discussions with Mr de Valera, I met individu-
> ally most of the Fianna Fáil ministers. All of them are exceedingly sym-
> pathetic, accessible and humane. They had not yet become 'respectable'.
> Most of them had been on the run when they were fighting for their
> freedom and would be shot at sight if they had been spotted. They had not
> yet [become] hardened bureaucratic ministers and there was no official
> atmosphere about them.[77]

It is reasonable to assume that these meetings consisted of nothing
more than the Irish ministers articulating their adherence to the principle of Indian independence, as well as expressing in general terms
their sympathy for Bose's position. However, this was not so:

> With the Minister for Agriculture I discussed how they were trying to make
> the country self-sufficient in the matter of food supply. It was interesting
> to know that wheat and sugar-beet were now being cultivated in large areas
> and the development of agriculture was making the country less dependent
> on cattle-rearing and therefore less dependent on the English market. I also

discussed with him the question of restriction of jute-cultivation in India and he gave me valuable suggestions as to how he would tackle the problem if he were put in charge.[78]

Bose stated that on the whole he found the work of the Fianna Fáil ministers of interest and of potential value to his countrymen, who themselves would soon have to tackle the problem of nation-building through the machinery of state. Pragmatic and profitable exchanges abounded between the two parties. Advice on looking to the future and tips on self-governance were imparted behind closed doors, in contrast to the preferred public rhetoric which centred on the two countries' shared history and experiences of the treacherous Empire. Such public talk had, admittedly, a dual purpose: to please the crowds and to irritate the British authorities. In his statement Bose also provided a summing-up of the situation in Irish politics as he saw it in 1936. Though short, it is a surprisingly accurate summation on the part of one who had visited the country only once, and it demonstrates Bose's ability to analyse the dynamics of complex political situations:

> The only unfortunate feature in Irish politics today is the breach between Fianna Fáil and the republicans, 25 of whom have been put in prison. The feeling of the government is that the republicans are too impatient and tactless and are blind to the realities of the situation – namely the existence of a pro-British party in the country and a partitioned Ireland in actual existence – which make it difficult if not impossible to declare a Republic at once. The members of the Fianna Fáil Party affirm it, but [say] that the actual declaration of it must depend on several factors or conditions.[79]

Bose was agreeably surprised to find that all Irish parties were equally sympathetic towards India and the people's desire for freedom regardless of their own internal differences. He also expressed his sense of fulfilment at having had the opportunity to carry out what he saw as useful publicity on behalf of India while in Ireland. He was suitably impressed to have been asked so often to speak on present-day conditions in India during his talks in Dublin. He concluded his 'Lausanne statement' by expressing an outlook that would have given a European or an Indian reader the impression of a very cosmopolitan 1930s' Ireland: 'outside their own shores the two countries which interested [the Irish] most were India and Egypt'.[80]

Letters to Mrs Woods

In his first letter to Mrs Woods after he had left Dublin, from Austria on 5 March 1936, we see evidence confirming IPI's report of the Bose–MacSwiney meeting. In fact he met with Mary MacSwiney again, on his return to Cork before he set sail for the Continent. Bose's letters to Mrs Woods had acquired a more affectionate tone, and it appears that the two had warmed to one another considerably:

> I cannot thank you sufficiently for your extreme kindness during my stay in Dublin and I therefore bring with me the most pleasant recollections. Your daughters were also extremely kind to me . . . please convey my grateful thanks to all of them . . . In a few days I shall write again to you as to what I think we should do – or could do – to continue this contact between India and Ireland . . . I do not know when we shall meet again. Bhavabhuti, one of our ancient poets, once wrote – 'Time is eternal and the earth is a vast expanse', so maybe we shall meet again – but perhaps not so unexpectedly as when I knocked against my prison-superintendent in [The] Shelbourne Hotel![81]

Mollie Woods seems to have been equally fond of Bose and was determined to keep the Indo-Irish connection alive. She replied promptly to Bose's first letter after his departure, sending press-cuttings and news from Dublin. He replied on 30 March, telling her how Ireland was still at the forefront of his mind:

> I often think of the days I spent in Dublin. It is like a dream and those [?days] went so quickly. I am grateful most of all to you for making my stay so interesting and pleasant. What I like most in you was that there was one spirit running through the whole family – one does not always find this.[82]

He went on to encourage Mrs Woods to continue being politically active, especially by trying to keep India a hot topic within Irish republican circles. However, interestingly, as a result of some experience he'd had in Dublin he expressed his doubts about the effectiveness of Maud Gonne MacBride:

> I am sure you will do useful work if you continue hammering. I am afraid that we can expect nothing from Miss M[83] and I am sorry that she has so much influence over Madame. However, you must go on doing your best and the result will certainly be encouraging to you.[84]

The Bose–Woods friendship had benefits other than the boosting of each other's egos via airmail, as may be seen from Bose's letter dated 31 March 1936.[85] When the passenger ship on which he was travelling docked at Port Said, in Egypt, Bose was prevented from disembarking. The British authorities seized his passport, and a policeman kept guard over him for the duration of the stay. Bose wrote:

> The incident is interesting – is it not? I did not know that I was a dangerous man even in Egypt. You may give publicity to the above incident, if you like. After this, you may imagine what sort of reception they will arrange in Bombay![86]

Even before she had met him, Woods had apparently been helping Bose with his propaganda campaign by drawing public attention to the Indian independence movement. In a letter of 20 February 1934 Bose told her how 'we are particularly grateful to you for the prompt reply to Mrs Cousins' article on her jail experiences. I was astounded to read it. Really I cannot understand her mentality.'[87] Margaret Cousins, after being sentenced to one year in prison for protesting the introduction of legislation which curtailed free speech in India, had gone on hunger-strike in support of Gandhi, then also imprisoned. Bose does not make clear what it was about her subsequent writings that he took issue with, but it more than likely related to her being more lenient about the Government of India than he would have liked. It must be empha-sised that Bose did not support Gandhi unquestioningly, as did many of his contemporaries. He was regularly frustrated by what he perceived as Gandhi's lack of urgency and that of the Mahatma's obedient and devout followers, Cousins being one. Bose was perhaps surprised that her Irish credentials did not automatically imbue her with more radical leanings. Bose also availed himself of the opportunity to air his views on domestic political problems when writing to Woods. He expressed his frustration at the more moderate element of the Indian National Congress who were in control of the estate of the late V. J. Patel, and in doing so alluded to Congress's perception of him in 1935 as perhaps being too radical. Bose was relying on the endowment of a quite hefty sum to carry out propaganda abroad. He complained that

> The probate was granted by the High Court of Bombay nearly fourteen months ago but the money is lying idle. The official party seems to be opposed to the idea that I should undertake the work. They were of course opposed to the late Mr Patel in his lifetime, but I never expected that meanness would go so far.[88]

Bose and Woods continued to correspond throughout 1937. Bose kept her informed of his circumstances in India, his imprisonments and internments at various times, as well as his health, which was again deteriorating. He told her that he had been trying to keep up to date on Irish affairs, and had managed to do so until the circulation of Irish papers in India had again stopped. The Indian papers, however, were cov-ering the new Irish constitution and he asked her to forward him a copy of the constitution, which she duly did. It appears that Mollie Woods's correspondence proved a useful propaganda device for Bose at home in India, and it came in handy during one of his stints in prison. In a letter from the Punjab dated 9 September 1937, he said: 'the cable you sent to India after my arrest last year was duly published in all the papers with a great deal of prominence. It was very kind of you to do so.'[89]

In late 1937 Bose, by this stage President-Elect of the Indian National Congress, as a result of a rapprochement with Gandhi, decided that he would undertake another trip to Europe. While there he would recuperate and write. This time, having written to the Secretary of State for India, the Marquis of Zetland, he was allowed to enter Britain.[90] He informed Mollie Woods of his intentions to travel in December. He had clearly grown to trust her confidence and abilities entirely, as he now had an important mission for her:

> The British Government have, at long last raised the ban of my entry into England – so I can come there. Can you please make enquiries *confidentially* if I can pay a visit to President de Valera when I am in England? It will be a courtesy call. The approximate date will be between the 16th and 19th January. Please treat this matter as *strictly confidential* and let not a soul know beyond the President and his Secretary. When you write back, please address the cover to Miss E. Schenkl,[91] Poste Restante, Badgastein and send it in a *sealed registered cover*. It is important and necessary to take this precaution, because I do not like that anybody else should know about this visit until I actually arrive in Dublin.[92]

He was particularly keen to get a picture of himself and de Valera as 'the Indian papers have been pressing for a photograph of President Dev. and myself when I meet him. They were extremely disappointed when I was in Dublin the last time.' In this letter, we see also how concerned Bose is about the British interception of his correspondence (which, judging by his IPI file in particular, was carried out with due diligence) when he noted at the end of the letter: 'PS I am enclosing the cover of your letter. I wonder if your seals were in this condition when the letter left Dublin?'[93] Mrs Woods immediately began to make the arrangements necessary for the meeting.

In one way, as it turns out, a meeting with de Valera was not to be as awkward a manoeuvre as he had anticipated. Like Bose, in January 1938 de Valera was in London, negotiating what was to become the Anglo-Irish Agreement of 1938. As this meeting could now take place in London, however, the chances of it remaining a secret were slim, to say the least, with both men being closely watched by the British. Sure enough IPI officials got wind of the meeting.[94] It seems possible, though, that they were caught off guard and were not aware of it until it actually took place, as they had mistakenly suspected de Valera of having arranged the rendezvous himself:

> Bose was received by President de Valera at the latter's hotel at midnight on Saturday 15th January: it is understood that the interview was at the request of the President of Éire, but this has not yet been confirmed: de Valera is at present heading a Delegation to London for Conversations about Trade and Defence, and it is possible that he wished to discuss trade

questions with the President-Elect of the Indian National Congress, whom he had received on the occasion of the latter's visit to Dublin some years back.[95]

Here we come to know, too, that IPI was aware of the Bose–Woods friendship although to what extent is not clear:

> Bose is also known to have been in touch by telephone with Mrs M. Woods of Dublin, with whom he was associated formerly in connection with the 'Indo-Irish League' – of which, incidentally, nothing has been heard for some considerable time.[96]

During his short trip to London Bose met an array of people, including the Labour politicians Arthur Greenwood, Ernest Bevin, Stafford Cripps and Clement Attlee, as well as some well-seasoned activists on Indian issues like Agatha Harrison and Harry Pollitt, the General Secretary of the Communist Party of Great Britain. However, Mihir Bose believes that 'another encounter probably meant more to him: a midnight meeting with Eamon de Valera at a London hotel'.[97] It is not known what transpired between the two men that night, but that they were both eager to meet is apparent.

There was one last alleged contact, albeit shrouded in uncertainty, between the two men before Bose's death. After the outbreak of the Second World War, with the age-old theory of the enemy's difficulty being an opportunity and the 1916 Irish Rising clearly in mind, Bose decided to embark on an elaborate mission. He would set up an Indian Government in exile which would embark on a propaganda campaign and instigate uprisings in India. With the Axis powers' help, by allowing captured Indian soldiers to align themselves with his newly styled Indian National Army (INA) he would eventually invade the country and dismantle the Raj once and for all. Bose's INA mission was ambitious, and, although appealing in principle, proved too far-fetched an idea for the Nazi Foreign Minister Ribbentrop to buy into.[98] Having escaped India in January 1941 (a masterstroke, considering he was under house arrest) Bose's 'plan B', not having been given the green light by the Russians, was to make for Berlin.[99] While based there for two years he received little support from the German Government, which put up with his presence only for its propaganda value. He was, however, allowed to set up a Free India Centre. During this time he also tried his hand with the Italians and paid visits to Mussolini. With still no success in acquiring support it appears that frustration got the better of him, as he is said to have taken to alcohol, cigarettes and beef for the first time.[100] Eventually Bose was transported by submarine to the Far East where he found General Tojo more accommodating and was helped in being allowed to recruit an army from Indian prisoners of war.[101]

The BBC Monitoring Service recorded five messages broadcast by Bose from Japan (some via Germany) to Ireland in late 1943 and early 1944. He had much to say about Ireland's influence on his thinking at this time:

> Of all the freedom movements we Indians have studied closely and from which we have received inspiration, there is perhaps none that can equal the Irish struggle for independence. The Irish nation has had the same oppressors and exploiters as ourselves. It has had the same experience of ruthlessness, brutality and hypocrisy as we have had . . . In 1916 Irish Republicans set up their provisional government on the eve of the Easter Rebellion. In 1943 India's freedom fighters set up their provisional government before launching their struggle for liberty. There was so much in common between us that it is natural that there should be a deep bond of affinity and comradeship between the Irish nation and ourselves.[102]

Most of these broadcasts started off by thanking President de Valera for having sent a congratulatory message to Bose's Indian provisional government. After the war Sir John Maffey was asked to enquire if the Irish Government could provide him with copies of any communications sent between the two men during those years. INA officers on trial in Delhi in 1945 had requested the documents, presumably for use as evidence that they had been fighting for an internationally recognised *Azad Hind* Government, although that is not made clear in the Dominions Office file in question. The Irish Department of External Affairs claimed that the only correspondence it had relating to Subhas Chandra Bose was a communication on file from the Japanese Consul to de Valera dated 17 November 1943, with an enclosed brief cable message from Bose declaring the formation of the Indian provisional government. External Affairs sent a copy of it to Maffey along with Joseph Walshe's short acknowledgment of its receipt to the Japanese Consul. De Valera had in fact refused recognition of Bose's provisional government in the Dáil in February 1944. The newly elected independent TD Oliver J. Flanagan, who had been openly pro-Axis in his utterances in the Dáil during the war, pressed him on the issue.[103] He asked the Taoiseach in his capacity as Minister for External Affairs if he was aware that a 'National Provisional Government for India has been established at Rangoon, Burma, and acts as government of the Andaman and the Nicobar Islands, and whether he will give recognition to this authority'. De Valera responded:

> I am aware of the existence of the body to which the Deputy's question refers. In conformity with the customary practise of neutral states, recognition has not been given during the course of hostilities to any new State or regime which owes its existence to the changing fortunes of the war.[104]

Flanagan responded briskly in a manner he knew would irritate de Valera: 'could the Taoiseach indicate why he will not recognise this government in view of efforts for recognition when the provisional government was established in this country?' De Valera was not drawn on the issue.

Bose had in fact received the good wishes of some in Ireland in his endeavours, but they were far from official, and we are aware of them through British wartime interceptions of diplomatic traffic. A decoded telegram from the Japanese Consul in Dublin detailed the activities of an obscure organisation called the Green Front in November 1943, an apparently national anti-partition movement, of which little is known.[105] The group met in Dublin on 5 November to commemorate the death of James Daly, who had been executed after the Connaught Rangers' mutiny in India in 1920.[106] Those known to have been associated with this group, according to Army Intelligence (G2), were Seamus O'Kelly of Sinn Féin and Martin Bell of Clann na Poblachta.[107] G2 also noted that this group had apparently been in contact 'with [the] London Branch of the Indian Revolutionary movement organised by Chandra Bose'. At the gathering they adopted a resolution sympathising with Bose's Indian independence movement:

> IRI Republicans (decoder please note this is not the so-called IRA), assembled on the day of remembrance of James Daly who was condemned by the British oppressors of India, congratulate Subhas Chandra Bose, Supreme Commander of the Indian National Army, on his splendid efforts. We look forward with confidence to the fight that the Indian National Army will wage, in emulation of the fight for freedom of the Army of the Irish Republic and under the leadership of the Independent Indian provisional government, for truth, justice and freedom.[108]

It is interesting to see that this group directly noted Bose's use of Irish precedents and that information regarding his activities was accessible to them at a time when strict wartime censorship conditions pertained. Also these activities provided the German propagandist Hans Hartmann with valuable material, as G2 was also in a position to note how in a broadcast talk he 'referred to a message of goodwill sent from Irish Republicans to Chandra Bose, and also material help from the Irish Govt. to the Famine'.[109] G2 was concerned about the matter and the head of military intelligence, Dan Bryan, added a note to the memo asking: '[H]ow did Germany get hold of this item?'[110] It seems probable that both 'Germany' (or more specifically Hartmann) and Bose received this information via the Japanese Consul in Dublin.[111] This particular communication led Bose to incorrectly assume that a message of support had been received from de Valera. As a result of this broadcast it is now widely believed that such a communication had been sent to Bose from de Valera during the war, when in fact it had not.[112]

Conclusion

Netaji Bose is generally thought to have died when his plane crash-landed on take off from the island of Formosa (Taiwan) in August 1945, three days after the allied victory over Japan.[113] The thorn in the side of the British Empire and the Raj was finally removed. Bose had died doing what he had always threatened to do, fighting the British with the sword, despite and against the wishes of his many pacifist contemporaries. Throughout his life Ireland had been a massive influence on him. As a teenager in Bengal he had read of Ireland's fight for freedom. He had experienced for himself the fruits of the Irish struggle when he had visited Dublin in 1936. He had met with and learnt from those who had participated in that fight and were then in government. He also exchanged ideas with some of the more militant Irish republicans and developed friendships that remained intact until his death. From the formation of an Irish-style Volunteer Force in Calcutta in 1928, to the propaganda campaign to gain recognition for Indian independence in the mid-1930s and the eventual armed struggle against the British during the Second World War, Ireland was an evident influence on Bose throughout his life. The British intelligence services, however, were preoccupied with communism during the inter-war period, so that the possible impact of such anti-colonial blueprints on Indian nationalists like Bose was not given due consideration.

Notes

1   Bose to Woods, 21 Dec. 1935, reproduced in Bose, *Letters, Articles*, p. 125.
2   *Netaji* (meaning 'great leader') is used nowadays as a respectful, honorific address.
3   French, *Liberty*, p. 202. On 14 May 1999 the Indian Government entrusted Justice (retired) M. K. Mukherjee of the Supreme Court with an in-depth inquiry into the disappearance of Netaji Subhas Chandra Bose: www.hindustantimes.com/news/specials/Netaji/deathstory.htm.
4   Bose and Collins also have something in common in death. Controversy has surrounded Michael Collins's death, with historians deliberating over whether he was murdered or if his shooting was an accident. For contrasting views see John M. Feehan, *The Shooting of Michael Collins: Murder or Accident?* (Cork, 1981), and Meda Ryan, *The Day Michael Collins Was Shot* (Dublin, 1989).
5   See 'Case against Benegal's Bose film in Bengal', *Times of India*, 12 May 2005; available: http://timesofindia.com/atricleshow/1107096.cms.
6   Eunan O'Halpin, ' "India's de Valera" or India's Casement? Subhas Chandra Bose and allied intelligence, 1939–45', paper presented at the Irish Conference of Historians, Trinity College, Dublin, 19–21 May 2005. In August 2005 a similar paper was given by O'Halpin at the Netaji Research Bureau, Kolkata; the revelation received front-page coverage throughout India: *Hindustan Times*, 15 Aug. 2005; available: www.hindustantimes.com/news/181_1462197,0008.htm.

7 M. Bose, *Lost Hero*, p. 12.
8 *Ibid.*, p. 15.
9 French, *Liberty*, p. 115.
10 M. Bose, *Lost Hero*, p. 36.
11 *Ibid.*, p. 31.
12 French, *Liberty*, p. 116.
13 Taken from 'a brief sketch of Bose's career', by Vickery, dated June 1935, BL, OIOC, IOR, L/P&J/12/215.
14 *Ibid.*
15 French, *Liberty*, p. 116.
16 See various miscellaneous IPI reports on Bose's activities in BL, OIOC, IOR, L/P&J/12/214 and BL, OIOC, IOR, L/P&J/12/215.
17 Taken from 'a brief sketch of Bose's career', by Vickery, June 1935, BL, OIOC, IOR, L/P&J/12/215.
18 M. Bose, *Lost Hero*, pp. 102–3.
19 Extract from Subhas Chanrda Bose, *The Indian Struggle 1920–34* (London, 1935) quoted in BL, OIOC, IOR, L/P&J/12/216.
20 General IPI update on Bose's activities in Europe in 1936, BL, OIOC, IOR, L/P&J/216.
21 Bose, *Indian Struggle*, pp. 397–9.
22 Andrew, *Secret Service*: see chapters 9 and 10.
23 IPI report on Bose's activities, 1933, BL, OIOC, IOR, L/P&J/12/214.
24 *Ibid.*
25 General IPI update on Bose's activities in Europe in 1936, BL, OIOC, IOR, L/P&J/12/216.
26 Manini Chatterjee, *Do and Die: The Chittagong Uprising 1930–34* (New Delhi, 1999), p. 56. Chatterjee has a section in the book titled 'Inspiration from Ireland', pp. 55–61.
27 *Ibid.*; and Durba Ghosh, 'Britain's global war on terrorism: containing political violence and insurgency in the interwar years', paper presented at the conference 'How Empire mattered: imperial structures and globalisation in the era of British imperialism', Berkeley, CA, April 2003; see also BL, OIOC, MSS EUR D 1194/4b, Grassley Collection, 'The Chittagong raid: terrorism in Bengal, 1927–37'.
28 Chatterjee, *Do and Die*, pp. 56–7.
29 *Ibid.*, pp. 60–1; for a side-by-side reading of both documents see pp. 305–7.
30 *Ibid.*
31 IPI report 'Subhas Chandra Bose and his contacts', 12 Feb. 1935, BL, OIOC, IOR, L/P&J/12/215. There is no record of this message in the NAI.
32 Bewley to Walshe, 9 April 1934, NAI, DFA, 19/50. This letter, which is reproduced in Appendix 4, provides an interesting insight into Nazi Germany in the mid-1930s, and also throws light on Bose's political astuteness; also see Bewley to Walshe, 22 Jan. 1936, NAI, DFA, 19/50A and *DIFP* 4, pp. 409–10.
33 *The Essential Writings of Netaji Subhas Chandra Bose*, ed. S. K. Bose and S. Bose (Oxford, 1997), pp. 8–9.
34 M. Bose, *Lost Hero*, (2004), pp. 315–16. A revised version of the biography was published in 2004.
35 Bose, *Letters, Articles*, p. 40; this letter, one of Bose's first to Woods, is reproduced in Appendix 5.
36 Bose to Woods, 9 Jan. 1936, NAI, DFA, 105/62; see also Bose, *Letters, Articles*, p. 132.
37 Memorandum of discussion between Eamon de Valera and John J. Hearne, 18 Aug. 1933, UCDA, P150/2303, and contained in *DIFP* 4, pp. 267–8.
38 Walshe to Ruttledge, 21 Aug. 1933, NAI, JUS, 8/443.
39 *Ibid.*, Ruttledge to Walshe, 23 Aug. 1933.
40 *Ibid.*, Duff to E. N. Cooper, Aliens Department, Home Office, London, 3 April 1935.
41 *Ibid.*, Cooper to Duff, 15 April 1935.

42 Bose, *Lost Hero*, pp. 95–7.
43 *Ibid.*
44 Report on Subhas Chandra Bose, 19 Oct. 1933, BL, OIOC, IOR, L/P&J/12/214.
45 Report titled 'Subhas Chandra Bose and his contacts', 12 Feb. 1935, BL, OIOC, IOR, L/P&J/12/215.
46 *Ibid.* The paragraph before the one pertaining to Ireland detailed how that January, Bose had met with and left a great impression on, the Italian leader Mussolini.
47 Vickery to Johnston, 14 June 1935, BL, OIOC, IOR, L/P&J/12/215.
48 *Ibid.*
49 *Ibid.*
50 See note on Bose's communist connections, 1935, BL, OIOC, IOR, L/P&J/12/215.
51 For further reading on 'the red scare' in Ireland see Dermot Keogh, 'De Valera, the Catholic Church and the "Red Scare", 1931–32', in J. P. O'Carroll and John A. Murphy, *De Valera and His Times* (Cork, 1983), pp. 134–59.
52 See chapter four.
53 *Irish Times*, 25 Jan. 1936; see also clippings contained in NAI, JUS, 8/443.
54 Immigration Office, Cobh, to Department of Justice, 1 Feb. 1936, NAI, JUS, 8/443.
55 Report on Subhas Chandra Bose, 13 Feb. 1936, BL, OIOC, IOR, L/P&J/12/216.
56 See above and Vickery to Johnston, 14 June 1935, BL, OIOC, IOR, L/P&J/12/215.
57 For further information on these men and the left-wing movement at this time see English, *Radicals*; O'Drisceoil, *Peadar O'Donnell*; Fearghal McGarry, *Frank Ryan* (Dublin, 2002) and O'Connor *Reds*.
58 Preceding details on Bose's activities in Dublin is an accumulation of information from BL, OIOC, IOR, L/P&J/216; NAI, JUS, 8/443 and contemporary press reports.
59 *Irish Times*, 4 Feb. 1936.
60 *Irish Independent*, 26 Feb. 1936.
61 *Irish Press*, 3 Feb. 1936.
62 Special Branch report, 14 Feb. 1936, NAI, JUS, 8/443.
63 *Ibid.*
64 *Ibid.*
65 O'Connor to Department of Justice, 4 Feb. 1936, NAI, JUS, 8/443.
66 Draft reply attached to Special Branch report by McGloin, 14 Feb. 1936, NAI, JUS, 8/443.
67 Report on Subhas Chandra Bose, 13 Feb. 1936, BL, OIOC, IOR, L/P&J/12/216.
68 O'Brien to Walshe, 29 Jan. 1936, NAI, DFA, P2/56.
69 Report on Subhas Chandra Bose, 13 Feb. 1936, BL, OIOC, IOR, L/P&J/12/216.
70 *Ibid.*
71 *Ibid.*
72 Two page secret report titled 'Anti-British activities in India', author unknown and dated with just the year 1936, BL, OIOC, IOR, L/P&J/12/216.
73 *Ibid.* This is a reference to Riuione Adriatica di Sicurita, the Italian insurance firm which would later be implicated in the post war investigations into the unpaid insurance claims of Holocaust victims.
74 Hanley, *The IRA*, p. 33.
75 Some of these letters are reproduced in Appendix 5.
76 Mrs Nehru was seriously ill and seeking treatment; she actually died while Bose was there on 28 February, Judith Brown, *Nehru: A Political Life* (Yale, 2003), pp. 120–1.
77 Bose, *Letters, Articles*, p. 351.
78 *Ibid.*, p. 352.
79 *Ibid.*, p. 351.
80 *Ibid.*, p. 352.
81 *Ibid.*, p. 149. This last jibe was in relation to a strange occurrence during Bose's trip to Dublin, where he bumped into a former prison officer he knew from one of his spells in prison. He seemingly had fond recollections of his Irish jail keeper, and was delighted to have seen him.
82 *Ibid.*, p. 169.

83 This more than likely refers to Maud Gonne MacBride's influence over the ageing Madame Despard, though why Bose should be so critical of her is not clear.
84 Bose, *Letters, Articles*, p. 169.
85 *Ibid.*, pp. 170–1.
86 *Ibid.*
87 *Ibid.*, p. 53.
88 *Ibid.*, p. 125.
89 *Ibid.*, p. 225.
90 M. Bose, *Lost Hero*, p. 117. As we know, Bose could have visited Britain at any time with his passport. The British authorities, anxious to keep up the pretence, had the British Consul in Austria stamp his passport with a 'fictitious endorsement' nonetheless.
91 This is Emile Schenkl, with whom Bose fell in love, in Vienna in 1933. He fathered their child and they later married. In May 2005 the inclusion of the marriage in a new film about Bose was one of the objections an Indian political group had to its release.
92 Bose, *Letters, Articles*, p. 236.
93 *Ibid.*, p. 238.
94 Vickery to Sir John Ewart, DIB, 20 Jan. 1938, BL, OIOC, IOR, L/P&J/12/217.
95 *Ibid.*
96 *Ibid.*
97 M. Bose, *Lost Hero*, p. 118.
98 French, *Liberty*, p. 204.
99 The circumstances surrounding Bose's escape, with significant new evidence relating to the famous 'Silver' double-agent case, were recently re-examined by Eunan O'Halpin in ' "India's de Valera" '.
100 French, *Liberty*, p. 204.
101 *Ibid.*, p. 205. French puts the number of voluntary INA recruits in the Far East at 10,000, other perhaps more accurate estimates go so far as to suggest 40,000: Leonard A. Gordan, *Brothers Against the Raj: A Biography of Indian Nationalists Sarat and Subhas Chandra Bose* (Calcutta, 1997), p. 498.
102 NAUK, Records of the Dominions Office (hereafter DO), 35/2059.
103 *Dáil Debates*, vol. 92, 16 Feb. 1944, O'Halpin, *Defending*, p. 223. It is also interesting to note how a week later Flanagan was putting pressure on the Government to provide a site for the erection of a memorial stone to the memory of the Connaught Rangers Mutiny in India in 1920: *Dáil Debates*, vol. 92, 23 Feb. 1944.
104 *Dáil Debates*, vol. 92, 16 Feb. 1944.
105 Japanese Consul General, Dublin, to Tokyo, 19 Nov. 1943, NAUK, Records of the Government Code and Cipher School (hereafter HW), 12/295. My thanks to Eunan O'Halpin for information on this document. It is interesting to note that the text of this decoding was shared with the US War Department. See chapter five for information regarding the Friends of India Society established during the war, for which this organisation may have been a front.
106 For further information regarding the Connaught Rangers' mutiny see Anthony Babbington, *The Devil to Pay: The Mutiny of the Connaught Rangers in India, July 1920* (London, 1991).
107 Handwritten note titled 'Evidence of Indian association to date', 10 Nov. 1943, Irish Military Archives (hereafter IMA), Army Intelligence (hereafter G2), G2/X/1317
108 Japanese Consul General, Dublin, to Tokyo, 19 Nov. 1943, NAUK, HW, 12/29.
109 Handwritten note titled 'Evidence of Indian association to date', 10 Nov. 1943, IMA, G2/X/1317. Hans Hartmann was head of the Irland-Redaktion German propaganda radio station which also broadcast Irish news and propaganda pieces. He was a Celtic scholar who had lived and travelled throughout Ireland in the 1930s, and was fluent in Irish. Also, see chapter four for information regarding the Irish Government sending monetary aid to Bengal during the famine.
110 *Ibid.*
111 See chapter four for further information regarding the Japanese Vice Consul in

Dublin and contacts with the Friends of India Society, a society whose membership overlapped with the Green Front's.

112 See for example French, *Liberty*, p. 207 and M. Bose, *Lost Hero*, p. 216.
113 French, *Liberty*, p. 209. As noted this is still highly disputed, see M. Bose, *Lost Hero*, pp. 248–53.

1 Philip Vickery as a young police officer at the Delhi *durbar*, 1911

2   Shapurji Saklatvala, Communist MP

3   Mollie Woods, founder member of the Indian–Irish Independence League

4   Maud Gonne MacBride, her daughter Iseult Stuart, Charlotte Despard and
Andrew Woods (husband of Mollie Woods), on Red Cross duty, Dublin

5   The Woods/Dey family (*standing, left to right*) Baby Woods, Mr H. L.
Dey, father of Tripura, Mollie Woods, Enda Woods; (*seated*) Andy
Woods and Tripura Dey

6 Political rally at College Green, Dublin: Maud Gonne MacBride and Charlotte Despard are seen seated on the left, 1932

7 Subhas Chandra Bose meeting George Lansbury, London, 1938

8   Frank Aiken and Eamon de Valera meeting Jawaharlal Nehru, Delhi, 1948

9   Eamon de Valera, Jawaharlal Nehru and Lady Mountbatten, Delhi, 1948

10   Eamon de Valera being introduced to Indira Gandhi, daughter of Prime Minister Nehru, with Frank Aiken in the background, Delhi, 1948

11   Group photograph taken on the occasion of Jawaharlal Nehru's visit to Ireland in 1956, featuring: (*left to right*) Maud Aiken, Phyllis O'Ceallaigh, Jawaharlal Nehru, President Seán T. O'Ceallaigh, the Indian Ambassador to Ireland Vijaya Lakshmi Pandit (Jawhralal Nehru's sister), Eamon de Valera; (*behind*) unidentified, possibly N. R. Pillai, Secretary General of the Indian Department of External Affairs, the President's *aides-de-camp*: Commandant Michael J. Hefferon and Colonel Sean O'Sullivan; Frank Aiken, Áras an Uachtaráin, Dublin

12 Sarat Chandra Bose (brother of Subhas Chandra Bose) and daughters
Rome and Chitra (*standing*), with his wife Bivabati Bose and Eamon de
Valera on the occasion of their visit to Dublin, 1948. Sisir Kumar Bose
took the photograph

13 The Indian flag and Sikh sword presented to Eamon de Valera in San
Francisco by the Revolutionary Ghadr Party in 1919

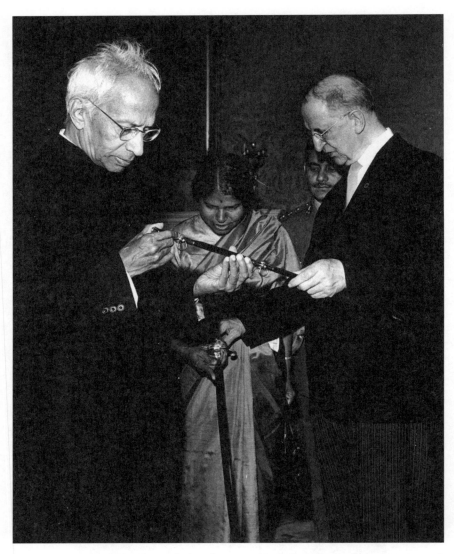

14   President Sarvepalli Radhakrishnan and Lakshmi N. Menon, Minister of State in the Indian Ministry of External Affairs, inspect the Sikh sword forty-five years after it was presented to Eamon de Valera, Áras an Uachtaráin, 1964

CHAPTER FOUR

The Second World War and the 'vanishing Empire'

Malik Rauf of the Berlin Radio then came to me and told me that all Indians must do something for the motherland and remarked 'Plight of England is an opportunity for India.' I was much impressed and gladly agreed to work for the motherland. I was asked to go to Éire to assist Irish National Army against Britain, as Germans had good relations with it. I accepted the suggestion and secretly reached Ireland with other co-workers.[1]

The onset of the Second World War furthered both Ireland's and India's national aspirations. In Ireland's case the decision to adopt the policy of neutrality provided the final realisation of independent action in foreign policy, and, on an international stage, it is considered by some Irish historians to have been a 'psychological necessity'.[2] However, a minority of radical nationalists remained who maintained allegiance to the Republic declared in 1916. They were disgruntled with the continuation of an impostor Irish Free State regime, and were willing to collaborate with Nazi agents to aid Britain's fall.

The decision made by the British Government during the war to grant India's freedom in its aftermath was one, Judith Brown has argued, 'made by a handful of British politicians as a by-product of war, not as a result of any prolonged discussion among India's rulers', and, crucially, by the end of the war Britain would become India's debtor, owing the country in excess of £1,300 million.[3] The war also provided radical Indian nationalists with opportunities to use Britain's difficulty as India's opportunity, as Ireland had done in 1916 and as seen in the previous chapter with Subhas Chandra Bose. But other motivated radicals, who were perhaps not as ambitious as Bose and were resident in Europe during the war, would help the nationalist movement in their own way and at their own pace. The war understandably resulted in increased surveillance by the British authorities of suspected subversives and it also saw greater surveillance by the Irish Government of Irish–Indian connections.

[127]

Lingering radicals

Towards the end of the 1930s, despite the fading Anglo-Irish trade war, de Valera was still considered quite the radical in British eyes and the British authorities continued to long for his departure from office. In the 1930s Prime Minster Baldwin shed some light on the problem when he remarked sardonically to the editor of the *Manchester Guardian* that 'there are three people . . . who are impossible to deal with – de Valera, Gandhi and Beaverbrook'.[4] When de Valera had come to power in 1932 the British Government had created an Irish Situation Committee (ISC) to evaluate and advise on the anticipated deterioration of the Anglo-Irish relationship. The Government was hindered by its lack of a representative in Ireland to keep it up to date on de Valera's intentions. There was only the Trade Commissioner William Peters to rely on for 'unofficial and sometimes improbable sources'.[5]

The ISC met regularly throughout the 1930s, and its work became all the more necessary with the outbreak of the economic war. The Secretary of State for Dominion Affairs, Malcolm MacDonald, a key member of the ISC, articulated feelings similar to those of Baldwin about dealing with de Valera, when, somewhat surprised by de Valera's business-like manner, he remarked that 'it is perhaps an indication of his present mood that in the course of [our four hour discussion] he never mentioned Oliver Cromwell or any other character or event which troubled Ireland prior to 1921'.[6] The tactic of bringing historical grievances into every discussion was one which IPI had accused Nehru of pursuing when it stated that 'he shares with Mr de Valera a habit of drawing upon the centuries for his arguments'.[7] The Secretary of State for India, the Marquess of Zetland, though not a permanent member of the ISC, was in 1936 a reluctant attendee, dourly reporting to the Viceroy Linlithgow, 'the following day I attended a long and dreary meeting of the Irish Situation Committee of the Cabinet'.[8]

However, Zetland became involved in a dispute with the ISC over a future declaration relating to Ireland's rights in the matter of secession from the Empire and the possible impact this would have on India. He thought the draft declaration, 'though drawn up only for the particular purposes of the controversy between the United Kingdom and the Free State, was in very general terms, which could easily be made applicable to other parts of the Empire'.[9] At a meeting in July 1936 he stressed that for many years the revolutionary elements in India 'had taken Ireland as their model, and when in 1921 it had appeared that the Irish extremists, as the reward of their resort to violence, were being given the substance of their demands, Indian opinion had been greatly affected'.[10] He remained concerned about this possible future declaration that

MacDonald thought 'the government might do well [to] keep up their sleeves [and] produce at some critical stage of the Free State negotiations'.[11] Zetland impressed on the ISC

> the unwisdom of making any public declaration to the effect that Ireland was mistress of her own house and could, if she desired to do so, leave the British Commonwealth of Nations without our attempting to resort to force to prevent her from going. I stressed the disastrous effect which any such public declaration would be likely to have in India, since India has always been ready enough to turn to Ireland as her model in so far as her subversive movements are concerned.[12]

Given these worries in the 1930s, it is interesting to note that by the late 1940s (and discussed in more detail in chapter five) India would again turn to Ireland for inspiration in relation to its 'secession from the Empire'.

Zetland was right to be concerned, as two years later, at the very conclusion of the economic war, during the negotiations which resulted in the Anglo-Irish Trade Agreement, the Irish Taoiseach was readily meeting with perhaps the most dangerous of all Indian radicals in his London hotel, then President of the Indian National Congress, Subhas Chandra Bose. De Valera would no doubt have willingly passed on pertinent information about his talks with the British authorities to the man whom he had received so cordially in Dublin two years earlier. These talks were proving quite successful, especially as Chamberlain was revealing himself to be more conciliatory in his approach to Ireland and dominions' affairs generally than any of his predecessors. In fact Bose was not the only Indian radical de Valera met that year.

In the autumn the 'patriot–journalist' and *Hindustan Times* reporter Chaman Lal paid a visit to Ireland. Lal had been brought to the Government of India's attention many years previously when he had been arrested and jailed four times in the 1920s in connection with the civil disobedience movement. IPI referred to him as 'Chaman Lal of Basil Blackett fame' (in order to differentiate him from another Indian of the same name, the left-wing *swarajist* Diwan Chaman Lal) in relation to an incident in 1928 when 'in a fit of nationalist ardour he threw his attaché case from the press gallery of the Legislative Assembly in Delhi on to the head of the late Sir Basil Blackett, the Finance Minister'.[13] Since then his widespread travelling (to Japan, North and South America as well as Europe) and his 'violently anti-British' writings ensured that IPI was monitoring his activities. Chaman Lal seems to have led the India Office on a merry dance throughout the 1930s. In April 1933 he had been given a passport (having been turned down on two previous occasions) on condition that he 'promise[d] that he would not do or say anything which would embarrass or annoy government'.[14]

On his arrival in the UK, India Office staff, initially convinced of his reformed character, actually assisted him by providing him with numerous introductions to journalistic circles in London. Yet concerns re-emerged when, in 1937, he was reported to be leaving Japan for America in order to arrange for the publication of his new book *The Vanishing Empire*, which, when it appeared the following year, was described by Vickery as 'thoroughly objectionable and quite rightly banned in India . . . even the Japanese were afraid of the political consequences following on the appearance of such a book'.[15] The India Office was perturbed at having had the wool pulled over its eyes by this Indian agitator and his passport was duly confiscated. The India Office was further vexed by the substantial publicity accorded to his visit to Dublin in August 1938.

The *Irish Press*'s view of Chaman Lal, while informed by essentially the same information, makes for quite different reading from his IPI file. Under the heading 'Ireland Inspires Indian Patriots' readers of the 31 August 1938 issue learned how Chaman Lal, 'the Indian Congress leader . . . attired in his national dress disembarked at Dun Laoghaire . . . bearing gifts for friends of India's struggle for freedom in Ireland'.[16] The report went on:

> For many years foreign correspondent of Delhi's *Hindustan Times* Mr Lal fell foul of the British authorities in India by reason of his activities in the Congress movement. He was imprisoned many times and his latest book, published in the USA, *The Vanishing Empire*, has been banned in India.[17]

Lal stressed that in all his lectures and writings he had instanced Ireland as 'a headline to other nations similarly placed' and stated that in India de Valera was seen as 'one of the greatest heroes of freedom . . . he inspired our youth to take a leaf from Ireland's book and to endure great sacrifice for the cause of their country's freedom'. The *Irish Press* clearly embraced the opportunity to give full coverage to these sentiments professed by the Indian patriot, who finished by saying, 'we regard Mr de Valera as one of the very few men who succeeded in a fight with the British'. It should be noted that reports of his visit were carried by two other daily newspapers, so this *Irish Press* article was one that would have interested the Irish pubic generally and not just Fianna Fáil supporters who, in the main, made up the paper's readership. According to Lal, in the course of his meeting with de Valera the following day, he had 'conveyed to him congratulations on behalf of the Indian youth and stated that they were very happy that Ireland had been able to solve some of her problems'.[18] He expressed his hope that Irish history would be replicated in India soon.

In a note to the India Office two weeks later, Vickery was able update Cecil Silver with new information about the meeting between Chaman Lal and the Taoiseach. Vickery had learned that Lal expressed to de Valera the opinion that 'opportunity might be taken of the present international crisis to adopt forcible measures against the government in India and asked him to accord his approval to measures of this kind being taken'. It no doubt entertained Vickery that his 'highly reliable source' reported that even 'Mr de Valera was rather taken aback at Chaman Lal's fiery utterances'.[19] We can only speculate as to the identity of Vickery's 'source'. However irritated IPI was at the publicity Lal received while in Ireland, something else that he obtained there was of far greater consequence and was no doubt the purpose of his visit.

In January 1939 Vickery again updated the India Office on Lal's movements, first refreshing Silver's memory of how 'last August he visited Éire and made some attempts to secure Irish support for a campaign against the Government of India'. Significantly, however, IPI had ascertained that 'while there he managed to secure a Mexican Certificate of Identity on which he subsequently travelled to Mexico, being fully aware that no British passport would have been granted to him for that purpose'.[20] From Cobh he had travelled to Vera Cruz and from there, he was able to travel to the US, where he remained throughout the Second World War. North America was not where the British authorities would want him to be, given the Indian activities of conspirators' there during the First World War.[21] To what extent, if at all, the Irish authorities had intentionally aided him to this end is not ascertainable. However, it is possible to conclude that the word going around Indian circles in Europe, especially after Brajesh Singh's successes a few years earlier, was that a trip to Ireland may well be of help in overcoming imperial passport and endorsement difficulties. As we saw in chapter two, the India Office had noted in 1932 that 'it might be serious if Indian suspects took to going to Dublin for their passports', yet six years later problems of this nature were still a concern, especially with war looming.

The impact of war

On 3 September 1939 Viceroy Lord Linlithgow declared war on India's behalf, stating that 'confronted with the demand that she should accept the dictation of a foreign power in relation to her own subjects, India has decided to stand firm'. As Patrick French has noted, the irony of Linlithgow's words must have been lost on him.[22] India's political leaders had not been consulted. The Congress Party's refusal to support the declaration, while crucially Jinnah and the Muslim League did, may have been otherwise but for the unfortunate manner with which the Government of India had tactlessly brought the country into the conflict.

Churchill's becoming Prime Minister in May 1940 further aggravated a Congress fully aware of his crass opinions about Indians and his antiquated imperialism. Throughout the war Churchill found himself under immense pressure from Commonwealth countries to grant independence to India or at the very least dominion status. Mackenzie King recorded in his diary how at a Canadian War Committee meeting in 1942 he himself had

> [u]rged quite strongly our endorsing self-government for India, agreeing at once to go as far as Britain would be ready to go. Also agreed to have a High Commissioner appointed to India from Canada to indicate our friendly attitude toward equality of status.[23]

More importantly, however, American opinion could not be ignored and was arguably one of the main forces in the decision to send Sir Stafford Cripps on his mission to India in 1942.[24] American hostility towards British imperialism at this time cannot be underestimated and the Raj was essentially losing what was left of its international legitimacy.[25] Many of these American concerns had been articulated as points in the Atlantic Charter of August 1941.[26] However, as the document was merely a declaration of common principles and not a binding treaty, Churchill could conveniently interpret these points as relating to Nazi Germany and not the British Empire. Just after the turning point of the war in North Africa, he declared: 'I have not become the King's First Minister in order to preside over the liquidation of the British Empire.'[27] However determined Churchill was to retain India, as the war continued Britain was finally forced to offer concessions, although, crucially, the Cripps mission promised independence only *after* the war and in return for the county's immediate cooperation in pursuit of it. As Gandhi famously stated this promise was too little and too late, likening it to 'a post-dated cheque on a bank that is failing'. There was also immediate displeasure at the choice of words, with Congress expressing distaste for the term 'dominion status'. The evolution of 'Commonwealth status' in the 1930s notwithstanding, Ireland after all was a dominion and yet had managed to remain neutral; India had wanted the same. Irish neutrality was another problem that Churchill would rather not have encountered in Britain's time of need, as earlier in the war it could have resulted in a German invasion of Ireland or an IRA–German collaborative nexus. Churchill would also bemoan the loss of the southern Irish ports, given back so readily by Chamberlain only a year before the war's start.

The outbreak of war resulted in increased activity on the part of IPI, which was worried that Indian radicals would exploit Britain's crisis to their own ends. A booklet entitled 'Suspect civilian Indians on the continent of Europe' was issued and updated every two months, with extra attention being given to those active in Vienna or Berlin suspected of establishing links with the Nazis.[28] Throughout the war Indians resident in the UK were monitored and given extra attention; this included many journalists and others sympathetic to India's cause who were considered dangerous by virtue of their anti-British espousals.

In the early 1930s an Indian law student, Dowlat Jayaram Vaidya, arrived in London and was given an introduction to the Communist Party of Great Britain on account of the interest he had shown in labour and communist activities in Bombay.[29] Vaidya's IPI file was quite sparse until the outbreak of the war by which time informants were submitting regular reports on his activities. This surveillance was primarily as a result of his nascent career as a journalist with the magazines *Life* and *Time* where he was in charge of their Eastern Department, but it was also attributable to his past associations with the LAI and his liaising with Krishna Menon, the Indian activist based in London, who later became a very significant figure whose career is looked at in more detail below.

It appears that Vaidya's office telephone was being tapped, a fact which throws light on both IPI's increased wartime remit as well as more general concerns over wartime censorship and the publication of pro-Indian independence propaganda. An interception regarding the Irish republican Geoffrey Coulter came to light in 1942. Coulter had been the assistant editor of *An Phoblacht* in the early 1930s, a left-wing cohort of Frank Ryan and Peadar O'Donnell who had been arrested several times during that decade. IPI believed that Coulter was *Life*'s correspondent in Ireland and phonecalls to him from the magazine's editor, the American journalist Stephen Laird, were being noted and passed on to IPI when he was in the process of submitting a piece relating to pro-Indian Irish sentiment in the wake of the failed Cripps mission.[30] Laird had informed him that he was 'anxious to say something about the Irish reaction to this India business', to which Coulter responded by telling him that 'study of the Irish newspapers discloses practically no quotation of foreign comment unfavourable to Congress or to Gandhi. Opinion here is 90 per cent pro both.'[31] Laird considered the opposite true of the British press and was delighted to hear such reports, but he nonetheless requested that Coulter's piece should 'elaborate that statement about Irish opinion being 90 per cent pro-Congress. Don't make it as flat as that.' Laird clearly thought that there were many Irish parallels that could be drawn to illustrate the gravity of the Indian situation:

> I am going to present the line that this may be an Easter 1916 for India and draw the parallel between the Moslem Hindu set-up and the North and South. Of course, the newspapers here are playing it all down and taking the line that it's pretty nearly over and has all been a flop, but so was Easter 1916 – at first.[32]

The transcription of the telephone conversation heightened IPI's curiosity, and less then two weeks later Vickery had acquired further information about Coulter for his colleagues. That information threw remarkable light on this somewhat obscure figure in the Irish republican movement, and was verified in a very short space of time.

> In June 1932 Coulter was a member of the IRA and had been assistant editor of *An Phoblacht* . . . [He] was assisting the Irish Revolutionary Worker's Party, though he was not a member . . . he was obviously left-wing IRA but in November 1933, the Éire High Commissioner reported that he had 'now disaffiliated himself from his Communist activities' . . . since 1933 little has been learnt about his political activities, but he has incurred some suspicion because he has worked in Éire under Erland Echlin, first for *Time* and then for *Newsweek*. Erland Echlin is an American, of pro-German sympathies who is now interned . . . the view of the Security authorities regarding Coulter is at present that he is 'a good journalist, who will try to spread news whether it is discreet to do so or not, and who generally has more sympathy with the left than with the right'.[33]

Vickery went on to note that there was nothing on record to show that Coulter was interested in India but in his opinion it was 'certainly a subject which would appeal to a man with an IRA background'. Throughout his career at IPI Vickery, as an Irishman, appears to have taken great pleasure in locating precise and up-to-date information about any Irish names and figures that appeared on file from time to time. He often overwrote and corrected any misspellings or inaccuracies relating to Ireland in other people's reports, and he always availed of an opportunity to show his true colours as a loyal Irish servant to the Crown, something revealed in his last note regarding Coulter: 'curiously enough, – or perhaps not so curiously, since many "Irish patriots" are not Irish, Coulter is an Englishman. He has been many years in Ireland'.[34]

V. K. Krishna Menon

A great deal of information about Irish and Indian politics was gleaned by tracing the activities of the Indian journalist D. J. Vaidya and those close to him. Another of his associates who had Irish contacts and was also of interest to IPI during the war was V. K. Krishna Menon. Menon, from Calicut in Kerala, had arrived in the UK in 1924 and was accepted as a research student at the London School of Economics. An IPI report dating from 1927 stated that he 'holds extreme political views and is anti-British in his conversation'.[35] He was the secretary of an organisation in London called the India League, which was considered the official 'instrument for the expression in [the UK] of the policy of Gandhi', so its agenda was, at first, one that pushed for the implementation of dominion status in India. It was originally called the 'Commonwealth of India League', founded by Annie Besant in 1920s. However, IPI correctly suspected Menon of having more extreme views than did Besant or indeed Gandhi in relation to attaining Indian independence: 'it is, however, a moot point whether Menon ever really approved of Gandhi's tenets in regard to non-violence'.[36] Gradually the organisation was taken over by more extreme Indian nationalists, like Menon, and the dropping of 'Commonwealth' from the title resulted in the attraction of 200 new members in 1932.[37]

In the late 1930s Menon became involved in local politics and was elected as a councillor for St Pancras. IPI were suspicious of his close connections with the CPGB as he attended the party's high level weekly meetings on India. This was a meeting of the CPGB's 'International Affairs Sub-Committee, an extension of the Colonial Committee which was divided into four bureaux dealing with Negro, Irish, Jewish and Indian problems respectively'.[38] IPI suspected that the India League's fall in membership by the late 1930s was a result of Menon's associations with the CPGB. However, in the long term he would become less involved in local politics in the UK because in 1935 during one of Nehru's trips to London the two men met and Menon was to become one of Nehru's closest friends and confidants, as well as India's first ambassador to Ireland.[39]

Throughout his time in London, and especially during the war years, Menon was liaising with Irish nationalists based in the UK. He often appeared on Irish republican platforms, and, interestingly, in doing so was not just availing of an opportunity to give voice to matters Indian. He had a genuine interest in Irish politics and was an enthusiastic contributor to the Irish republican movement in London. He was a frequent visitor to Scotland where the police kept a record of his political activities; when he spoke in Glasgow in 1942 the police reported that the meeting of the India League had been attended by 1,500 people.[40] On Easter Sunday 1938 he took part in an 800-strong march from Paddington Green to Trafalgar Square in commemoration of those killed in the Easter Rising.[41] The following year he was one of the speakers at an open-air meeting, held in Stepney, east London, the purpose of which was to canvass support for the campaign to release Frank Ryan who had been captured and imprisoned in Spain while serving in the International Brigade. Scotland Yard noted that Menon prefaced his address by 'alluding to his personal acquaintance with Ryan. He knew the latter in his student days, when he was an indefatigable worker for Irish autonomy.'[42] The two had more than likely met through the LAI in the early 1930s, though there is little evidence of a real friendship between them, and neither appears to have been heavily involved in the IIIL, though Menon would have known Despard who often spoke on India League platforms. He claimed that Ryan's objective was permanent world peace, and that he had sacrificed a brilliant academic career in pursuit of it by commanding a section of the International Brigade. Menon told the crowd that 'to suffer his imprisonment without protest was a crime against democracy, and the British Government's hand should be forced by a well-supported petition, so that a strong demand might be sent to Franco for Ryan's release'.[43]

In December he was again with his Irish activist friends at a Connolly Club meeting on Grays Inn Road. Peadar O'Donnell, who tackled the sensitive question of 'Conscription for Irishmen?', was the 'special guest' speaker. Also present were members of the Anti-Partition League and Menon, who spoke on behalf of the India League. The purpose of the meeting was to commemorate the life of the Irish anti-Treaty republican Liam Mellows, who had been executed during the Irish Civil War. During the early years of the Second World War Menon continued to attend Irish nationalist meetings at which, in the light of the crisis developing in India attendant on the failure of the Cripps mission, he spoke with more urgency. At another Connolly Club meeting, this time in Birmingham, held to commemorate James Connolly, Scotland Yard noted the aggressive nature of his speech and made a connection between this and his overt left-wing leanings. This, along with his continued interest in Ireland, was of concern to the wartime British authorities:

> Menon alleged that Britain's refusal to grant autonomy to India and her attitude towards the Irish problem were incompatible with her war aims. He had always taken a keen interest in the struggle for the complete independence of Ireland because the Irish and the Indians were fighting the same enemy – British imperialism. Their efforts, however, formed but a part of a world-wide struggle for true democracy and freedom, which would only be won when the workers of all lands dropped their racial and religious differences and united to overthrow capitalism.[44]

He would often speak on Irish platforms without making reference to India. In September 1942 he attended a Connolly Club meeting held to support the demand for a reprieve for IRA prisoners sentenced to death in Belfast for the murder of a Royal Ulster Constabulary officer. Six IRA volunteers had been arrested and their death sentences had prompted a public outcry throughout Ireland. The US Minister to Ireland, David Gray, recorded that the 'hysterical reprieve agitation culminated in large and general demonstrations throughout Éire'.[45] Clearly the campaign for their reprieve (in the event, only one of the six, Thomas Williams, was hanged for the murder) had attracted interest even in London, and Scotland Yard noted the presence at the rally of Indian nationalists, and in particular Menon,

> who did not refer to the Indian Political situation, said there had been continual animosity between England and Ireland for over 300 years, and the execution of the six IRA men would further embitter the Irish people against Britain. He considered that deputations to the Home Secretary on the matter would be futile and the only effective action would be to win over public opinion to demand reprieves.[46]

IPI kept open Menon's file even as the transfer of power was approaching. An India Office report admitted that while 'the target set for IPI' was altering, it was 'essential to be aware of the activities of such persons as Krishna Menon and of other persons of even more dubious record'.[47]

As will been seen, given his political background and his interest in Irish affairs, it was apt that Vengalil Krishnan Krishna Menon (despite the controversies that dogged his future diplomatic career) was to be the first Indian Ambassador to Ireland.[48]

Sir Charles Tegart

An incident involving an Irish former IPI officer ruffled some feathers in the Dublin Government during the Second World War. Charles Tegart had worked for IPI in Europe and the US during the First World War, refused the headship of the organisation in 1923 and became instead Chief Commissioner of the Calcutta Police. Tegart gained quite a reputation in India, where he was regarded as one of the most successful officers of the Indian Police, and several attempts were made on his life. In his obituary *The Times* recalled 'the coolness with which he faced the repeated attempts on his life', the failure of which 'gave rise to the legend among the anarchists that he was invulnerable'.[49] People praised Tegart's bravery and dedication and, as Michael Silvestri has noted, his Irishness was singled out for mention. The Governor of Bengal, Lord Lytton, joked that attempts to assassinate Tegart would prove futile as he was an 'Irishman' who 'for all we know may be a Sinn

Féiner at heart. He is the last man, therefore, to be deficient in sympathy with the cause of Indian nationalism.'[50] However the reality could not have been further from the truth, and such a quip, if anything, merely highlights some English administrators' suspicions in relation to loyal Irish servants of the Crown in the wake of the Irish revolution. Tegart was knighted in 1926 and he retired in 1931. His retirement was an active one: he served on the Council of India for six years and the lecture he gave on 'terrorism in India' to the Royal Empire Society in 1932 was considered the definitive statement on Indian armed resistance against the Raj.[51] He spoke of the Indian 'terrorist movement' in terms not unlike contemporary descriptions of the more recent 'war on Islamic terrorism':

> Terrorism had different leaders, though they had penetrated the Congress machine in Bengal. The rank and file were generally students. Its network was happily not spread all over India; it relied for its efficiency on secrecy; it burrowed underground; there was no outward sign of it. It emerged and struck its victims suddenly and again disappeared from view.[52]

Tegart had also served in Ireland at the time of the war of independence, from July to November 1920, and was one of several officers of the Indian Police transferred to reinforce British intelligence networks there.[53]

The son of a vicar and raised in Dunboyne Co. Meath, Tegart was educated at Portora Royal School, Enniskillen, and at TCD, joining the Indian Police in 1901 at the age of 20. He is famously known in relation to a defensive structure used in Palestine in 1930s. He had been sent there in the aftermath of the Arab rebellion of 1936 as an advisor on 'suppressing terrorism . . . to prevent bands fleeing from justice, smuggling arms, or entering for terrorism and agitation across the frontiers between Palestine and Syria, Transjordan, and the Lebanon'.[54] The structure adopted on his advice became known as 'Tegart's Wall',[55] a protective barbed-wire fence (almost 50 miles long), reinforced with police posts, searchlights and pillboxes, which ran along the Syrian and Transjordan frontiers. Considered one of the first ever defensive fences established by the British, Tegart's idea was a last-resort security measure, and one that has been utilised since in Northern Ireland and elsewhere.

In July 1940 the Irish High Commissioner in London, John Dulanty, received an urgent and secret communication from Joseph Walshe. Dulanty was told to contact Lord Caldecote, Secretary of State for Dominion Affairs, and to relate to him the following:

> Certain persons have of late made rather frequent visits to Ireland. These visits did not seem to be connected with any normal business transaction

which might explain their frequency . . . well founded rumours have reached the government that these persons have been talking to Deputies and other Irish citizens in a manner likely to be detrimental to the interests and general well-being of the Irish State. The visits have given the definite impression that there was interference in the internal affairs of our country.[56]

Walshe observed that because 'these persons had been invariably in London immediately before the visits to Dublin', the suspicion was that they were 'acting with, or on behalf of, some British political group'. He went on to say that the 'Irish Government would be very glad to obtain the help of the Secretary of State for Dominion Affairs in putting an end to further visits', as they were particularly perturbed that these visits 'coincided with a campaign in the Press of Great Britain and in a section of the American Press' against Ireland's neutrality. He also warned the British Government that the continuation of such activities could 'end in a serious breach of the real friendship and goodwill which exists between our two countries' and that 'the excellent work of the British Representative in Ireland could be brought to nought by well-meaning busybodies who are ignorant both of the history of Ireland and of the abiding determination of its people to work out their own destiny'.[57]

Clearly Tegart's reputation among Irish political circles was not as favourable as in Britain. We know from Dulanty's response that 'certain persons' was in fact a reference to Tegart: 'On reading the words "certain persons" Lord Caldecote said, "What is the meaning of this? I know of only one person. I suppose this refers to Tegart?"'[58] Dulanty agreed, and he continued to make enquiries about Tegart in London. Sir Patrick Kelly, formerly Commissioner of Police in Bombay, was a countryman and long-term friend of Tegart. They had joined the ICS together. After a conversation with Kelly, Dulanty reported to Walshe: 'Sir Patrick Kelly has certainly the nationalist outlook and he and Tegart he said had much in common when discussing Irish nationalist questions.'[59] Kelly also informed Dulanty, however, that Tegart was much more successful 'on the political side than on the administrative', and that the Government 'appreciated his particular gifts because they have employed him on one piece of work or another ever since he left India . . . His work in Palestine, for example, was entirely political.' Crucially, when asked about whether he had any knowledge of Tegart's recent movements, Kelly responded that he did not, but 'would not be surprised to find him on a government "mission" as in Palestine'.[60] It was at the request of Colonel Valentine Vivian, a colleague from his days in the Indian Police, that Tegart had been 'keeping an eye on events in Éire'.[61]

[139]

Tegart's previous career in intelligence was enough to have the Irish Government on edge, and with reason. Tegart had in fact reported to Whitehall in June 1940 that there was a significant amount of U-boat activity off the coast of Ireland and that the IRA was making preparations for a German invasion.[62] Such reports would have encouraged Churchill's preoccupation with a fifth column threat in Ireland. Indeed, Tegart's report has been described as a seminal influence on British strategic policy on Ireland.[63] Caldecote claimed to have taken up the matter of Tegart's frequent trips with the permit authorities and thought that they were 'now firmly refusing permits to anyone outside the limited categories of persons entitled to travel'.[64] However, given Tegart's links with British intelligence he would have in all probability remained within this category. Tegart would have readily done all he could to help the British with their 'Irish problem' as, according to another former Indian Police colleague J. C. Curry, Ireland's refusal to enter the war on the side of the Allies was a source of much confusion to him. Tegart's wife later related: 'as the weeks went on and Éire remained neutral [he] became more and more disturbed'.[65]

Henry Obed and Axis intrigue

Ireland's neutrality threw up an unexpected difficulty for the British authorities in relation to the detention and eventual release of an Axis collaborator who happened to be Indian, Henry Obed. As Eunan O'Halpin has pointed out, while causing neutral Ireland intense difficulties, espionage, sabotage and subversive operations attempted by Axis agents there during the Second World War were on a very small scale compared with those carried out in other neutral states in Europe and Latin America.[66] Nevertheless, it was a security problem that had to be tackled with the utmost care on the part of the Irish authorities. Obed was a subject of great concern to the British authorities for more than twenty years. As was seen in chapter one, he was a well-known subversive, long suspected of smuggling drugs and arms from Europe to India, and it is possible that at one stage he had done business with the young Roddy Connolly.[67] Originally based in Hamburg, he eventually set up shop in Antwerp, under the cover of a curious live animal import and export business. He was an elusive character. Neither the Belgian nor the Indian Government (he regularly travelled to and from India with his consignments) were ever able to find proof of his criminal activities, although he was interned by the former after the outbreak of war. In 1936 his solicitor wrote to the India Office, detailing his good business standing and character, and demanding an unrestricted passport for him.[68]

IPI apparently lost track of Obed from 1936 until he resurfaced in 1940, in the unlikeliest of places, County Cork, with two German–South African accomplices. He did not remain at large for long.[69] Many of the locals took note of his presence in the rural vicinity of Tralaspeen on the early morning of 7 July 1940, not because of his bewildered, mute friends, clutching large suitcases, but because of the elderly Obed's white Gandhi cap and his thick Indian accent.[70] He asked one local '[I]s this west Cork?' The unsuspecting boy gave the men directions, and was rewarded with a bar of chocolate – he told the Garda that Obed 'pronounced the word "Chock-ol-ate" '.[71] Eventually the three men were given a lift in the local creamery lorry, but were spotted by an observant Garda and arrested. In their possession was 'a quantity of explosives – two suitcases containing eight incendiary bombs and five canisters of explosives – and also £800 in cash'.[72] After his arrest Obed, who was interviewed separately, denied all knowledge of his two companions' intentions and professed to be unconnected with their expedition. A G2 officer noted:

> His story, that he is only an honest Indian, was magnificently told. I nearly believed him, until Captain Lohan made the discovery (not adverted to by the Garda) that *all* the money was in sequence as to its serial numbers.[73]

To gain favour with his interrogators he told them that he had 'been in the United States when Mr de Valera was there in 1920 . . . he had sold statues of Terence MacSwiney in New York at the time'.[74] Initially G2 was suspicious that the landing of the two South Africans and an Indian might be a 'British-made "German Plot" ', as the head of G2 was asked by Joseph Walshe to be present for the three prisoners' examinations once they had arrived in Dublin. In his report to Walshe he stated: 'I assumed that the main purpose of my attending the proceedings was to ascertain if a British "plant" or frame-up was involved of such a kind as to embarrass the government and to prejudice our neutrality.'[75] Presumably suspicions arose due to all three coming from Commonwealth countries with no immediately apparent Nazi connections, especially in Obed's case. However Bryan immediately ruled this out and felt that the two South Africans' objectives lay in England.[76]

In London IPI unearthed Obed's file, which disclosed that the Belgian authorities had arrested Obed when Belgium entered the war, and he was taken to Lille. IPI surmised that 'presumably therefore he was released by the Germans, when they occupied that town and was given this further mission'. Vickery was somewhat amused by the not-too-convincing report that 'they had landed in Kerry (Toe Head) from a trawler coming from Brest, in error for the United Kingdom!'.[77] The details of the landing of the trawler *Soizic* were duly passed on to the British. Given the Irish authorities' initial suspicions in relation to this case, this is a prime example of Anglo-Irish cooperation in the sphere of security at a time when public perception of relations between the two countries was quite otherwise.[78] Evidence of the tense atmosphere between some of the leading politicians was seen earlier in relation to Sir Charles Tegart. However, agreement in relation to intelligence cooperation had been reached in 1938 and in keeping with this the British authorities were given all the details surrounding the *Soizic* case, including information regarding a letter found on Obed's person addressed to a fellow Indian, Sardar Bahadur Khan.[79] Khan had been living in Dublin since at least 1937 when 'he was issued with a Pedlar's certificate at Store Street Station'.[80] He left for England early in 1939 with the intention of 'taking up a seafaring position' but ended up working for a construction company in Liverpool. Obed was apparently unaware of his departure and had intended to make contact with Khan in Dublin.[81] The passing on of this information to the British resulted in the arrest and questioning, in Liverpool, of Khan and two other Indians, 'who it was thought might be implicated in Obed's intrigues'. They were even transported to London for close questioning before being released.[82]

IPI acknowledged the irony of his being arrested in Ireland after all those years at large when they were unable to find any concrete evidence of arms-trafficking. It was, however, satisfied that he had been tried by an Irish military tribunal and sentenced to seven years' penal servitude. Obed had a difficult time while in prison in Ireland as he had chronic bronchitis. He kept his distance from his German fellow prisoners, of whom he said: 'they seldom or ever speak to me or I to them. We have nothing in common. I am by no means a sympathiser of Hitler and they know this.'[83] He befriended instead IRA prisoners, especially Owen McDermott, whose family in Baldoyle wrote to Obed and forwarded letters from his wife.[84]

In the aftermath of the war difficulties arose relating to the release of Axis agents who had been arrested in Ireland, but particularly Obed. IPI noted in July 1945 that Obed had 'presumably earned some remission of this sentence, for the question of his release is now being considered by the Éire government', and IPI was aware of how anxious the Irish authorities were to know what the British would do with Obed if he returned to the mainland. Vickery was adamant that no undertaking be given as to how he would be treated, as he had reason to believe that 'the Éire government [wanted] an assurance that Obed will not again be prosecuted'.[85] The Home Office insisted that he not be allowed to land in Great Britain and the India Office was unwilling to send him back to Europe, because Obed would more than likely seek refuge with his wife in Belgium.[86] It was feared that he would not be reprimanded by the Belgian authorities and so would return to his nefarious activities: the outbreak of communal disturbances in India provided a ready market for the arms he smuggled. The preferred option was to have him returned direct to India, but the Irish authorities had made it clear in 1946 that they would not foot the bill, and at that point the matter reached an impasse.[87] Norman Archer (of the office of the UK Representative to Éire) was inclined to believe that there was more to Irish difficulties in relation to the release of Obed than met the eye when he noted:

> The cynic might say that the Éire government, in order to meet criticism from the humanitarians, are anxious to send Obed to his wife and former home in Antwerp, and are raising legal difficulties as to our proposal that he should be deported directly to India.[88]

Finally in 1947, and after much deliberation between Frederick Boland of the Department of External Affairs, and the Dominions and Foreign Offices in London, arrangements were agreed on with regard to the handing over of all the Axis agents still in Ireland. Obed, however, remained an anomaly and the legal concerns that the Irish authorities had voiced were acknowledged in British inter-departmental correspondence.

> The Home Office do not want him in the United Kingdom and the only satisfactory destination for him is India. Since he is a British subject it is doubtful whether the Éire authorities have legal power to deport him and *for obvious political reasons we do not wish to suggest that they should.*[89]

So Irish hesitations had less to do with aggravating the British authorities on Obed's behalf, and more to do with not creating a precedent that could impact adversely on Ireland's Commonwealth status. While the British themselves were aware of this, they had their own agenda to pursue:

> Now that they [the Irish] have brought themselves to take firm action, we feel that the United Kingdom authorities would put themselves in a very false position if they refused to take Obed off Éire's hands when the Éire authorities are willing to put themselves to some trouble to get rid of him. Although Obed may be less dangerous than some of the others, it remains true that his presence in Éire is an embarrassment to us and that if we miss this opportunity we may find it difficult to shift him later.[90]

Following protracted correspondence between Dublin and London, Obed was eventually flown to London whence he was deported back to

India and not to his wife in Antwerp, as he had hoped. When India became independent Obed wrote a letter of petition to Nehru, which resulted in his passport being granted. The letter, written in 1948, throws some interesting light on his activities during the Second World War:

> Malik Rauf of the Berlin Radio then came to me and told me that all Indians must do something for the motherland and remarked 'Plight of England is an opportunity for India'. I was much impressed and gladly agreed to work for the motherland. I was asked to go to Éire to assist Irish National Army against Britain, as Germans had good relations with it.[91] I accepted the suggestion and secretly reached Ireland with other co-workers.[92]

Whether this should be interpreted as Obed attempting to put a more positive nationalist gloss on his activities to influence Nehru is debatable. What is clear, though, is that he did in fact befriend Irish republicans, either accidentally or intentionally, and had more in common with them than with his erstwhile Nazi cohorts.

Obed met with an unexpected end in 1952, in a manner which had little to do with his life-long subversive activities. He was murdered by his wife, some five years after their reunion, who suspected him of having an affair with the daughter of a local police official.[93]

De Valera and the Bengal famine

The war was a contributory factor to the disastrous famine in Bengal which broke out after the province's worst harvest of the century, in 1943. Because of an increase in the demand for rice to feed Indian soldiers, poor distribution of food and a lack of imports, the ensuing malnutrition and disease resulted in the death of up to 3 million people over a three-year period. The new viceroy, Lord Wavell, appointed at the famine's height, was greatly disturbed by what he saw on his inaugural reconnaissance tour of the worst affected areas, but he was somewhat more perturbed by the inertia displayed by both Government of India personnel and London in response to demands for help. Churchill was inclined to believe that the Bengal famine was a statistical invention.[94] Wavell even threatened resignation over the issue, and the proliferation of reportage throughout Europe and America of the increasingly desperate situation did not do the British war effort any favours.

The Bengal famine received extensive press coverage in Ireland, being particularly poignant as it was only two years before the centenary of the great Irish famine. In November 1943 after several months of reports depicting the horrific conditions in Bengal and other Indian provinces affected, de Valera moved a vote in the Dáil to donate £200,000 towards Indian famine relief. It came in the wake of a telegram from the Mayor of Calcutta, Syed Badrudduja, urgently asking for help:

> Bengal's 60,000,000 in grip of unprecedented tragic famine. Epidemics exacting heavy tolls in rural areas. Children, women worse affected. Mayor's fund rendering medical aid, catering free meals for children, diet on extensive scale. Eagerly expect best co-operation to save human lives.[95]

The donation, quite a significant amount for Ireland to contribute given the difficult wartime economy, would coincide with a drive for funds by the Irish Red Cross, asking the public to raise a further £500,000. De Valera was reported to have said that 'he was asking the Irish people, who had been helped in their hours of necessity by other peoples, to make a generous contribution'. The entire House met the decision with unanimous and enthusiastic approval. William Norton, the Labour Party leader, was particularly vocal:

> We in this country ought to know what famine means. The famine of 1847 left a mark on this country and on its people, on its industries and on its development, and that mark is with us to-day . . . I understand that the records of assistance which we got at that time will show that many people then resident in India contributed generously to the relief of famine in the Ireland of 1847. It is India's turn to-day.[96]

Even more appreciative of the motion proposed by de Valera was Jim Larkin, who spoke passionately on the issue:

> When I came in and got this notification that the government, at last, after many weeks, had risen to an appreciation of the needs of the multitudes of enslaved peoples in British India, I thought that at last there was some justification for their continuance as a government. It is a most gracious gesture.[97]

He further flattered de Valera and his Government, saying that he felt 'deeply gratified that the spokesman of the Irish race is sending a word of comfort and making a gesture of help to the enslaved millions in British India'. De Valera returned the compliment to Larkin in making a further appeal to the Irish people: 'I am sorry I have not the eloquence of Deputy Larkin to enforce the appeal but I am making it sincerely, and making it with the full responsibility of my position.'[98]

The British reaction to this gesture on the part of the Irish Government was predictably, but perhaps understandably, cynical. Enquiries were made by IPI as to whether the money was being paid directly to the Indian Red Cross or, more worryingly, to the Mayor of

Calcutta. Badrudduja had worked with Subhas Chandra Bose in the Calcutta Corporation and was an ardent supporter of the radical nationalist. The Bengal famine was considered to have been something of a last straw and was a major factor in alienating citizens once loyal to the King and Emperor. Also, it is thought to have been a significant influence on the decision of those Bengalis who subsequently joined the ranks of the INA. Money on this scale ending up in the wrong hands could prove devastating to British rule. The Secretary of State for India, Leo Amery, harboured such a fear, and expressed as much to Wavell: 'Meanwhile de Valera has got his Dáil to vote £100,000 through the Irish Red Cross to Indian famine relief. I can only hope it goes straight to your fund and not to people like Joshi and Mrs Pandit.'[99]

Amery was concerned also about the possible repercussions that publicity of this nature could have on the Government in London. He asked Wavell: '[D]o you feel yourself that Indian public opinion will make an invidious comparison with the Government here if we do not do something of the same sort on a reasonably large scale?'[100] Amery stressed to Wavell the crucial point that 'in these matters psychology counts so much that I should very much like to know your view'.

Another worry concerned the effects that the Government's limited appeal for aid for the famine might have on London-based Indian political factions, as it left 'the field open to a variety of other funds, and more particularly Krishna Menon's fund . . . which is of course being used to re-establish Menon's much weakened position in this country'. Menon's India League was one of many Indian political organisations in London attempting to raise funds, and publicity, for famine relief in Bengal. One of them, the Council for the International Recognition of Indian Independence, run by Amiya Nath Bose, set up its own famine committee.[101] The Council was the quickest off the mark in sending a telegram of thanks to the *Irish Press* after the news of de Valera's donation and it was duly published on the front page under the heading 'Famine Committee Thanks Taoiseach'. The telegram read: '[We] are profoundly grateful to you for your subscription to the Mayor of Calcutta Fund . . . [We] are also raising funds in Britain for transmission to Mayor of Calcutta. We feel the Mayor has effective organisation for distribution.' The wording here suggests that Amiya Nath Bose and his colleagues were hoping that the donation would in fact end up with the Mayor and not with the Red Cross.

IPI, which was monitoring the activities of the Council, noted that

[Amiya] Bose has been extremely elated because the *Irish Press* (de Valera's Party organ) published on its front page the cable sent to de Valera by the Council . . . He has been making jubilant statements to the effect that the Éire contribution is being sent to the Mayor of Calcutta: he regards this as the work of his Council and is pluming himself hence on 'another victory over the India League'.[102]

The Council was buoyed by the Irish publicity and attempts were made to obtain more by sending a delegation to the Irish High Commissioner, John W. Dulanty. Amiya Nath Bose apparently thought that

> Indian women members of such a deputation would be effective and that Shah's inclusion as a Muslim would also be a good advertisement. He [felt] that Mr Dulanty would be compelled to notify the Foreign Department of the government of Éire of the names of the delegation etc., and that far more would get into the Éire papers by this means than would be the case if merely direct telegrams of thanks to Mr de Valera are sent.[103]

Vickery wasted no time cutting Bose and his cohorts down to size in his notes, as he gleefully added:

> As it happens his elation is unjustified because it has been decided to send the money . . . not to the Mayor of Calcutta but to the Indian Red Cross! So far as is known, the latter is a loyal branch of the British Red Cross, which will make for a wise and equitable distribution of the Éire fund.[104]

Indeed, later on Dulanty unwittingly got drawn into some of this Indian factionalism when he attended the annual dinner given by one of the political groups, Swaraj House. The chairman, Dr Gangulee, described as an 'extremist' by IPI, expressed gratitude at the 'large sum of money contributed by Éire for famine relief in India', but, IPI went on to note, 'he grew more and more excited, and shouted that India would be free no matter who willed otherwise'. IPI was happy to note Dulanty's startled reaction to the evening's proceedings, saying that he gave 'an extremely cautious speech . . . spoke for five minutes and left the gathering at the end of his speech'.[105]

The decision to donate money to Indian famine relief was not a hasty one. De Valera had made calls to the Indian Red Cross enquiring whether, given that Ireland was not in a position to donate actual food, hard cash would be of any use. Assured that it was, he donated as much as was possible under the strained political and economic circumstances that nearly four years of war had produced.[106] The following month Wavell sent Amery an update. The picture he painted was bleak:

> The Red Cross are using the Éire money for the purchase of woollen blankets partly from Provinces whose Air Raid Precaution . . . organisations are being wound up, and partly from Army stocks . . . from a financial point of view it is, I think, still true that the difficulties in Bengal concern supplies rather than money, and that charitable contributions, however generous, would only be a drop in the ocean of public expenditure.[107]

The Friends of India Society and allied intrigue

Another group was set up in Ireland during the emergency which, among other things, raised money for famine relief in India, the Friends of India Society (FOIS).[108] The FOIS came to the attention of G2, Irish Army Intelligence, in 1943 when a TCD student, Sheila Dutt, sent a telegram from the 'Indian Association Dublin' to Gandhi wishing him 'long life' on his 'successful termination of fast to lead motherland to complete freedom'. Colonel Dan Bryan of G2 noted in pen on the intercepted telegram that he wanted 'to know something about this association' and directed that Dutt be watched.[109] Dutt and her mother, Mrs Indu Dutt, were from Decca in Bengal, and they had arrived in Ireland from Calcutta on 19 October 1939. Sheila had been accepted on to a degree course in modern languages at TCD. Initially resident at 58 Merrion Square, by 1944 they had relocated to Northumberland Road.[110] Over the next few months it became clear that the Dutts were members of a group that was founded that year by a Mr and Mrs Hurley-Beresford, who had relocated to Dublin from London after the outbreak of the war.

G2 was unable to uncover much information about the couple except that Mr Hurley-Beresford ran the Hotel Advisory Bureau at Amiens Street Station and that his wife, Geraldine, was the daughter of an ex-Brigadier General of the British Army and ex-wife of a naval officer. Suspicions abounded about the couple from early on. The business was not thought to be 'particularly flourishing'. They were noted as unable to pay for a drink one week, yet the following week were 'suddenly flush with money', buying clothes from the well-known drapers Kevin & Howlin, paying with cash, and able to arrange 'for a fleet of taxis to drive home their guests' from a party in their house.[111] Geraldine Hurley-Beresford was the main organiser for the FOIS and was soon attracting Indians and other interested people resident in Dublin to attend monthly lectures held at the Contemporary Arts Gallery, 133 Baggot Street, and parties and fundraising nights she organised at members' homes. The FOIS was formed, allegedly, to promote good relations between India and Ireland, without reference to politics; it put on entertainments and provided insights into Irish cultural life for Indians visiting Dublin . However, although many of the lectures given were seemingly quite innocuous, like the one themed 'Arts and Crafts from India' and given by Dr Said Yasin, a veterinary surgeon working at TCD, other lectures were more overtly political. At one of the latter, in 1945, on the life of Jawaharlal Nehru, listeners were informed that Nehru had great admiration for 'the Sinn Féin and Suffragettes movements, had visited Ireland on two occasions [and]

[148]

stated that the 1916 Rebellion and Casement's speech from the dock had a profound affect on [him]'.[112] Among those present at this lecture was Hanna Sheehy Skeffington; G2 also noted a Mr Woods as a regular attendant at FOIS meetings, more than likely a reference to Tony, son of Mollie Woods, the founder of the IIIL some ten years earlier. However, there was some concern over the FOIS's apparent connections with London-based Indians.

In the wake of the coverage of the Bengal famine in the European press, the Hurley-Beresfords announced that a FOIS social evening would be held at the Country Shop, St Stephens Green, on 16 October 1944. The door receipts would 'go towards the relief of distress in India', and one Sylvia Stephenson, an English woman about whom G2 could find out very little, would ask for subscriptions to a fund 'for the purpose of erecting a memorial to Mrs Gandhi . . . and that any subscriptions received would be forwarded to London'.[113] (The previous February Gandhi's wife, Kasturbai, had died in prison in India.) The money collected, which amounted to £11 10 6d, was duly forwarded to Nehru's sister, Vijaya Lakshmi Nehru, by Stella Webb of the FOIS.[114] Dan Bryan was concerned about such activities and noted in relation to this report:

> Having regard to British difficulty and general touchiness where the 'Indian Problem' is concerned and to the membership of the Friends of India Society . . . this activity seems to open up the possibility of the very type of embarrassment for the State which was anticipated from the Society's existence here. It is difficult to see what action can be taken, if indeed any action is considered necessary and desirable.[115]

However, of greater concern were the people whom Hurley-Beresford had recruited into the FOIS, and especially the society's connection with an Axis diplomat. As early as May 1943, when G2 was attempting to ascertain whether there was in fact an Indian association in Dublin, the following was noted (more than likely as a result of phone-tapping by G2):

> Mrs Hurley-Beresford 25 Sth Frederick Street in conversation with Ichihashi [Japanese Consul] confirms by reference the existence of an Indian Society or association of some kind in which Ichihashi is interested. Latter is providing literature and books for the lectures by Mrs Hurley-Beresford (purpose of not stated).[116]

Ichihashi went on to attend several, if not all, of the meetings organised by the FOIS throughout 1943 and 1944. In fact on two separate occasions, as a result of his association with 'Irish subversive elements' in the run up to D-Day, Ichihashi received a strong warning from Joseph Walshe. Walshe reported to de Valera that the Consul 'got as pale as a

Japanese can, and looked astonished and very guilty'.[117] The warnings
had little effect as Ichihashi continued to associate with the FOIS. In
1945, it was reported that 'Mrs Hurley-Beresford entertained the
Japanese Consul to tea in her flat . . . the tea was tête-à-tête', and after
the meeting she suggested changing the name of the FOIS to 'The
Friends of India and Asiatics Society' so that it would enable Ichihashi
to speak 'on such countries as Siam, Ceylon, Manchuria and Korea'.[118]
These connections alarmed the Irish authorities and Dan Bryan saw
fit to send a letter to Joseph Walshe informing him of Ichihashi's
activities:

> I am sending herewith a note on a recent meeting of the Friends of India
> League which was held in the Country Shop, Stephen's Green, the atten-
> dance at which, you will observe, included Ichihashi. While the ostensi-
> ble purpose of this meeting was social and charitable, its underlying idea
> and the tendency of this organisation generally cannot but be held parti-
> san. It is therefore thought that the presence of Ichihashi could hardly be
> explained away as being entirely social or charitable.[119]

Also in attendance, along with Ichihashi, at one memorable FOIS party
in 1944 was one-time IRA Chief of Staff Seán Harrington and another
right-wing IRA member, Joseph O'Kelly, who, G2 duly noted, was
sporting a swastika badge.[120] Karl Petersen, the German Legation's
press attaché, who was a particular object of Allied attention for
his alleged espionage activities, was also present.[121] So were several
German internees, who afterwards were 'warned by the German
Legation against having anything further to do with the Hurley-
Beresfords' activities following the incident of their missing the bus
after (the) previous party'.[122] The German Legation seemingly harboured misgivings in relation to the Hurley-Beresfords, as did the Irish
authorities.

Although the Japanese Vice-Consul was more than likely liaising
with this Indian group in the light of Japanese support of Subhas
Chandra Bose's separatist mission in the Far East, there was something
more pressing about the FOIS's existence, and Axis participation in its
activities, as far as Dan Bryan was concerned. He noted in his letter to
Walshe that he had 'some reason also for believing that the British
(were) watching the activities of this organisation'. Other information
on file seems to support Bryan's suspicion. Peadar O'Donnell had
informed the G2 agent 'F' that the Hurley-Beresfords and Sylvia
Stephenson, another FOIS member as seen earlier, who recently arrived
in Dublin from the UK, were all previously employed with the UK
Ministry of Information.[123] Moreover, it seems that other FOIS
members were uneasy with the Hurley-Beresfords' manner and their

'predilection for malicious gossip'.[124] Mrs Hurley-Beresford apparently made regular trips back to London throughout this period, evidenced by a Garda report in which she is said to have mentioned that on a recent visit to England she had met some 'very prominent Indians who were delighted to hear the existence of the society in Éire'. She hoped that the society would come together and invite some of these Indians across in order to see how interested Irish people were in the Indian cause.[125]

Very suddenly, however, and coinciding more or less with the end of the war, the activities of the FOIS simply ceased. By 1946 most of those involved in the FOIS had evidently left Ireland, including the Dutts who returned to India on Sheila's graduation. The Hurley-Beresfords had spoken of travelling to China. Bryan noted in May 1946 that 'this society seems to be moribund' and inconclusively, but believably, the FOIS G2 file ends with a note by Bryan saying simply that it 'still remains open whether Mr or Mrs or both are/were British agents'.[126] Given that very few Indians resident in Ireland associated with the FOIS, and those who did were more interested in the cultural aspects of the society; that it was established by an English couple who had arrived from London in 1943 (the very year that Bose's INA mission with Japanese support was instigated); and that the Hurley-Beresfords liaised mainly with the staff of the Axis legations in Dublin, it seems possible that FOIS was in fact a British intelligence front created to probe links between Indians and Axis diplomats and supporters in Ireland.

Conclusion

Radical Indian nationalists such as Krishna Menon remained tuned into Irish affairs throughout the war. Loyal Irish servants of the Crown who had experience in both countries, such as Sir Charles Tegart and Philip Vickery, did all they could in their capacity as intelligence agents to help the British war effort while struggling to understand why Ireland and India would not. IPI's increased wartime remit revealed further radical Indo-Irish contacts. British authorities were concerned by de Valera's donation of significant amounts of money to aid relief of the Bengal famine. Understandably, much more of a concern for the British, however, was Indo-Axis collaboration as seen in the chapter three and as evidenced in this chapter by the wartime activities of Henry Obed, who was ostensibly sent to Ireland to liaise with the IRA. The British intelligence services by this stage were aware of the attraction that Irish–Indian anti-imperialism could have for other potential subversives, and it is quite possible Britain initiated the establishment of the Friends of India Society in Dublin in an effort to monitor the activities of Axis representatives in the safe-haven of neutral Southern Ireland, even though Irish Army Intelligence was readily cooperating with its British counterparts.

The Second World War brought with it irreversible changes to the imperial political landscape. By its close, although not yet independent republics, Ireland and India were edging ever closer to their goal. Their wartime records, in Ireland's case by remaining neutral, in India's by Congress fervently protesting against India's participation in the conflict without its consent, had a critical impact on even the most conservative of British politician's imperial resolve. Neither country would have been happy with the most progressive of imperial accolades, dominion status. Complete independence was clearly the only way forward where India was concerned, and in Ireland's case nomenclature remained the only stumbling-block.

Notes

1 Extract from letter to Jawaharlal Nehru from Henry Obed, 18 Feb. 1948, IMA, G2/X0375. Obed was an Indian subversive, resident in Europe in the 1920s and 1930s, who was suspected by the British intelligence services of trafficking arms to India. He became a German agent on the outbreak of the Second World War and, as discussed in more detail below, was captured in Ireland in 1940.
2 For example, see Lee, *Ireland*, pp. 262–4.
3 Judith Brown, *Modern India: The Origins of an Asian Democracy* (New York, 1994), pp. 319–20.
4 Deirdre McMahon, *Republicans and Imperialists* (Yale, 1984), p. 140.
5 Nicholas Mansergh, *The Unresolved Question: The Anglo-Irish Settlement and its Undoing* (London, 1991), p. 282.
6 Memo of talk with de Valera, 7 July 1937, BL, IOIC, IOR, L/PO/6/97.
7 Report, Jan. 1936, L/P&J/12/293.
8 Minutes of ISC, 16 July 1936, BL, IOIC, IOR, L/PO/6/97.
9 *Ibid.*
10 *Ibid.*
11 *Ibid.*
12 Zetland to Linlithgow, 31 July 1936, BL, IOIC, IOR, L/PO/6/97.
13 IPI note on Chaman Lal, 30 Aug. 1946, BL, OIOC, IOR, L/P&J/12/470. By this stage Blackett had died in a road accident in Germany aged just 53.
14 Vickery to Dibdin, 3 May 1938, BL, OIOC, IOR, L/P&J/12/470.
15 *Ibid.*
16 *Irish Press*, 31 Aug. 1938.
17 *Ibid.*
18 *Irish Press*, 1 Sept. 1938.
19 Vickery to Silver, 15 Sept. 1938, BL, OIOC, IOR, L/P&J/12/470.
20 Vickery to Silver, 19 Jan. 1938, *ibid.*; it is not clear how Chaman Lal could have obtained such a document in Ireland which, at the time, did not have diplomatic relations with Mexico.
21 See Introduction, this book, and Popplewell, *Intelligence*.
22 French, *Liberty*, p. 120.
23 William Lyon Mackenzie King Diaries, 5 March 1942, available: http://king.collectionscanada.ca.

24 See for example Amery to Linlithgow, 2 March 1942, in the twelve-volume *The Transfer of Power, 1942–1947*, ed. P. N. S. Mansergh and E. W. R. Lumby (London, 1970–82) (hereafter *TOP*), vol. 4, p. 295; and Amery to Linlithgow, 10 March 1942, *ibid.*, pp. 401–4.
25 Brown, *Modern India*, p. 330.
26 For the full text of the Atlantic Charter see: www.yale.edu/lawweb/avalon/wwii/atlantic.htm.
27 Read and Fisher, *Proudest*, p. 314.
28 French, *Liberty*, p. 121; and see various files dating from the Second World War in BL, OIOC, IOR, L/P&J/12 category.
29 History sheet of Dowlat Jayaram Vaidya (no date, but ends c. 1942), BL OIOC, IOR, L/P&J/12/478.
30 Recently declassified US documents show that Laird had in fact been a Soviet spy since the 1930s and provided Soviet agents with information during the 1940s: John Earl Haynes and Harvey Klehr, *Venona: Decoding Soviet Espionage in America* (London, 1999).
31 Transcribed telephone conversation, London to Sutton, Dublin, 14 Aug. 1942, BL, OIOC, IOR, L/P&J/12/478.
32 *Ibid.*
33 Vickery to Silver, 29 Sept. 1942, *ibid.*
34 *Ibid.*
35 Report on V. K. Menon, Dec. 1927, BL, OIOC, IOR, L/P&J/12/323.
36 Fact sheet of V. K. Menon, 10 June 1940, *ibid.*
37 Extract from Scotland Yard report, 16 March 1932, BL, OIOC, IOR, L/P&J/12/448.
38 Report on Menon and the CPGB, no date, BL, OIOC, IOR, L/P&J/12/646.
39 See chapter five for further discussion of Menon's appointment as Ambassador to Ireland.
40 Special Branch reports, Jul. to Dec. 1942, Edinburgh, Scottish National Archives, HH55/54. My thanks to Eunan O'Halpin for this reference.
41 Extract from Scotland Yard report, 20 April 1938, BL, IOIC, IOR, L/P&J/12/323.
42 Extract from Scotland Yard report, 23 Aug. 1939, *ibid.*
43 *Ibid.*
44 Extract from Scotland Yard report, 14 May 1941, *ibid.*
45 Memo on State of Ireland, 10 Oct. 1942, British Diplomatic Files, available: www.fdrlibrary.marist.edu. One of the five men reprieved, Joe Cahill, went on to become chief of the IRA in the early 1970s.
46 Extract from Scotland Yard report, 2 Sept. 1942, BL, IOIC, IOR, L/P&J/12/323.
47 French, *Liberty*, p. 267.
48 As late as 1972 the Special Branch at Heathrow took note of Menon's intended visits to Ireland, surmising in June 1972 that he was planning to attend a World Peace Congress in Belfast. This information was made available recently when his Metropolitan Police file was released. My thanks to Eunan O'Halpin for this information.
49 *The Times*, 8 April 1946.
50 Quoted in Michael Silvestri, ' "An Irishman is specially suited to be a policeman": Sir Charles Tegart and revolutionary terrorism in Bengal', in *History Ireland* (winter, 2000), p. 40.
51 *Ibid.*, p. 41.
52 *The Times*, 2 Nov. 1932.
53 Silvestri, ' "An Irishman" ', p. 41.
54 *The Times*, 28 May 1939.
55 Robert Fisk, *In Time of War: Ireland, Ulster and the Price of Neutrality, 1939–1945* (London, 1983), p. 121.
56 Walshe to Dulanty, 17 July 1940, NAI, DFA, A6.
57 *Ibid.*
58 Dulanty to Walshe, 9 Aug. 1940, *ibid.*
59 Dulanty to Walshe, 20 Aug. 1940, *ibid.*

60   *Ibid.*
61   Fisk, *In Time of War*, p. 121.
62   O'Halpin, *Defending*, p. 227.
63   Fisk, *In Time of War*, pp. 121–4, 161; and G. R. Sloan, *The Geopolitics of Anglo-Irish Relations in the Twentieth Century* (London, 1997), pp. 202–3.
64   Dulanty to Walshe, 9 Aug. 1940, NAI, DFA, A6.
65   Taken from the memoir written by K. F. Tegart, 'Charles Tegart: memoir of an Indian policeman', p. 295, contained in BL, OIOC, MSS EUR C 235. My thanks to Eunan O'Halpin for this reference.
66   O'Halpin, *Defending*, p. 240.
67   See chapter one.
68   Information from various reports in Obed's quite substantial IPI file: BL, OIOC, IOR, L/P&J/12/477.
69   O'Halpin, *Defending*, p. 242. For further information regarding other Axis agents interned in Ireland during the war see O'Halpin, *Defending*, chapter 6; also see O'Halpin, *MI5 and Ireland, 1939–45* (Dublin, 2003) and Mark Hull, *Irish Secrets: German Espionage in Ireland, 1939–1945* (Dublin, 2003), pp.1–126.
70   Garda report, 'Landing of three foreigners at Tralaspeen Strand, Castletownsend, Co. Cork', 7 July 1940, IMA, G2/X/0375. Obed, who had the better English, apparently took the initiative and stopped to ask various locals for directions.
71   *Ibid.*
72   Vickery to Silver, 20 July 1940, BL, OIOC, IOR, L/P&J/12/477.
73   G2 report on Obed, 12 July 1940, IMA, G2/X/0375.
74   'Report to Secretary' (Department of External Affairs), 9 July 1940, *ibid.*
75   *Ibid.*; the head of G2 until May 1941 was Liam Archer.
76   G2 refers to the South Africans Herbert Tributh and Dieter Gartner, as Germans throughout their reports. Although both were 'ethnic Germans' they were in fact, born in South West Africa and had only relocated to Germany to go to University in the late 1930s. See Hull, *Irish Secrets*, pp. 121–2.
77   IPI incorrectly noted Toe Head as being in Kerry.
78   Eunan O'Halpin, 'MI5's Irish memories: fresh light on the origins and rationale of Anglo-Irish security liaison in the Second World War', in Brian Girvin and Geoffrey Roberts (eds), *Ireland the Second World War: Politics, Society and Remembrance* (Dublin, 2000), pp. 133–51.
79   Incorrectly spelt 'Behadar' in IMA, G2/X/0375 and, subsequently, in Hull, *Irish Secrets*, pp. 123–5.
80   Garda report, 'Re: Sardar Behadar KHAN', 8 July 1940, IMA, G2/X/0375.
81   *Ibid.*
82   Vickery to Silver, 20 Aug. 1940, BL, OIOC, IOR, L/P&J/12/477.
83   Quoted in Hull, *Irish Secrets*, p. 243.
84   Note from 'conversation with journalist Kirwan who visits Mountjoy for Prisoners' Welfare purposes', 12 July 1940, and various correspondence on file, IMA, G2/X/0375.
85   Vickery to Silver, 27 July 1945; and IPI to Gibson, BL, OIOC, IOR, L/P&J/12/477.
86   Dominions Office memo, Aug. 1946, BL, OIOC, IOR, L/P&J/12/477.
87   IPI to Hanchet, 14 Dec. 1946, *ibid.*
88   Archer to Price, 5 Dec. 1946, *ibid.*
89   Price to Moore, 11 April 1947, *ibid.*
90   *Ibid.*
91   He clearly meant the IRA.
92   Obed to Nehru, 18 Feb. 1948, IMA, G2/X0375.
93   Hull, *Irish Secrets*, p. 255.
94   See French, *Liberty*, pp. 181–4; and Read and Fisher, *Proudest*, pp. 339–40.
95   *Irish Press*, 12 Nov. 1943.
96   *Dáil Debates*, vol. 91, 11 Nov. 1943.
97   *Ibid.*
98   *Ibid.*

99   Amery to Wavell, 19 Nov. 1943, *TOP*, vol. 4, p. 486; the £100,000 refers to the initial instalment of the donation paid to the Irish Red Cross.
100 *Ibid.*
101 Amiya Nath Bose was a nephew of Subhas Chandra Bose.
102 Report on Indians in the UK, Nov. 1943, BL, OIOC, IOR, L/P&J/12/646.
103 *Ibid.*
104 *Ibid.*
105 Extract from Metropolitan Police report, 19 Dec. 1946, BL, OIOC, IOR, L/P&J/12/658.
106 *Dáil Debates*, vol. 91, 11 Nov. 1943.
107 Wavell to Amery, 9 Dec. 1943, *TOP*, vol. 4, p. 532.
108 The FOIS was also referred to by the Irish authorities as the 'Indian Association', the 'Friends of India League' or the 'India League'. It is possible that it was also the 'Green Front', a group referred to in chapter three, that sent messages of support to Subhas Chandra Bose. An entire file detailing the activities of the FOIS can be found in the Irish Military Archives, titled 'Indian Association', G2/X/1317.
109 Note by Bryan, 2 March 1943, IMA, G2/3203.
110 Extract from report, Oct. 1944, contained in IMA, G2/3203 and G2/X/1317.
111 Undated notes by 'Terry', possibly May 1943, IMA, G2/X/1317.
112 Garda report, 3 Jan. 1945, *ibid.*
113 Extract from weekly report, 6 Sept. 1944, IMA, G2/3503 and also contained in IMA, G2/X/1317.
114 Webb to 'Lakshmi [sic] Pandit', 29 Nov. 1944, IMA, G2/X/1317.
115 Note in ink, 22 Sept. 1944, *ibid.*
116 G2 memo headed 'Evidence of Indian Association to date', dated 10 Nov. 1943; the Hurley-Beresford conversation noted in the memo dates from 25 May 1943: IMA, G2/X/1317. Ichihashi was in fact the Japanese Vice-Consul; some confusion surrounded whether both Vice-Consul and the Consul, Beppu, were associated with the group, but it appears that in the main it was Ichihashi who attended meetings and met with the Hurley-Beresfords.
117 O'Halpin, *Defending*, p. 240; see also Walshe to de Valera, 27 May and 1 June 1944, NAI, DFA, A2.
118 Again, Ichihashi, the Vice-Consul, was confused with the Consul: Garda report, 10 March 1945, IMA, G2/X/1317.
119 Bryan to Walshe, 23 Oct. 1944, IMA, G2/X/1317; also see O'Halpin, *Defending*, p. 240.
120 Notes on interview with 'F', 17 Oct. 1944, IMA, G2/X/1317.
121 O'Halpin, *Defending*, p. 209.
122 Notes on interview with 'F', 17 Oct. 1944, IMA, G2/X/1317.
123 *Ibid.*; whether O'Donnell was aware of the identity of 'F' is not made clear, but it is unlikely.
124 *Ibid.*
125 Garda report, 6 Dec. 1945, IMA, G2/X1317.
126 Notes by Bryan, no date (possibly early 1946), *ibid.*

CHAPTER FIVE

A Commonwealth republic

> Mr de Valera emphasized that he had always been most careful to state that he did not wish to leave the Commonwealth so long as it was understood that no allegiance to the Crown of England was involved. The Indian Commonwealth solution would have exactly met his position, and he was clearly angry at Mr Costello's action.[1]

At the time these words were written both Ireland and India were independent republics, one within the Commonwealth, the other outside it. However, a lot had happened to change the political landscape of both countries before the formal declarations of their republican status were made. In both countries one-time revolutionaries had become statesmen. De Valera and Nehru were to meet in India in 1948, not as radicals but as bone fide politicians, during a period in history when both men would finally witness the formations of the republics for which they had fought for so long, but under circumstances that neither would probably have anticipated or chosen. In their new-found role as national statesmen they would face their toughest battle yet as, in the end, both republics did not arrive proudly on the world stage with revolutionary flair, but were born slowly and apprehensively, bearing the deforming birthmarks of partition, an unwelcome testament to the long, ravaging road to independence and the irreversible effects it had had on each country's domestic politics.

Tribulations in the aftermath of war

On 14 June 1945 Wavell announced plans to reconstitute an executive council and to hold a conference of Indian leaders in order to discuss these initiatives. The following day all of the Congress leaders who had been imprisoned in the wake of the 'Quit India Movement', declared an unlawful organisation in 1942, were finally released. Known as the 'Shimla Conference', its failure to reach an agreement was followed in

July with a shock Labour victory in Britain and Clement Attlee became Prime Minister. Amery was replaced by the staid 74-year-old Frederick Pethick-Lawrence as Secretary of State for India (and now also for Burma), an appointment which somewhat dampened Congress's initial delight at Churchill's fall from government. Ominously, a British ICS man and later historian, Hugh Trevor Lambrick, had made an astute observation in his diary in relation to India–Ireland parallels:

> Why do not Congress speakers see the irony, and indeed absurdity, in their invoking the example of Ireland – her long struggle for Home Rule, and England's eventual surrender? Nothing could be more damaging to their own cause. The lesson of Ireland for India can be summed up in one word – Ulster.[2]

In a similar twist on the Irish parallel, at the famous Minto Park meeting in March 1940 when the Lahore Resolution was adopted by the All-India Muslim League, Jinnah compared the unhappy union of Britain and Ireland to the yoking together of Hindus and Muslims.[3] The war years had seen the rapid rise of Jinnah's Muslim League articulating quite specific demands declaring that 'Pakistan is a question of life or death for us'.[4] Handing India its independence, be it dominion status or otherwise, had become as complicated as ever. This was something that Wavell thought was lost on his London cohorts who had, understandably, been preoccupied during the crucial war years. Both the British Government and India's Congress hoped that, if pushed to concede Muslim demands, any geographical truncation in order to establish Pakistan would prove too small and weak to survive, an argument often used in relation to the partition of Ireland. With this in mind, and in the wake of yet another failed mission by Cripps the previous year, in March 1947 Congress decided to accept partition as the price of retaining a strong central administration for an independent India.[5]

In the meantime, Indian politicians were still keen to adhere to Irish precedents insofar as India's developing relationship with Britain and the Commonwealth was concerned. The newly appointed Irish Minister Plenipotentiary to Australia, Dr T. J. Kiernan, reported to Frederick Boland in 1946 that he had met with Nehru's nephew in Australia, who informed him that India was not represented at a recent Commonwealth trade meeting in London, partly in the belief that Ireland would not be represented. He also enquired of Kiernan's diplomatic status, much disputed at the time, and said that 'undoubtedly India would follow any line of action [Ireland] take[s] to get proper recognition of its diplomatic representative abroad'.[6] The same month Kiernan had a more amusing encounter to recount in relation to India and inter-imperial etiquette. He had attended a dinner along with the British, Canadian and New Zealand representatives at the house of the High Commissioner for India Sir Raghunath Paranjpye. Instead of seating his guests at one table the High Commissioner had small tables each holding four people, thus rendering any hierarchical seating arrangements redundant. In a speech after the dinner he explained why he had decided on this unusual seating plan.

> [He] had been in a difficulty about precedence as between the British High Commissioner who is the senior representative of the dominions and the new Irish representative who is also a Minister, and to solve his difficulty he had hit on the small tables plan.[7]

Partition remained an unwanted cross that Southern Ireland had to bear but it also impacted greatly on its imperial status, something which was becoming a source of increasing confusion for many in Ireland, Britain and the rest of the Empire alike. De Valera however was not as bemused, as he was the author of the very source of this bewilderment, the Executive Authority (External Relations) Bill, which was approved by the Irish Cabinet in December 1936, when famously the Taoiseach took advantage of the constitutional uncertainty caused by the abdication of King Edward VIII. The concept of 'external association' with Britain, where Ireland was associated with the Crown for purposes of common external concern only, was not a new one. It was an idea that had in fact risen before the Anglo-Irish Treaty of 1921 as a suggestion communicated to the Irish delegation by de Valera before they left for London. Arguably, at this stage de Valera's formula to end the centuries' long Anglo-Irish allegiance dilemma was in its embryonic stages and too subtle a proposition to hold much weight with either the delegation itself or, more to the point, the British. However, de Valera did not let the idea die. It resurfaced and was fleshed out in all its ambiguous glory on the night of 10 December 1936 when the text of the Bill was approved. The next day it became legislation.[8]

Bizarrely, depending on interpretation, Ireland either remained or ceased to remain a member of the British Commonwealth of Nations with the implementation of the External Relations Act. The Irish Government proceeded on the assumption that Ireland was an entirely sovereign, independent country, while Britain and the Commonwealth, interpreting the maintenance of the symbolic role of the monarch as a gesture of solidarity towards them which implied a desire on the part of the Irish to remain in the Commonwealth, conducted relations on the assumption that Ireland was not a foreign country. Crucially, however, neither was insistent on its own interpretation.[9] As the years went on, however, this lack of clarity became a target for de Valera's opponents who, convinced that Ireland was in fact a republic, questioned the purpose of the Act's existence. De Valera's brainchild was deliberately defective, but the motivation behind it was less complex. He had assured concerned members of the Dáil that the Bill did not contain any proposition to sever the connection with the Commonwealth. This was something that had to be stated, as the South's departure would result in a further distancing from Ulster's Unionists, and would provide them with as definitive a reason as they had ever had against the reunification of the country. How could they go into discussions with a Southern Government that was unwilling even to remain a member of the Commonwealth? As de Valera saw it, the end of partition was attainable only so long as Ireland remained in the Commonwealth, however tenuous the link.[10] As yet, there was no such thing as a republic within the Commonwealth, and so the declaration of an Irish republic was not on the cards, at least for as long as he remained in power. No doubt, other less immediate repercussions were also apparent: common citizenship and travel rights, as well as preferential trade agreements, would all be in jeopardy for the sake of nomenclature. Was it worth it? De Valera lost his first election in sixteen years in February 1948 and his opponents, who went on to form Ireland's first inter-party Government, seemed to think it was.

De Valera's anti-partition tour

The controversial circumstances surrounding the repeal of the External Relations Act are well documented elsewhere, but by the time of de Valera's anti-partition world tour the statute remained in place, if only by a thread.[11] India was the last leg of this propagandising and fundraising tour. Free from the constraints of office for the first time in sixteen years, de Valera spent a considerable amount of time in the USA, Australia and New Zealand. The Dominions Office in London kept a file on de Valera's tour, which indicates how anxious it must have been to counteract adverse publicity. In relation to his trip to the USA, despite the significant amount of publicity it received, the Dominions Office was somewhat happy to note:

> Reports hitherto received from the United States suggest that Mr de Valera's United States tour had little effect in influencing general United States opinion on the Irish partition issue . . . Mr de Valera after beginning moderately (it is believed that the United States government had counselled moderation during his tour), gradually adopted in his public speeches an increasingly violent anti-British attitude on the Irish partition question.[12]

Sir John Maffey, now Lord Rugby, the UK representative to Ireland, did not pull any punches in his summary of how news of the anti-partition tour was apparently being received in Dublin, where the new inter-party Government was attempting to settle down to business:

> There is some restiveness here at Mr de Valera's posing as leader and spokesman of the country in spite of his defeat at the polls in the recent elections. He seeks to refurbish his personal glamour in the political field here and to cause the Costello government the maximum of embarrassment.[13]

As far as the Australian leg of the tour was concerned, de Valera 'continued his anti-partition propaganda' there, but the Dominions Office reported that he had 'apparently received less publicity and less sympathy than he might have hoped'. The countries taken in by the tour, however, had substantial Irish populations, so a certain amount of publicity was guaranteed, which leads one to conclude that the decision to visit India must have been a politically strategic one.

India had been partitioned only recently and, like Ireland's, it was a domestic as opposed to an international partitioning, was also carried out along religious lines and likewise coincided with the transfer of power from Britain. The similarities were clear. De Valera was now to meet the newly appointed statesman Nehru, whose career reflected many aspects of his own. Having recently adopted constitutional nationalism at the expense of partition, the one-time revolutionary was preparing a warm reception for the one-time Irish freedom fighter who had inspired so many Indians over the years. Naturally the Dominions Office was anxious to keep track of de Valera's movements and utterances, but they were less concerned about the effect his tour would have on public opinion in relation to partition in Ireland or India, and more concerned with the impact that his visit could have on Indian policy in relation to the Commonwealth, which had yet to be clarified. An India outside the Commonwealth could prove problematic for Britain, and taking advice from the author of the External Relations Act was not exactly top of their list of preferred methods to elucidate matters. The Commonwealth Relations Office warned the British High Commissioners in both India and Pakistan in advance of de Valera's visit that it might have the effect of encouraging 'yet further examination in India (and perhaps Pakistan) of the possible applicability of solution on lines similar to those adopted in Éire to the problem of the future position of India and Pakistan in the Commonwealth'.[14] The effect of his opinion in relation to partition was a secondary concern: 'anything which Mr de Valera says about the partition question may also be used to draw an analogy between that and the partition of India into two dominions last August'.[15]

De Valera and Frank Aiken arrived in Calcutta on the morning of 14 June where they were received by the Governor of Bengal, Chakravarthi Rajagopalachari, an Indian National Congress stalwart who shortly afterward went on to succeed the Earl of Mountbatten as Governor General of India, the first ever Indian to hold the position. They met with Subhas Chandra Bose's brother Sarat Bose, who also had a keen interest in the Irish independence movement, as he had met with Maud Gonne MacBride in Paris in 1914.[16] A good relationship was clearly struck up as a few months later Sarat wrote to both de Valera and Aiken in relation to a new English daily that he was establishing entitled *The Nation*, which, he told them, would stand for 'the complete independence of India, free from British or any other foreign influence or control and the ending of autocratic rule in the Indian States'.[17] He hoped that they would be in a position to recommend to him a suitable candidate, preferably a member of the Dáil, who would be willing to take up the position of the paper's 'Éire correspondent'. Interestingly, an Irish friend of his in India had suggested Seán O'Faolain and Sarat Bose asked for Aiken's opinion of him.[18] Clearly Sarat felt there was a need for coverage of Irish politics in India, but crucially the information had to come directly from Irish sources. This was especially so where the coverage of partition was concerned. He said that the correspondent would have to send 'a newsletter every week covering news, political and otherwise, which [were] likely to be of interest to the Indian reader and also political trends in Éire *vis-à-vis* Northern Ireland and the UK'.[19]

After lunch on June 14 de Valera and Aiken travelled to Delhi, to Government House, where they stayed for the next two days with Jawaharlal Nehru. The following day a pre-recorded speech by de Valera was broadcast from Delhi, full of the type of rhetoric that would have greatly pleased his Indian listeners:

> For more than 30 years many of us in Ireland have followed with deepest sympathy the fortunes of the people of India in their efforts to secure freedom. We regarded the people of India as co-workers and allies in a common cause and we rejoiced exceedingly when India's right to independence was fully acknowledged.[20]

He went on to express the hope that further ties would be established between Ireland and India and that the contacts would not cease now that both countries had achieved their independence: 'We hope that before long formal diplomatic relations will be established between our two countries and official representatives exchanged. So the two peoples may become still better acquainted with each other, and that the existing bonds of friendship may be strengthened.'[21]

It was perhaps such sentiments about imminent diplomatic exchanges that ruffled the feathers of the newly elected coalition Government in Ireland, as noted earlier by Lord Rugby. Sir Terence Shone, High Commissioner to India, kept the Dominions Office informed of de Valera's every utterance during his trip. Firstly, he noted that, generally, in the course of 'various speeches during his passage through India, Mr de Valera emphasised the interest which the people of Ireland had always had in India and their pleasure in India's recently acquired freedom'. He noted with care de Valera's exact remarks on Ireland's relationship with the Commonwealth, as clearly he too was aware of the implications that de Valera's advice to Nehru could have on India's soon-to-be-decided republican status:

> As regards Ireland's position in the Commonwealth, Mr de Valera said that, although Éire was an independent republic, she was externally associated with the states of the British Commonwealth because the Irish people felt that such an association met the sentiments of certain elements in their population and was not inconsistent with Éire's national position and interests as a republic.[22]

Here we see de Valera acknowledging that the External Relations Act was designed primarily with partition and Ulster Unionism in mind. The Dominions Office was clearly concerned that the expression of such sentiments in Delhi could induce Nehru to attempt to create a similar set of circumstances in India in the hope that it too would lead to an end to partition or, worse for Britain, an India outside the Commonwealth. Shone noted that it was for India 'to decide whether or not the devil she knew was better than the devil she did not know'.[23] In such circumstances the British Government would have to formally review its stance on whether republican status was compatible with Commonwealth membership. Tellingly, Shone reported to the Dominions Office:

> Although Mr de Valera emphasised throughout that his pronouncements referred solely to Éire and were not proffered in regard to India's future attitude, it was inevitable that his remarks about Éire's relationship with the Commonwealth should give rise to some deliberation on India's own future relationship with the Commonwealth.[24]

He was correct in his assumptions. In fact, the previous year, while still in office, de Valera had already impressed on an Indian delegation (sent over to study Ireland's constitution) 'the desirability of some sort of external association'.[25]

Sir Benegal Narsing Rau was the Indian Constituent Assembly's constitutional advisor and was heavily involved in the process of drawing up the new Indian constitution. He was one of India's foremost jurists and had served briefly as Prime Minister of Jammu and Kashmir from 1944 to 1945, and was to be India's representative on the UN Security Council from 1950 to 1952.[26] In October 1947, while visiting Canada and the USA on a constitutional fact-finding mission, Rau got in contact with John J. Hearne, the Irish representative in Ottawa. Hearne had been the architect of the 1937 Irish constitution and it was in that capacity that Rau wished to meet him. Hearne organised a meeting for him with the Secretary of the Department of External Affairs, Frederick Boland, who happened to be in Washington at the time, Rau's next port of call. He provided Rau with a letter of warm introduction to Boland. He told the Secretary:

> Sir Benegal informs me that many of the provisions of our Constitution are being incorporated in the new draft Indian Constitution. He consulted me about the provisions relating to the President, the Council of State, Personal Rights, Social Policy, and so on. He has an amazing knowledge of our system. You know how able Indian jurists are.[27]

Hearne spoke very highly of Rau and was more than happy to facilitate his investigations. He gave a lunch for him, inviting all the High Commissioners in Ottawa, as well as the President of the Exchequer Court, who was 'the best jurist on the Canadian bench'.[28] In a personal letter to Boland, anticipating Rau's arrival in Washington, Hearne implored:

> Do please see Sir Benegal. He wants to talk to you about an Indian Republic externally associated etc. . . . I hope this is not an imposition but I thought that as this distinguished Indian jurist was going to Washington you would be glad to see him.[29]

Rau wished to ascertain how the provisions the Assembly planned to 'borrow' from the Irish constitution were 'working in the country of their origin' and it was for that reason that Rau was arranging to visit Dublin to consult de Valera in person before returning to India.[30] While talking to Boland he was seemingly particularly interested in the constitutional position of the President and about the workings of the External Relations Act.[31] While in Dublin he would meet not only with the Taoiseach but with the Department of External Affairs' legal advisor and the Attorney General.[32] On his return to Dublin Boland was keen to have suitable arrangements in place for Benegal's visit there, and, interestingly, in a minute to the legal advisor, Michael Rynne, he had this to say:

> I hope we can arrange a [suitable] programme for Sir B Rau. He is mainly interested in the 1936 Act, but I hope we can persuade him to the idea of connected action by Ireland and India towards getting rid of the King

business altogether . . . the principle of connected action seems to me worth securing because if India goes for 'External Association', as she seems likely to do, what she does and does not do – and the manner in which she does it – may be of practical consequence one way or the other from our point of view.[33]

In December 1947 the Government of India's Information Services released a newsletter in which they detailed Rau's research and the resulting implementation of the proposed amendments to the draft constitution in the wake of his talks with Irish politicians. In it Rau quotes de Valera, in what seems to have been a reflective mood:

> Referring to his talks with the Irish Premier, Mr de Valera, Sir B. N. Rau disclosed the satisfaction with which the Irish Premier greeted the birth of New India. 'I used to think,' remarked de Valera, 'that Mahatma Gandhi's creed of non-violence was a mistake, but now when I contrast the way wherein your country has achieved its freedom with that of other countries I think you had divine guidance.'[34]

Significant concerns existed throughout the Commonwealth about Rau's research during 1947–48. John Kearney, the High Commissioner for Canada in India, was on a sojourn at home when he attempted, on two occasions, to obtain further information about Rau's investigations from John J. Hearne. He told Hearne in no uncertain terms that 'the policy of the Canadian Government was to keep India in the British Commonwealth of Nations'.[35] In the first of these discussions, Hearne related, Kearney had

> seemed eager to have a full account of my conversation with Sir Benegal Rau in October . . . I made it clear, however, that I had expressed no view to Sir Ben on the question as to whether India should, or should not, leave the British Commonwealth of Nations.[36]

Kearney, Hearne noted, had been critical:

> He doubted the wisdom of my omission to express an opinion . . . He pressed me as to whether Sir Ben had then asked me the direct question . . . Mr Kearney said that Sir Ben may well have understood my silence as meaning that, in my view, India should leave the Commonwealth.[37]

Hearne stated that he had not asked Kearney whether the Canadian Government was urging Pandit Nehru to keep the Crown as the link with the British Commonwealth, but he 'was sure that that must be so, and that our Executive Authority (External Relations) Act 1936 is pointed to as a model'.[38] Clearly, Nehru and fellow politicians and administrators, such as Rau, were more than familiar with the precedent of 'external association' and had seriously considered adopting it. Terence Shone noted an interesting analogy drawn by the *Bombay*

Chronicle about de Valera's pronouncements on Commonwealth association when he was in India, which, though 'definitely vague', suggested
that Ireland, while remaining in the Commonwealth, was aspiring to the
achievement of 'the lotus in the mud pond, which lives in and thrives
through the mud and yet remains untouched and unsoiled by it'.[39]

One-time revolutionaries: de Valera and Nehru

Nehru gave a dinner in honour of de Valera in Delhi. Several Cabinet
ministers attended, as well as Lord and Lady Mountbatten. Nehru and
de Valera clearly had a lot to talk about and they initiated a respectful
correspondence when de Valera returned to Ireland. Nehru informed
him that many of his fellow Indians were gravely disappointed at the
brevity of his stay: 'there were so many people who were anxious to
meet you. But it was difficult to find the time for this and many of them
are rather annoyed with me because of this.'[40] He also felt the need to
reiterate how significant the visit was for many Indians:

> For a long time past, several generations of Indians have followed closely
> and with deep sympathy events in Ireland. We have drawn inspiration
> from many of the happenings there and you have been admired by vast
> numbers of our people. For them it was an event that you visited India
> and their only regret is that they could not take advantage of your visit.[41]

Nehru noted in a subsequent letter that he longed to visit Ireland again
as he had gone 'there once a very long time ago when . . . a student'.[42]
This was more than likely during his first year of study at Trinity
College, Cambridge, as in 1907 Nehru had written to his father about
a visit to Ireland, asking him:

> Have you heard of the Sinn Féin in Ireland . . . it is a most interesting
> movement and resembles very closely the so-called extremist move-
> ments in India . . . this movement is causing consternation. They say that
> if its policy is adopted by the bulk of the country, English rule will be a
> thing of the past.[43]

De Valera, for his part, kept up to date with Indian affairs, and he wrote
a congratulatory letter to Nehru in September 1948, after the resolution
of the ongoing Hyderabad dispute. Some of the Princely States were initially unwilling to acknowledge the new status quo that the transfer of
power and partition had brought, one of the larger states, Hyderabad,
being one. Its majority Hindu population had a Muslim ruler, the Nizam
of Hyderabad, who wanted the state to remain independent of both India
and Pakistan. His immense wealth and large army complicated matters.
The unstable situation resulted in sporadic communal riots in the state
throughout 1947, with Mountbatten attempting to placate the Nizam

and Sardar Patel, now Deputy Prime Minister, vehemently insisting that India could not accept 'a snake in its belly'.[44] After Mountbatten's departure Nehru's approach hardened and, encouraged by Patel who undoubtedly had a hard-line attitude to the situation, on 13 September 1948 the military annexation of Hyderabad, code-named 'Operation Polo', was authorised. Although it took only four days to complete and the state was incorporated into India for good, it had been a risky military move, and the Indian chiefs of staff had even tried to prevent Patel from giving the order.[45] On 18 September de Valera wrote to Nehru: 'I hasten to send you my congratulations on the happy termination of the Hyderabad dispute. I know what a cause of anxiety it was to you. I know also that you will be generous in victory.'[46]

This is an interesting correspondence: as Judith Brown has noted, there was considerable international unease at the use of force, not least in Britain where Attlee had to work hard to counter the Conservative Party's criticisms of the Indian Government's treatment of a former princely ally of the Raj.[47] In dealing with the Hyderabad dispute *The Times* thought the use of violence was 'deplorable':

> Its present use of force against a weaker neighbour which resists its claims comes badly from a government that owes its existence to the principles embodied in the Charter of the United Nations, and seems likely to strain still further relations with Pakistan.[48]

Such coverage undoubtedly aggravated Nehru and his ministers. De Valera was probably a lone voice of support from the West and, given that he was in the unique position of having experienced the domestic partition of his own country and the problems it posed, it must have pleased Nehru that de Valera approved of the radical military action that he had taken. Nehru replied:

> The Hyderabad affair has been much misinterpreted in the English papers. It has in fact led to very substantial gains in peace and security in India. The whole atmosphere has been cleared and the various religious communal groups have a sense of security and fellow feeling. I think ultimately it will lead to far better relations with Pakistan. It was very good of you to congratulate me on the happy termination of the Hyderabad dispute.[49]

Sardar Patel also wrote to de Valera as, due to illness (he had suffered a heart attack the previous March and was confined to bed), he had been unable to meet him during his Indian sojourn. Sardar had wanted to greet de Valera personally, 'not merely as a friend but as a valiant fighter of freedom's battle and a great patriot',[50] and he considered it a great pity that ill-health had prevented him from 'having the pleasure and privilege of thereby fulfilling one of my most ardent wishes ever since

Vithalbhai told me in such nice terms about you'.[51] This is of course a reference to his late brother and co-founder of the IIIL, V. J. Patel, who, Sardar assured de Valera, always had 'a very soft corner in his heart for you'.[52] Although Vithalbhai had long since passed away, the memory of his Irish connections lived on through his younger brother, who was now India's new Deputy Prime Minister. Other interesting Indian figures had come forward when news of de Valera's Indian visit was first aired. Many Indian doctors who had studied in Ireland were anxious to welcome de Valera to their country, many others were keen to ask him if he could find them a position in an Irish hospital, including Sarat Chandra Bose's son, Sisir Kumar Bose, who wanted to study paediatrics in Dublin.[53]

There are many notes from Irish citizens who had settled in India, especially from the religious community, and a particularly intriguing letter from an Indian Christian, Joachim Alva, who seemingly had befriended de Valera while in India.[54] Alva was appointed the Sheriff of Bombay shortly afterwards, 'the first from the Indian Christian community to be appointed to this post', and in his lengthy letter he informed de Valera of other Christians who had been appointed to important positions since the transfer of power, like the Finance Minister Mathai and the Minister for Health Rani Amrit Kaur. Another letter is also of particular note. P. S. T. Sayee, a lawyer from south India, had been in Ireland studying law in 1915–16, when he had first met de Valera. He was aware that the former Taoiseach might not remember him, so he refreshed his memory:

> I underwent training along with the Irish Volunteers in Dublin. I contributed on Indian Nationalism to Irish Volunteer. And I was intimately associated with your National Leaders of those glorious days . . . After the Rebellion of 1916 it became impossible for me to continue to stay in Dublin. I therefore left for Bray along with Mr Desmond Fitzgerald and his family. After some time he was arrested and taken away and I found my way somehow back to India.[55]

He was sorry that de Valera 'had chosen to be the leader of the opposition', yet he thought he would find it amusing to know that his successor, John A. Costello, 'is none other than my old tutor in Law in 1915 and 1916 in Dublin'.

The Mountbattens had de Valera and Nehru as their lunch guests on 15 June.[56] It was in fact one of the Viceroy's last official functions in his capacity as Governor General of India, as he was succeeded a week later by Rajagopalachari. It is perhaps somewhat fitting, although clearly not orchestrated, that de Valera was the Viceroy's last guest, given the part played by Ireland in the break up of the British Empire. It is also poignant that he and Nehru were together at this point in time, one successfully transformed revolutionary present for the other's debut as his country's leading statesman. Like de Valera he would hold the portfolio of Minister for Foreign Affairs in conjunction with the Prime Ministership. Nehru was also bringing many of his fellow revolutionaries with him into the new Government, as had de Valera in 1932, and there was no better person to give advice on how to cope with the country's transition to independence. De Valera and Mountbatten, however, got on famously, and Mountbatten wrote to him shortly after the trip telling him, 'my wife and I enjoyed having you and Mr Aiken to stay with us in Delhi, and I shall never forget our interesting conversations'. He was writing from his new residence in Mullaghmore, Co. Sligo. He had just 'completed putting electric light and the proper fresh water system into Classiebaun Castle and hope[d to] furnish it, and to be able to come and spend some of our holidays here . . . all the people are so friendly'.[57] Given these utterances, it is tragic to recall that the elderly Lord Mountbatten was killed at his Irish retreat by an IRA bomb in 1979.

A Commonwealth Prime Minister's visit to Dublin

The controversial announcement of the Government's intentions to declare Ireland a republic and to leave the Commonwealth in 1948 was a short-sighted manoeuvre which, fortuitously for Ireland, resulted in the British Government maintaining its 'most favoured nation' status the following April. Given Ireland's proximity to Britain and the large Irish community resident and working on the mainland, it was arguably sheer practicalities that dictated the outcome. Many British politicians thought that Ireland should have been more harshly penalised for this move and that 'most favoured nation' status not be granted, but Britain was unable to comply because of pressure from other Commonwealth countries that had substantial Irish populations. Rumour spread swiftly in the early months of 1949 that Ireland was, however, to be reprimanded legislatively by the British, with articles to that effect appearing in various British newspapers. During these tense months of Anglo-Irish relations Krishna Menon kept John W. Dulanty up to date with what India was being told in relation to the ongoing difficulties, which, as it turns out, was very little. 'The British Government', he said, 'had conveyed to India information with regard to the conversations that passed between [Ireland] and them, but no actual consultation with India had taken place.' Menon was even instructed to pass on to Dulanty in London a cable sent by Nehru expressing 'the fullest sympathy of India so far as the Irish government is concerned', with Nehru urging Menon to 'tell Dulanty to assure his government that if there is any way in which we can be of help we will be glad to consider any suggestion'.[58] However, in April 1949, at a Commonwealth conference in London, the Indian Government affirmed its desire to maintain its country's full membership of the Commonwealth and to accept the King as 'a symbol of the free association of its independent member nations'.[59]

Nehru had spent many days in discussion with the British and no doubt in the previous months had been made aware of the implications that staying out of the Commonwealth would possibly have for India, whose geographical location could result in it not being granted most favoured nation status. He may also have been made aware of the British Government's plans for retaliation against the Irish decision, as less then two weeks later the British Parliament would pass its Ireland Bill. There, written in British law for the first time, was the legislative threat alluded to earlier, a constitutional guarantee to Ulster Unionists that under no circumstances would the unity of Ireland be achieved without their Parliament's consent. The Southern Government had received no official notification of the intended legislation, and was furious.

As the epigraph to this chapter illustrates, de Valera, too, was angry, but for another reason. He considered that putting up with the ambiguous external relations legislation for a while longer might have allowed Ireland to achieve a status similar to that of India – a republic within the Commonwealth. Under such circumstances, de Valera thought that there was a possibility of ending partition as opposed to ensuring it. Nehru was taking those considerations into account and had not fully made up his mind in relation to Commonwealth membership. For, when H. S. Malik was India's representative in Canada (before being posted to France), he told Hearne that he had asked the Prime Minister for instructions on what to say should he be asked what the final decision was likely to be and Nehru replied:

> Tell them that I don't know the answer to that question. Tell them that the decision will largely depend upon the conduct of the British in the meantime. If they try to interfere with us in any way; above all if they do so through Pakistan and the use of partition of the country for the purpose of keeping their finger in our affairs, India will certainly quit the Commonwealth in 1948.[60]

Nehru's comments were prophetic, though in relation to Ireland, and it seems that only he could prevent history repeating itself in relation to India.

Nehru availed of the opportunity to visit Ireland for the second time after his gruelling trip to London in April 1949, when the Anglo-Indian discussions had ended and India had declared its intention to remain in the Commonwealth. He had postponed his departure for home from London in order to make the visit.[61] He arrived in Dublin for the day on 28 April 1949 with, among others, Krishna Menon and John Dulanty. The Taoiseach John A. Costello, as well as de Valera and Frank Aiken, were at the airport to meet him. Considering the previous day's announcement, it is interesting to note the protocol adopted by the British, Australian and Canadian Governments, each of the Commonwealth countries sending a representative to greet Nehru.

Shortly after arriving Nehru was taken to Áras an Uachtaráin where he was received by the President. A delegation of the Indian League in Dublin arranged for an afternoon reception at the Shelbourne Hotel in honour of his visit.[62] Later he had the privilege of being the first distinguished stranger to be received on the floor of the Dáil, where he was welcomed with rapturous applause. Both Costello and de Valera met him at the foot of the stairs and escorted him across the floor to the Ceann Comhairle from where he was introduced. At the airport later that evening he told an *Irish Press* reporter that 'ever since my childhood, I have thought of Ireland, and for many years her past history has been interlinked with ours because of our struggles for freedom. We have tried to learn much from the experience of Ireland.'[63] Nehru went on: 'I hope that those bonds may long continue. I am sure they will keep us together in many ways for the good of both our countries and for the larger cause of world peace.'[64]

Early the following week the recently appointed Prime Minister of Pakistan, Liaquat Ali Khan, visited Ireland. Kahn's visit was a much less publicised and more subdued affair than Nehru's. It also threw up an unwelcome problem. At a Cabinet meeting the question of whether Khan would also be received on the floor of the Dáil was brought up.[65] It was decided that 'the Prime Minister of Pakistan should be received on the floor of the Dáil if time should permit him to visit the Dáil'. There was a caveat, however, recorded by the Department of the Taoiseach's Assistant Secretary Nicholas Nolan, who noted:

> I understand, however, that the feeling of the government was that, as Mr Liaquat Khan is not up to the international status of Mr Nehru, it would be far better if things could be so arranged that Mr Liaquat Khan was not received on the floor of the Dáil – although it was realised that the reception of Mr Nehru a few days before created an embarrassing precedent.[66]

Khan was in Dublin only for the day of 3 May, and as he spent most of the afternoon at the Royal Dublin Society's Spring Show with the Minister for Agriculture and independent TD, James Dillon, it was noted that 'by the time that was over, it was too late for Liaquat Khan to pay a visit to the Dáil'.[67] This incident was as much a demonstration of the first coalition Government's inexperience in office as it was of Ireland's official attitude towards the newly created Pakistan.

In July 1949 the Indo-Irish relationship had come full circle and the culmination of the countries' shared histories was the appointment of V. K. Krishna Menon as Ambassador to Ireland. As an accreditation it was symbolic for several reasons. Menon, as was seen in chapter four, had many radical Irish contacts and had been keenly interested in the Irish independence movement throughout his many years as an activist in London. And it was fitting that it should have been India, its old anti-imperialist ally, whose ambassador was the first to be appointed to the newly declared Republic of Ireland. During the presentation of his Letters of Credence in Dublin, President Seán T. O'Ceallaigh was most expressive:

> Only those who know the Irish people intimately – who know our deep and sincere friendship for your country and the anxious sympathy with which we followed its long struggle for national freedom – will understand how much this occasion means to us in Ireland . . . the bonds which unite India and Ireland are of no conventional or material order. Our commercial and economic relations are not yet of special importance . . . nevertheless the bonds of sympathy and understanding which exist between our two countries are not weaker, but stronger, for the fact that they are based, not on community of interest in the material sphere, but on the unshakable attachment of our two countries to the ideals and spiritual values which we hold common.[68]

Ireland also helped India to establish a new Commonwealth precedent, as Menon's appointment provided India with a speedy expression of its newfound independence as a republic within the Commonwealth. As a matter of principle India had not consulted their fellow members of the Commonwealth, and Menon's credentials were addressed to the President of the Republic of Ireland.[69]

Menon's role was a dual one as he was already India's High Commissioner in London, and since Ireland had left the Commonwealth the previous year joint accreditations were no longer appropriate. However, the Irish Government felt that in the circumstances, Menon's nomination by the Indian Government should be accepted, and the Irish Department of External Affairs issued a statement agreeing 'to waive for the time being, their objections to a joint accreditation in this case'.[70] The Irish Government, it seems, were correct to make the exception. Three years later Boland, who had replaced Dulanty, reported on Menon's controversial 'retirement' as Ambassador to both the United Kingdom and Ireland.[71] He was aware of existing concerns that Dublin might become 'a diplomatic suburb of London by the accreditation to us of people already accredited and resident here', but he went on to note:

> In the particular case of India, I think there is a good case in favour of taking the man from London . . . at moments of controversy, they are inclined to side with us . . . India is particularly interested in Ireland and on more than one occasion, we have had evidence that the Indian High Commissioner here has taken a benevolent interest on our behalf when matters affecting us were discussed at Commonwealth conferences or meetings . . . the value of taking the Indian ambassador from London is that it gives us a means of ensuring that the Indian delegation at Commonwealth conferences here, some of which may be discussing matters of consequence to us, will be fully informed of our views and interests.[72]

The following month, August 1949, Menon, who by now had acquired a reputation as a difficult character, was causing a stir in relation to his impending departure by attempting to hold on to his posting in Ireland when it had already been agreed that his successor, Bal Gangadhar Kher, would take over the reins in both London and Dublin. Menon even circulated a rumour that Dublin had accepted the principle of joint accreditation in his case specifically only 'because of his national record'.[73] Somewhat amusingly, and perhaps an occurrence possible only among Irish and Indian diplomats who were once revolutionaries, there ensued a battle for who had the best national record, with the Indian representative to France, H. S. Malik, urging on Con Cremin that

> Mr Kher would have an even stronger claim [than Menon] for an exception in his favour as his national record is quite outstanding and he is in this respect far ahead of Mr Krishna Menon. He mentioned as an example that Mr Kher had been imprisoned by the British on at least six different occasions for his nationalist activities.[74]

As it was an ill-founded rumour originating with his own colleague, Kher need not have worried. Menon's reputation had, by that stage, become quite damaged and his replacement was most acceptable, especially to London. However, Menon did not vacate his Irish posting quietly and, as Boland saw it, he then 'began intriguing in an effort to retain the appointment of Indian ambassador to Dublin'.[75] Boland informed Dublin that during one meeting Menon had become 'rather excited and agitated. I have no doubt but that Mr Menon uses narcotic stimulants. Mr Menon began a long discourse of which it was rather difficult to grasp the point.'[76] Menon was determined to blacken Kher's name, claiming him to be a 'scheming politician' who was under the impression that Britain and Ireland were the same country.[77] Menon's attempts to undermine his appointment in Boland's eyes came to nothing: after meeting him, the

Irish representative remarked that Kher was 'a very different type from Mr Menon. He is deeply versed in the literature of Irish nationalism and the prospect of becoming Indian ambassador to Ireland is plainly for him a moving personal experience.'[78] As Boland had suspected, Menon was by this stage addicted to the barbiturate Luminal, use of which was clearly affecting his day-to-day functioning, and this particular incident was far from being the most controversial during this period of his long and otherwise most impressive career.

When they met in April 1949, Nehru and de Valera spoke not only of a shared history but of a hopeful future in which the two countries worked to ensure that their relationship would bring about more pragmatic results, especially in the area of trade. Attempts had been made by India in this regard as early as 1947 when a government advisor, Mr Shulka, visited the Department of Industry and Commerce in Dublin. Shulka is reported to have explained

> that his present visit was of an exploratory nature, and he enquired whether it would facilitate trade if an Indian representative was appointed here, or a branch of the High Commissioner's Office in London was opened in Dublin with corresponding representatives on behalf of the Irish government in India. He was informed that such questions were under consideration at the present time by the Minister for External Affairs, and that undoubtedly such direct representation would be useful. He explained that there was very strong feeling of friendship for Ireland in India and that the new Indian government would be very anxious to develop trade and do anything possible to help this country.[79]

A mutually beneficial trade relationship was all that either country had left to offer in the post-war and post-imperial age, but given the geographical distance between them it would be difficult. As noted elsewhere, it was more than likely the nationalist economic policies of protectionism adopted by both countries that somewhat ironically hindered any later development of a trade relationship between the two.[80] At any rate it could hardly replace the urgent excitement and mutual empathy that had characterised the hitherto contra-imperial friendship that various aspects of each country's nationalist elites had embraced and thrived on. It was only when Ireland joined the UN in 1955 that opportunities for cooperation on international affairs between the two countries became practicable. The following year Nehru visited Ireland again, but this time it was a more leisurely stay. One of the highlights was a trip with Frank Aiken and President Seán T. O'Ceallaigh to the Abbey Theatre to see a production of Seán O'Casey's *Juno and the Paycock*.[81]

It must be remembered that it was not until 1964 that an Irish Embassy was established in India. In 1961 Jawaharlal Nehru's sister, Vijaya Lakshmi Pandit, then High Commissioner to the UK, 'made it known that her brother was extremely anxious to see an Irish representative appointed to New Delhi and expressed the hope that the government might take a decision to this effect soon'.[82] A government memorandum on the topic dating from March 1961 noted in response: 'It is, of course, the recognised and virtually invariable principle that dip[lomatic] rep[resentation] is on a reciprocal basis', and that it

> had always been the intention of successive governments to have a representative accredited to India one day. This intention, implicit in the acceptance of an Indian ambassador in 1949, derives from the historic ties between the two countries, the mutual sympathy felt in each over a long period for the struggle of the other to secure independence from the same power, the importance of India in the Asian continent, and the place in world affairs which India assumed despite partition immediately on attaining independence. That a representative has not hitherto been appointed is due solely to considerations of finance and personnel.[83]

These difficulties were explained to Madame Pandit at the time. She expressed her appreciation of these factors but reiterated her brother's strong desire to have an Irish representative in New Delhi. When informed of the matter the Minister for External Affairs, Frank Aiken, was

> satisfied that to delay further the opening of a diplomatic mission in India is likely to give serious offence to the Indian government and that for this reason it is necessary to take the step. Apart, however, from this aspect of the matter, there are, in the Minister's view, cogent reasons why a mission should now be opened in India.[84]

The main reasons cited here were India's significant place in world affairs, both as a large, democratic and powerful country of the Asian Continent and as a country that had assumed greater prominence in the UN in the preceding years. The following September, however, little development had been made in establishing an Irish mission in India, and further pressure was exerted by the outgoing Indian Ambassador Mr Changla. This time his views were expressed to the Taoiseach, Seán Lemass. Changla is reported to have

> pressed very strongly for the establishment of an Irish diplomatic mission in India. I told him that I personally was very definitely of the opinion that this is something that we must do. I explained that I discussed it with you and that you had drawn attention to the difficulties of filling a new ambassador post at this time because of pending retirement.[85]

Lemass was aggravated by Aiken's apparently lax attitude to the appointment of an Irish representative to India, and ended his correspondence on the matter somewhat curtly by impressing on Aiken that 'it is undesirable to delay this matter for much longer. It is for you to take the initiative. I do not anticipate any difficulty from the viewpoint of the Minister for Finance.'[86] An Irish Ambassador to India, William Warnock, was finally nominated in 1963 and appointed in early 1964.[87] To mark the occasion, that same year, at President de Valera's insistence, the Indian President Dr Sarvepalli Radhakrishnan visited Ireland.[88] During his visit the 82-year-old de Valera proudly produced the sword presented to him by members of the revolutionary Ghadr movement in San Francisco in 1919.

Conclusion

Just before the Second World War India was not even a dominion and Ireland was about to initiate a policy of neutrality that could have resulted in an aggressive reaction from its neighbour who was embarking on a period of uncertainty and great difficulty. One wonders how British politicians felt, a mere six or seven years later, about the wholesale transformation of Indian and Irish revolutionaries into statesmen and diplomats. The hurried repeal of the External Relations Act in 1949 had a detrimental effect on both Ireland's domestic and foreign relations, and the repercussions for its relationship with Britain could have been much worse had it not been for their geographical proximity. As de Valera noted, the Indian Commonwealth solution that was reached the very same year could have suited Ireland's independent position and possibly paved the way for an Ireland within the Commonwealth. Whether this in turn would have facilitated the reunification of the country, however, is a discussion beyond the confines of this study. What is certain is that the British Government was apprehensive of de Valera's capacity for influencing the newly instated Indian Government, as the Dominions Office had opened a file on the subject when it became aware that his anti-partition tour would include India. In any event, whether or not talks with de Valera ever influenced Nehru and his Government's decision, India made history by becoming the first republican Commonwealth country.

Notes

1 Memorandum of conversation of Labour MP Ungoed-Thomas at lunch with de Valera and Aiken at the Council of Europe, 5 Sept. 1949, NAUK, DO, 35/3941; Nicholas Mansergh in conversation with de Valera, Feb. 1952, noted that he said 'if in office, Éire happy to accept Indian solution – would have striven for it': see Mansergh, *Nationalism*, p. 185.
2 C. H. Philips and Mary Doreen Wainright (eds), *The Partition of India: Policies and Perspectives, 1935–47* (London, 1970), p. 511.
3 French, *Liberty*, p. 123.

4   *Ibid.*, p. 216.
5   McMahon, 'A larger and noisier Southern Ireland', p. 172; for further reading on partition in India and Ireland see Fraser, *Partition*.
6   Kiernan to Boland, 5 Dec. 1946, NAI, DFA, Canberra Embassy series, box 5.
7   Kiernan to Boland, 9 Dec. 1946, *ibid.*
8   For further reading on the exact circumstances surrounding the enactment of the External Relations Act see Ian McCabe, *A Diplomatic History of Ireland 1948–49* (Dublin, 1991), pp. 16–19; also see various relevant documents in *DIFP* 4, pp. 530–9.
9   Mansergh, *Unresolved Question*, p. 308.
10 Mansergh, *Nationalism*, p. 186.
11 See McCabe, *Diplomatic History*; and David McCullagh *A Makeshift Majority: The First Inter-Party Government, 1948–51* (Dublin, 1998). De Valera began the tour in March 1948, six months before Costello's declaration of intent to repeal the External Relations Act.
12 Telegram, Commonwealth Relations Office, to UK High Commissioner in India and UK High Commissioner in Pakistan, 2 June 1948, NAUK, DO, 35/3930.
13 *Ibid.*
14 *Ibid.*
15 *Ibid.*
16 See Bose to Woods, 7 Dec. 1933, reproduced in Appendix 5.
17 See Sarat Chandra Bose to Frank Aiken, 21 Aug. 1948, UCDA, Frank Aiken Papers (hereafter P104), P104/4806; and Sarat Chandra Bose to de Valera, 21 Aug. 1948, UCDA, P150/2955. Unfortunately the de Valera and Aiken Papers do not throw any light on whether this request had been followed up.
18 O'Faolain was an IRA member turned writer and social commentator.
19 Sarat Chandra Bose to Frank Aiken, 21 Aug. 1948, UCDA, P104/4806; and Sarat Chandra Bose to de Valera, 21 Aug. 1948, UCDA, P150/2955.
20 'Radio talk by Mr de Valera from New Delhi', 15 June 1948, UCDA, P150/2955. It is not clear from what station the speech was broadcast.
21 *Ibid.*
22 Shone to Dominions Office, 9 July 1948, NAUK, DO, 35/3930.
23 *Ibid.*
24 *Ibid.*
25 Mansergh, *Nationalism*, pp. 188–9; McMahon, 'A larger and noisier Southern Ireland', p. 182
26 Encyclopaedia Britannica online: www.britannica.com/eb/article-9062785/Sir-Benegal-Narsing-Rau.
27 Hearne to Boland, 31 Oct. 1947, NAI, DFA, 305/41
28 *Ibid.*
29 Hearne to Boland, 31 Oct. 1947, marked 'Personal', *ibid.*
30 Rau to Boland, 6 Nov. 1947, *ibid.*
31 Minute, Boland to Rynne, 13 Nov. 1947, *ibid.*
32 Woods to O'Connell, 24 Nov. 1947, *ibid.*
33 Minute, Boland to Rynne, 20 Nov. 1947, *ibid.*
34 Government of India Information Service's 'News in brief', 30 Dec. 1947, *ibid.*
35 Hearne to Boland, 2 Jan. 1948, *ibid.*
36 *Ibid.*
37 *Ibid.*
38 *Ibid.*
39 Government of India Information Service's 'News in brief', 30 Dec. 1947, *ibid.*
40 Nehru to de Valera, 18 June 1948, UCDA, P150/2955.
41 *Ibid.*
42 Nehru to de Valera, 15 July 1948, UCDA, *ibid.*
43 Jawaharlal to Motilal, 12 Sept. 1907, quoted in Dorothy Norman, *Nehru: The First Sixty Years*, vol. 1 (London, 1965), p. 12; see also Sarvepalli Gopal, *Jawaharlal Nehru: A Biography 1889–1947*, vol. 1 (London, 1975), p. 22.

44 French, *Liberty*, pp. 369–71; and Brown, *Nehru*, pp. 210–11.
45 French, *Liberty*, pp. 369–71.
46 De Valera to Nehru, 18 Sept. 1948, UCDA, P150/2955.
47 Brown, *Nehru*, p. 211.
48 *The Times*, 14 Sept. 1948.
49 Nehru to de Valera, 26 Sept. 1948, UCDA, P150/2955.
50 Sardar Patel to de Valera, 13 June 1948, P104/4806.
51 *Ibid.*
52 *Ibid.*
53 Sisir Kumar Bose to Aiken, 2 Feb. 1949, UCDA, P104/4806.
54 For example, see Archbishop Mulligan of Delhi-Shimla to de Valera, 16 Dec. 1948, UCDA, P150/2955 and various letters to de Valera from Irish Catholic associations and communities on file in the Aiken Papers, UCDA, P104/4806; also see Alva to de Valera, 14 June 1949, UCDA, P150/2955.
55 Sayee to de Valera, 12 June 1948, UCDA, P104/4806. Desmond FitzGerald's son, the former Taoiseach Dr Garret FitzGerald, does not know of Sayee and was always under the assumption that his father made the trip to Bray on his own: Dr FitzGerald in correspondence with the author.
56 *Irish Press*, 16 June 1948; see also 'Extracts from press reports and comments for week ended 24 July 1948', NAUK, DO, 35/3930.
57 Mountbatten to de Valera, 24 Aug. 1948, UCDA, P150/2955.
58 Confidential report, Dulanty to Boland, 1 Feb. 1949, NAI, DFA, 305/14/36.
59 Deirdre McMahon, 'Ireland and the Empire–Commonwealth, 1900–48'. in Judith M. Brown and W. M. Roger Louis (eds), *The Oxford History of the British Empire*, vol. 4: *The Twentieth Century* (Oxford, 1999), pp. 161–2.
60 Hearne to Walshe, 23 Sept. 1947, NAI, DFA, 305/41.
61 *Irish Press*, 29 April 1949.
62 *Ibid.*
63 *Ibid.*
64 *Ibid.*
65 Further items list, 2 May 1949, NAI, DT, S 14524, A.
66 Note, 4 May 1949, *ibid.*
67 *Ibid.*
68 Translation of President's reply, no date, NAI, DT, S 14461, A1.
69 MacCabe, *Diplomatic History*, p. 95.
70 *Ibid.*, and see also NAI, DT, S 14 461 A1 and BL, IOIC, IOR, L/P&S/3/420 file on Menon.
71 Menon was suspected of having effectively resigned under pressure from Nehru after his involvement in the corrupt purchasing of arms for the Indian army while in London.
72 Boland to Nunan, 23 June 1952, NAI, DFA, P236.
73 *Ibid.*, Cremin to Nunan, 11 July 1952.
74 *Ibid.*
75 *Ibid.*, Boland to Nunan, 18 July 1952.
76 *Ibid.*
77 For further examples of difficulties that Kher had encountered with Menon in relation to his appointment see various letters on file in NAI, DFA, P236 especially Boland to Nunan, 1 Aug. 1952.
78 *Ibid.*
79 Memorandum of F. J. Hegarty, Department of Industry and Commerce, 5 Jan. 1947, NAI, DFA, 317/98.
80 Brian Girvin, 'Political Independence and democratic consolidation', in Holmes and Holmes, *Ireland and India*, p. 141.
81 See file on this visit, NAI, Office of the Secretary of the President (hereafter, PRES), P 4276.
82 Unsigned memo for Government, 2 Mar. 1961, NAI, DT, 96/6/265.
83 *Ibid.*

84 *Ibid.*
85 Lemass to Aiken, 10 Sept. 1961, NAI, DT, 96/6/265.
86 *Ibid.*
87 Fact sheet on Warnock's nomination, 12 Nov. 1963 and credentials signed by de Valera, 27 Feb. 1964, NAI, DT, 96/6/265.
88 For further information on this visit see NAI, DT, S 17563.

Conclusion

In modern times Irish people have both sustained and undermined the British imperial system, and in both colonial and post-colonial studies Ireland is presented as a unique phenomenon, as it can be viewed, paradoxically, as both 'imperial' and 'colonial'.[1] This study, however, has concentrated on the latter characteristic as the 'imperial' has received more attention than the 'colonial' in the few recent historical studies that have been carried out in relation to Ireland and India exclusively. As mentioned in the Introduction, throughout many general histories of Ireland and India, there appear numerous comparisons and fleeting references to a long-established and acknowledged relationship between both countries' nationalist movements; however, a study devoted to analysing this association was nowhere to be found. Thus far, in Irish and Indian historiography, that the two nationalist movements are analogous has been taken for granted. There is clearly scope therefore for scholarly attention to the history of Indo-Irish radical discourse. This brings me to the main purpose of this study, which has been to add empirical detail to this neglected anti-imperialist–nationalist nexus. The exact nature of the connections made between figures from both revolutionary movements, like de Valera and Nehru and Subhas Chandra Bose, have hitherto remained indistinct, and other established contacts, especially those made within communist circles, were simply unknown.

This study also illuminates the role of figures and organisations previously considered somewhat obscure in both Indian and Irish history. Individuals like V. J. Patel, Brajesh Singh, Mollie Woods and Charlotte Despard emerge as quite significant figures in their respective movements, people who have been given little attention in their own right. Woods especially should be singled out for attention as she cultivated close friendships with both Patel and Bose and encouraged Indo-Irish collaboration in the hope that both sides could learn from their respective experiences. These were agitators who attempted to add an aspect of global finesse to local nationalist politics and successfully established their own tailor-made organisation in the shape of the IIIL, while simultaneously participating in the LAI, an internationally successful communist front organisation that was winning over nationalist converts in the colonies. Ironically as a result of travelling abroad and thinking 'outside the box' while attempting to draw attention to their national struggles, many of them have since been neglected by their country's revolutionary histories. The LAI is also an organisation about which little was known, and while this study has not attempted to detail its entire history, it shows how effective it was as a means by which Indo-Irish connections were established and flourished in the inter-war period. It also demonstrates how the Comintern policy of attempting to solicit broadbased support in the colonies by advocating tolerance towards the non-communist Left and colonial nationalist movements, was successful but short-lived, and its abandonment was followed by the LAI's rapid decline.

This study also reveals a significant amount about IPI, an agency about which very little is known and one almost entirely overlooked in intelligence historiography. Detailed analysis of the organisation's files discloses considerable unease on the part of the British authorities about the activities of Indian radicals in continental Europe, and in the UK and Ireland. The amount of surveillance carried out reveals just how apprehensive its officials were about Indian subversive activity. This increased concern was legitimate, given the rapid expansion of Indian nationalist centres outside of India and British intelligence's experience with Indian radical activity in the US during the First World War.

It is also safe to conclude that an overemphasis was placed on Indians with communist leanings at the expense of those driven by purely separatist ideals and those who were involved in the smuggling of anti-imperialist literature and arms-trafficking to India, people like Henry Obed, an Axis conspirator, who was not as closely monitored as he might have been had he displayed communist leanings. However, IPI did become aware of the flourishing Indo-Irish nexus of the late 1920s and 1930s in the guise of the formation of the IIIL and thought it a development that warranted monitoring. The agency also became greatly perturbed when it became apparent that some Indian subversives were deliberately taking advantage of Ireland's ambiguous imperial status by travelling to Dublin or Cork, safe in the knowledge that further passport endorsements would be granted to them there, something which would not have happened in the UK. Networking among Indian and Irish radicals during the Second World War not only warranted sustained surveillance by British intelligence concerned about collaboration and fifth-column threats, but it was a nexus considered legitimate enough to mimic in order to facilitate Axis monitoring – as chapter four showed it is feasible that British intelligence agents established the FOIS in Dublin.

Although some of Subhas Chandra Bose's biographers have noted that he took heart from Ireland's history, the full impact of Ireland as an influence on his thinking has, to date, been severely underestimated. While Bose was seen to vacillate between supporting communist and fascist ideology whenever it best suited his basic political goal of Indian independence from Britain, the one consistent inspiration for him throughout his political life was the Irish revolutionary movement. As a young adult he read books written by Dan Breen and Terence MacSwiney, and he set up a volunteer force in Calcutta modelled on its Irish namesake. He travelled to Ireland and in so doing fulfilled a long held dream. He met with de Valera not only in Dublin in 1936 but in London two years later. In the wake of his visit to Ireland he continued to write to and receive letters and Irish press cuttings from his fond friend Mollie Woods, up until the outbreak of the Second World War. After his death, Bose's correspondence with Woods was even taken up by his Austrian wife Emile Shenkl. He clearly had the 1916 Rising in mind when he embarked on his over-ambitious INA mission, as we know from the broadcasts he made during the war from the Far East to a city thousands of miles away that he had visited some years earlier. And his trip to Dublin was significant in its own right, as it was an opportunity for a recently elected revolutionary, de Valera, to court another radical not looked on favourably by the British authorities, and to provide him with a welcome akin to a mini-state visit. Bose also met with Irish ministers and discovered how the realities of independence and the day-to-day running of government were being put into practice.

If throughout the 1920s and 1930s the developing Indo-Irish radical nexus was a symptom of the decline of the British Empire, the transfer of power in India was the final illustration of its demise, and it was appropriately witnessed by Eamon de Valera, the Viceroy's final guest. Two years later, in 1950, de Valera was invited to be the chief speaker and to unfurl the national flag at a formal reception in Birmingham to celebrate the declaration of India as a republic, something he never got to do for his own country. When the organisers were asked why they had not asked a fellow Indian, their response was unequivocal, and it succinctly describes the Indo-Irish parallels of the first half of the twentieth century that spawned the multi-faceted relationship which is described in this study:

The answer is, firstly, there is a bit of Irish in every heart, but with us Indians there is more. We and the Irish had strong ties of friendship. We suffered under the same tyranny for many centuries. They had the Black and Tans; we had the massacre of Amritsar. They had de Valera and Casement and MacSwiney; we had Gandhi and Nehru and Bose. They had Sinn Féin; we had our National Congress. They had the IRA; we had the INA. It is not only for the smile and the shamrock we know Ireland. It is for the toughness of their leaders and for the rebellion in their hearts against all injustice and all inhumanity.[2]

Notes

1 Jeffery, *Irish Empire*, p. 1.
2 *Irish Press*, 26 Jan. 1950.

BIOGRAPHICAL NOTES

Frank Aiken (1898–1983)
TD, succeeded Liam Lynch as chief of staff of the IRA in April 1923 and issued the cease-fire orders which ended the Civil War. Founder member of Fianna Fáil in 1926. Served as Minister for Defence from 1932 to 1939; Minister for Land and Fisheries, June to November 1936; Minister for the Coordination of Defensive Measures, 1939–45; Minister for Finance, 1945–48; Minister for External Affairs, 1951–54, and 1957–69; Minister for Agriculture, March to May 1957 and Tánaiste, 1965–69. Accompanied de Valera on his anti-partition world tour, March–June 1948.

Frederick Boland (1904–85)
Entered the Department of External Affairs in 1929. Junior administrative officer, 1930–31. First Secretary, Paris Legation, 1932–34; Head of the League of Nations Section of the Department of External Affairs, 1934–36; Principal Officer in charge of Foreign Trade Section, Department of Industry and Commerce, 1936–38; Assistant Secretary, Department of External Affairs, 1938–46; Secretary, Department of External Affairs, 1946–50; Ambassador to Britain, 1950–55; Permanent Representative to the United Nations, 1956–64.

Sarat Chandra Bose (1889–1950)
Born in Calcutta, brother of Subhas Chandra Bose. Barrister and nationalist politician. Became President of the Bengal Congress in 1936 and served as a member of the All-India Working Committee, 1936–47; became a leading member of the Forward Bloc. Met with Maud Gonne MacBride in Paris in the early 1900s and became a friend of Eamon de Valera, having met him for the first time in 1948.

Subhas Chandra Bose (1897–1945)
Born in Cuttack. Prominent in the Indian independence movement and a physical force nationalist. Worked under Chittaranjan Das (co-founder of the Swarajya Party) in the Calcutta Corporation. Suspected of terrorist activities, and arrested and imprisoned, October 1924 to May 1927 and again in January 1930. Following his release in September 1930 was elected Mayor of Calcutta. Along with Nehru was one of the radical, left-wing leaders of the Congress Party. From 1933 to 1936 was a roving ambassador for Indian independence in Europe;

[183]

visited Ireland in February 1936 established links with the Irish republican community, especially the Woods family. President of the Indian National Congress, 1938, and elected for a second term in 1939 only to resign and form an independent party, the All-India Forward Bloc. He escaped house arrest and arrived in Germany in spring 1941; travelled via submarine to Japan and with Axis help founded the INA and the 'Azad Hind' Government in the Far East in October 1943. Died in an air crash in Formosa (Taiwan), August 1945.

Margaret Cousins (1878–1954)

Born in Co. Roscommon. Theosophist, suffragist and activist for Indian and Irish independence. Married the theosophist James Cousins in 1903. They were joint founders along with Francis and Hanna Sheehy Skeffington of the Irish Women's Franchise League in 1908. She and her husband emigrated to India in June 1913. Founded the Indian Women's Association, 1914; founded the All-India Women's Conference, 1928. Arrested and imprisoned for protesting at the introduction of legislation curtailing free speech, December 1932 to October 1933. Elected President of the All-India's Women's Conference, 1939.

Roddy Connolly (1901–80)

Son of James Connolly. Was beside his father in the General Post Office during the 1916 Rising. Attended the Second World Congress of the Comintern in Moscow where he was a member of the Commission on the National and Colonial Question, July 1920. Founded the Communist Party of Ireland, September 1921. During the Civil War aligned himself with the republican leadership. Travelled throughout Europe in the early 1920s and liaised with the Indian communist M. N. Roy. Affiliated with Republican Congress, 1934. Joined the Labour Party in the 1940s; later TD for Louth and chairman of the Labour Party.

Charlotte Despard, née French (1844–1939)

Born in Edinburgh. Suffragist, nationalist and novelist; sister of Field Marshal Lord French who became Lord-Lieutenant, Viceroy of Ireland in 1918. Radicalised by her experience of the conditions in the London slums. Became a member of the Independent Labour Party. In 1907 she was one of those who broke away from the Women's Social and Political Union and formed the Women's Freedom League. Moved to Ireland in 1910; became active in labour politics and joined Sinn Féin. A member of several Indian societies in London where she met Gandhi in 1914. One of the founder members of the IIIL in 1932. Became a member of the Communist Party of Ireland in the 1930s.

Eamon De Valera (1882–1975)

Born in New York. TD, nationalist politician and statesman. Commandant of the Third Battalion of the Irish Volunteers during the 1916 Rising. Imprisoned in England, 1916–17. Elected member for East Clare in July 1917; elected President of Sinn Féin in October 1917. Imprisoned in England, 1918–19. President of Dáil Éireann, 1 April 1919 to 2 January 1922, a post he referred to as 'President of the Irish Republic'. In America from 11 June 1919 to 23 December 1920. Opposed the Anglo-Irish Treaty and served with the Third Dublin Brigade of the republican forces during the Civil War. Arrested by Irish Free State troops and imprisoned, August 1923 to July 1924. TD for Clare, 1923–59. Resigned Presidency of Sinn Féin in March 1926. Founder of Fianna Fáil in May 1926; became leader of the Opposition in Dáil Éireann in August 1927; President of the Executive Council and Minister for External Affairs, 1932–37; President of the Council of the League of Nations and Acting President of the Assembly of the League of Nations, 1932–33. Taoiseach and Minister for External Affairs, 1937–48. Minister for Education, September 1939 to June 1940; Minister for Local Government, August 1941; Taoiseach, 1951–54 and 1957–59; President of Ireland, 1959–73.

John Dulanty (1881–1955)

Born in Liverpool. Joined the British Civil Service in 1914. Managing director of Peter Jones, Ltd, 1919–26. Irish Trade Commissioner in London, 1926–30; Irish High Commissioner in London, 1930–49; Irish Ambassador to Britain, 1950.

Brajesh Singh Lal (–1966)

Born in Kalakankar (date unascertainable). Indian nationalist activist and committed communist. Brother of the Raja of Kalankar and M. N. Roy's right-hand man and financier during the 1930s. Fell out with Roy and travelled to Europe in 1932. Along with his brother he visited Ireland regularly and supported the IIIL and befriended the Woods family. Controversially obtained an Empire-wide emergency passport in Dublin when this would not have been possible in the UK. By the 1960s was working for the Foreign Languages Publishing House in Moscow where he met and soon after married Stalin's daughter, Svetlana Alliluyeva. He died in 1966. Alliluyeva travelled to India with his ashes and while there sought political asylum at the US Embassy.

Maud Gonne MacBride (1866–1953)

Born in Hampshire. Nationalist activist and founder of Inghinidhe na hÉireann in 1900. Muse and friend of W. B. Yeats. Married Major John

[185]

MacBride in 1903. After their marriage separation she went to Paris until his execution in 1916 when she returned to Ireland. Formed the Women's Prisoners' Defence League during the Civil War and was imprisoned by the provisional Government. Friend of Charlotte Despard and a founder member of the IIIL in 1932.

Seán MacBride (1904–88)

Born in Paris; son of Maud Gonne MacBride and Major John MacBride. Anti-Treaty republican activist and lawyer; leading member of the IRA from the late 1920s and throughout the 1930s, part of which time he served as director of intelligence. Attended the Congress of Oppressed Nations in Brussels, February 1927 and the LAI World Congress in Frankfurt, July 1929; member of Saor Éire. Joint founder of Clann na Poblachta in 1946. Formed part of Ireland's first inter-party Government as Minister for External Affairs, 1948–51. Founder member of Amnesty International, of which he was Chairman from 1973 to 1976, and UNESCO. Nobel Peace Prize winner, 1974; Lenin Peace Prize winner, 1977.

(Sir) John Maffey (Lord Rugby) (1887–1969)

Colonial administrator and diplomat. Served in India for 25 years, primarily at the North West Frontier, where he was Chief Commissioner from 1921 to 1924; Governor-General to the Sudan, 1925–33; Permanent Under-Secretary of State for the Colonies, 1933–37; UK representative to Éire, 1939–49.

V. K. Krishna Menon (1897–1974)

Born in Calicut. Joined Annie Besant's Home Rule movement in India before travelling to England in 1924. Became General Secretary of the India League, 1929. Member of the socialist group on the St Pancras Borough Council. Established a strong friendship with Nehru in the 1930s. During this time he was an active Labour Party member involved in several Irish societies in London. Following the transfer of power he was appointed High Commissioner to the UK, 1947–52. Became India's first Ambassador to Ireland, 1949. Elected to the Upper House of the Indian Parliament, 1953; Minister without Portfolio, 1956–57; Minister for Defence, 1957. Resigned from the Congress Party in 1967.

Jawaharlal Nehru (1889–1964)

Born in Allahabad. Barrister, socialist, nationalist politician and statesman. President of the Indian National Congress, 1929, 1936, 1937 and 1946. In Europe 1926–27, accompanying his wife who was seeking treatment for her health. He attended the first meeting of the LAI in February 1927. Spent most of the period from 1930 to 1936 in prison for his involvement in the civil disobedience campaigns; imprisoned again during the Second World War, October 1942 to June 1945. India's first Prime Minister and Minister for Foreign Affairs, 1947–64.

Henry Obed (–1952)
Born in Lucknow (date unascertainable). Indian subversive suspected of arms- and drugs-trafficking. Ran an import and export business in Hamburg, 1922–24. He then moved to Antwerp and established a live animal import and export shop. Avoided arrest and conviction by both the British and Belgian authorities for over twenty years. Eventually arrested in Cork, July 1940, as one of a party of three Axis agents who had landed with sabotage equipment; imprisoned in Ireland, 1940–47. He later claimed that his intention was to establish contact with the IRA. He was murdered in 1952 by his wife, who suspected him of having an affair.

Art O'Brien (1872–1949)
Born in London. President of the Gaelic League in London, 1914–35; President of the Sinn Féin Council of Great Britain, 1916–23; co-founder of the Irish Self-Determination League of Great Britain, of which he became Vice-President, 1919–22, and President, 1922–24; Sinn Féin Representative in London, 1919–22. Opposed the Anglo-Irish Treaty. Managing editor of the *Music Trades Review*, 1924–35. Minister to France, 1935–38.

Peadar O'Donnell (1893–1986)
Born in Co. Donegal. Left-wing republican and novelist. IRA commander of Donegal Brigade, 1921–22. Imprisoned during the Civil War. Elected TD for Donegal in 1923. Editor of *An Phoblacht*, 1926–29; and member of the Army Council of the IRA, 1925–34. Attended LAI executive council meeting in Brussels, December 1927, and the LAI World Congress in Frankfurt, July 1929. His arguments against the payment of land annuities to Britain became Fianna Fáil policy in 1932. Formed Republican Congress in 1934; Editor of the *Bell*, 1946–54.

Donal O'Donoghue (1897–1957)
Born in Co. Cavan. Left-wing republican. Member of the IRA Dublin Brigade; interned during the Civil War. Attended the Congress of Oppressed Nations in Brussels, February 1927; an executive council meeting of the LAI in Brussels, December 1927 and the LAI World Congress in Frankfurt, July 1929. Editor of *An Phoblacht* in the 1930s.

Married Cumman na mBán activist Sighle Humphreys in 1935; editor of *Republican Review*, 1938–39; founding member of Clann na Poblachta in 1946.

Vallabhbhai Sardar Patel (1875–1950)

Born in Gujarat. Lawyer, nationalist politician and brother of Vithalbhai J. Patel. Joined the civil disobedience campaign and successfully organised the Bardoli campaign against British tax increases, 1927–28. President of the Indian National Congress, 1931; served as Home Minister, Minister of States and Deputy Prime Minister, 1947–50.

Vithalbhai Javerbhai Patel (1871–1933)

Born in Gujarat. Nationalist politician, elder brother of Vallabhbhai Sardar Patel. President of the Indian Legislative Assembly, 1925–30. Fierce critic of Gandhi. Spent much time in Europe in the 1920s and early 1930s as a propagandist for Indian independence. Subhas Chandra Bose was his protégé at this time. He visited Ireland on four occasions, 1919, 1927, 1932 and 1933, and befriended many Irish republicans. Co-founder in 1932 of the IIIL.

(Sir) David Petrie (1879–1961)

Born in Scotland. Entered the Indian Police in 1900. Director of the Intelligence Bureau (DIB), 1924–31; Chairman of the Public Services Commission in India, 1932–36; Director General of MI5, 1940–46.

M. N. Roy (1887–1954)

Born in West Bengal. Communist leader, revolutionary and writer. In the wake of the partition of Bengal came into contact with militant nationalists. Sought German help for Indian independence during the First World War. In 1915 Roy went to Batavia to rendezvous with Germans in an attempt to land arms in India. These schemes, however, failed and he fled to America in 1916; absconded to Mexico in 1917 and met the Soviet emissary, Michael Borodin. Having visited Moscow in 1920 he eventually settled in Berlin in1921 as a Comintern agent; editor of the *Vanguard*. Liaised with Roddy Connolly in 1922 and possibly facilitated him in the purchasing of arms. Returned to India in 1930 and was imprisoned for six years. Joined the Indian National Congress upon his release in 1936 and organised a league of Radical Congressmen. His support of the Allied war effort controversially resulted in he and his followers resigning from Congress. Spent his last years writing critical analyses of communism, fascism and liberalism and began the humanist movement in India.

Frank Ryan (1902–44)

Born in Limerick. Joined the IRA in 1921 after the War of Independence and was interned during the Civil War. Took up a scholarship to UCD upon his release and became involved with the UCD Republican Club and the Dublin IRA. Attended the Congress of Oppressed Nations in Brussels, February 1927; an executive council meeting of the LAI in Brussels, December 1927 and the LAI World Congress in Frankfurt, July 1929. Editor of *An Phoblacht*, 1929–33. Member of Republican Congress and editor of *Republican Congress*, 1934. Volunteered to fight for the Spanish Republic in 1936 and became the highest ranking Irish officer in the International Brigades; wounded at the battle of Jarama, 1937. After a brief visit to Dublin he returned to Spain and was captured by Italian troops in 1938; imprisoned and sentenced to death. An international campaign succeeded in having his death sentence commuted. In 1940 German military intelligence negotiated his release into their custody and he was taken to Germany. Suffered a stroke and died in Dresden in 1944.

Shapurji Saklatvala (1874–1936)

Born in Bombay. MP, communist, and political activist for Indian and Irish independence in the UK. Was the third Indian person and the second member of the Communist Party of Great Britain to become an MP. Moved to England in 1905; joined the Independent Labour Party, 1910; co-founder of the Worker's Welfare League, 1917; joined the People's Russian Information Bureau, 1918. Joined the CPGB, 1921. Labour MP for North Battersea, 1922–23; from 1924 to 1929 he was a Communist Party MP. Had extensive Irish contacts in London including Charlotte Despard and Art O'Brien. Travelled regularly to Ireland to speak at political rallies, attending the Republican Congress meeting in Rathmines, September 1934.

Hanna Sheehy Skeffington (1877–1946)

Born in Co. Cork. Feminist and republican activist. Married the socialist, pacifist and journalist Francis Skeffington in 1903. They were joint founders along with James and Margaret Cousins of the Irish Women's Franchise League in 1908. She was imprisoned in 1912 for a window smashing offence. She carried supplies during the 1916 Rising during which her husband was shot dead. She joined Sinn Féin in 1918; Editor of the *Irish Citizen* until 1920. Remained a prominent figure in feminist and republican circles nationally and internationally despite an unsuccessful campaign as an independent candidate for Dáil Éireann in 1943.

(Sir) Charles Tegart (1881–1946)

Born in Co. Derry. Educated at Trinity College Dublin. Joined the Indian Police Service in 1901. Appointed Commissioner of Calcutta Police in 1926. Was asked to take over the headship of IPI in 1926 but declined. Retired from the Indian Police Service, 1931; served on the Council of India, 1931–37; offered the post of Inspector General of the Palestine Police in 1937, but declined and instead accepted a short-term post to organise the police force to combat terrorism there. Controversially worked in Ireland for the British intelligence services during the Second World War.

(Sir) Philip Vickery (1890–1987)

Born in Co. Fermanagh. Educated at Trinity College, Dublin. Joined the Indian Police Service in 1909. Was sent in 1915 to work under John Wallinger's fledgling intelligence agency which monitored Indian nationalist activities in Europe. Went to America and Canada to carry out surveillance of Indian radicals in 1919, remaining there until Wallinger's retirement in 1926, when he returned to London and took over the agency, by then formalised as IPI. He remained head of IPI until its closure in 1947; Commonwealth Relations Office, 1952–62.

Joseph Walshe (1886–1956)

Solicitor. Served on the Irish delegation in Paris, November 1920 to January 1922; Secretary to Dáil Ministry of Foreign Affairs, February 1922 to August 1922; Acting Secretary, Department of External Affairs, September 1922 to August 1927; Secretary, Department of External Affairs, August 1927 to May 1946; Ambassador to the Holy See, May 1946 to September 1954.

Mary (Mollie) Woods (1869–1954)

Born in Monasteraden in Co. Sligo. Irish nationalist activist. She married Andrew Woods and moved to Dublin; from 1917 was associated with Maud Gonne MacBride and Charlotte Despard. Worked for Michael Collins during the War of Independence, and her family's home in Morehampton Road became a safe house for various left-wing republicans in the wake of the Civil War. Founding member of the Women's Prisoners' Defence League. Co-founder of the Indian–Irish Independence League in 1932 and friend to many Indian nationalists who visited Ireland throughout the 1930s, including: V. J. Patel, Brajesh Singh Lal and Subhas Chandra Bose. Woods kept up regular correspondence with Bose until his death, after which his Austrian wife Emile Shenkel began corresponding with her.

APPENDIX 1

'Britain in Ireland', *Anti-Imperialist Youth Bulletin*, May 1931

Ireland has guided the Imperialists in their treatment of the workers and peasants of other countries. 300 years of the fanning of racial and religious hatreds, of the use of armed violence, bribery and corruption among the Irish peasantry taught the Empire builders how best to maintain their hold over the colonies.

The English conquest of Ireland meant that the clansmen were reduced to serfs. Huge tracts of land in Ulster were given to English and Scottish settlers, at nominal rents. The natives were evicted. In parts of Ireland the Irish were registered, like natives in South Africa. Any unregistered person was arrested. Tillage farming became unprofitable. Arable land was turned into sheep farms.

Time and time again the Irish rebelled. Massacres, burning and pillage were the replies of the British Imperialists.

Ireland is important to England, both as a source of exploitation and as a strategic centre in times of war. The Easter Rising of 1916 put mortal fear into the hearts of the British Imperialists and they attempted to smash the Irish working class movement by the execution of Jim Connolly.

Between 1919 and 1921 the Irish youth fought for their freedom, but they were betrayed by their native capitalists, and today Ireland is still chained to British imperialism, although a "Free State" in name.

But the young Irish workers and peasants, with their standards of life being attacked through the effects of the world crisis, are beginning to organise against both native and foreign exploiters. We send our greetings to them and pledge ourselves to aid them in their struggle.

APPENDIX 2

Resolution of Dublin mass meeting of the League Against Imperialism

This Mass Meeting of Dublin Anti-Imperialists sends greetings to the workers of Great Britain and calls on them to resolutely oppose the aggressive action of the British Tory government against the people of Ireland, who are striving for freedom from the stranglehold of Imperialism and Capitalism which has impoverished the mass of the people and partitioned our country.

We call on the workers of Great Britain and throughout the British Empire to demand that all British Military and Naval Forces be withdrawn from the whole of Ireland.

We call on our race in Britain and throughout the British Empire to protest against the shameless Imperialist attack on the Irish people; we appeal to them actively to associate themselves with all genuine anti-Imperialist activities within their reach so that the Imperial stranglehold on this nation may be broken and Irish life so organised that our exiled brethren may come home to a free united Irish Republic where capitalist exploitation and its attendant evils and unemployment and slumdom shall have been for ever abolished.

APPENDIX 3

Indian–Irish Independence League constitution

NAME: Indian–Irish Independence League.

OBJECT: The object of the League will be to help by every means possible to secure the complete national, social and economic independence of the people of India and Ireland.

THE METHODS to be adopted will be:

1 Organising in Ireland and where else possible a complete boycott of British goods and concerns.
2 Establishing an Indian Information Bureau to spread the truth about the Indian struggle, and to counteract Imperial lies generally.
3 Taking steps necessary to link up the Indian and Irish movements in order to make effective the fight against the common opponent – the British Empire.
4 Exploring all possibilities of effective economic and trade alliance between Ireland and India, in order to defeat British Imperialism in its attempts to isolate and attack India or Ireland in the economic field.
5 Calling upon sympathisers of India and Ireland all over the world to establish similar Leagues.

APPENDIX 4

Irish Legation
Berlin
Tiergartenstrasee 34A
9 April 1934

Secretary
Department of External Affairs
Dublin

I have had a long visit from Mr Bose, the Mayor of Calcutta, who is again in Berlin. He tells me he hopes to go to Ireland in May. I impressed upon him that he should let me know the exact date and port, so that there would be no difficulties about his landing. He promised to do so.

I mention his visit, as his impressions of government circles here are of a certain interest. He states that he finds them strongly pro-English, and inclined to be hostile to India. He mentioned a recent speech in which General Goring stated that he had refused to receive Gandhi or his representatives. He also referred to passages in Hitler's book in which he pronounced himself opposed to Indian independence. His view is that the racial theory is at present allowed to outweigh all other considerations, and that consequently England as a Germanic people can do no wrong . . . According to Mr Bose, any change of orientation on Germany's part can only come about slowly and as a consequence of hard facts. He regards the people as on the whole friendly to Indian aspirations and not particularly enamoured of England; the governing classes on the other hand are the only ones which count, and their whole policy is based on friendship with England. He stated that even among the people in general he had noticed lately a less sympathetic attitude, which he ascribes to the agitation against the Jews and coloured peoples. His general diagnosis of the situation is that the German works from theory to fact, and if his theory depends on friendship with England he will believe that such friendship exists in spite of any facts to the contrary.

As regards India, Mr Bose regards the time for passive resistance as definitely past. He blames Gandhi for not having done any propaganda in the Indian army, and says that that will be their task for the next few years. He is frankly a believer in physical force, but says that some years of propaganda will be necessary before the country is ready.

I gave him a letter of introduction to you, but was careful to warn him that I did not know whether the President would be able to receive him on account of the many claims on his time.

C. Bewley

APPENDIX 5

C/o American Express Company
Nice (France)
7 December 1933

Dear Mrs Woods,

Thank you so much for your letter of the 3rd November. I am sorry for the delay in replying to it.

It was good of you to send the sympathetic message of Irish friends to the Indian Press. I am sure it will be greatly appreciated. I remember that in September 1929 the family of Terence MacSwiney sent a short but magnificent message on the occasion of the death from hunger strike of Jatin Das in Lahore Prison. The message was received with grateful appreciation.

Thank you very much for the invitation to come to Ireland. I have been longing to visit Ireland for years and I hope to do so before I return to India. In my part of India (Bengal), recent Irish history is studied closely by freedom-loving men and women and several Irish characters are literally worshipped in many a home. At present I am not allowed to visit the United Kingdom – nevertheless I shall be permitted by the Irish Free State government to visit Ireland (Free State). But I want to keep this fact a *strict secret*. Some friends of mine in London are trying to secure permission for me to visit England. But if the British government come to know that I am planning to visit Ireland, it will put their back up and they will never issue a passport for my visit to England. Until the question of my visiting England is finally decided, one way or the other, I desire to keep quiet regarding my intention to visit Ireland.

For Madame Gonne MacBride I have a message from my brother whom I met in prison before I sailed for Europe. My brother met Madame in 1914 in Paris and ever since then, has been one of her admirers. I dare say Madame does not remember my brother. He has been in internment since February 1932. My brother went with Mukherji, an Indian friend of his, to visit Madame.

I duly received a copy of your bulletin and I liked it. Do you get any of the Indian papers (in English) regularly? If you get them, would it be possible for you to pick out the interesting news – or would it be necessary to supply you with the news in ready form? How often do you publish the bulletin? I am anxious to supply you with information about India.

Kindly let me know which papers in Ireland are likely to publish interesting news, exposing the true character of British Imperialism. *Irish Press* of Dublin is Dev's paper – I think. Which is the organ of the I.R.A.? We shall try to send some news from time to time, if you could supply me with a list of the friendly Irish papers and journals.

[195]

I hope letters are not secretly censored in Ireland *nowadays*, as they are in India. It is necessary for me to know that.

With deepest regards,
I am
Yours sincerely
Subhas C. Bose

Kurhaus Hochland
Badgastein (Badgastein)
(Austria)
5 March 1936

Dear Mrs Woods,

You must be thinking what a funny man I am to leave Dublin and, as it were, disappear from the picture altogether. Well, I cannot sufficiently apologise for my fault. I have been passing through a whirlwind since I left Dublin and only now have I been able to settle down to a quiet rest.

After leaving Dublin I saw Miss MacSweeney [*sic*] the same night. I am glad that I took that train from Dublin because the boat was due the next morning. I could not therefore see Miss MacSweeney again the next morning.

The sea was rather rough and I was sick all the time. I had to give up the idea of writing a long letter to you from the boat.

Then as soon as I reached Paris, I had a round of engagements and people round all the time. When I retired at night, I felt too tired to write a long letter. Then I left Paris and went to Lausanne to see Mr and Mrs Nehru. Mrs Nehru was seriously ill and she died while I was at Lausanne. We had to make the arrangements for the cremation etc. – and we were kept busy all the time. Mr Nehru will be flying to India soon, he has to preside over the National Congress which will meet at Lucknow early in April. From Lausanne, I came here for a rest and also for bath-treatment. The baths here are very effacious [*sic*] as a 'pick-me-up'. I feel pretty badly shaken up as a result of continuous travelling and also some amount of worry. This rest will do me good and then I intend taking the boat from Marseilles about the 20th March.

Towards the end of my stay in Dublin, I used to get peculiar pain in the inside which was continuous. I never had this before. I did not speak to anyone about it, because I did not like to cause worry. The pain disappeared a few days after I arrived in Paris.

I cannot thank you sufficiently for your extreme kindness during my stay in Dublin and I therefore bring with me the most pleasant recollections. Your daughters were also extremely kind to me and, of course, Enda was my guardian angel. Please convey my grateful thanks to all of them.

I do not know when we shall meet again. Bhavabhuti, one of our ancient poets, once wrote – 'Time is eternal and the earth is a vast expanse', so maybe we shall meet again – but perhaps not so unexpectedly as when I knocked against my prison-Superintendent in Shelbourne Hotel.

In a few days I shall write to you again as to what I think we should do – or could do – to continue this contact between India and Ireland. Have you had any talk with Mme. MacBride since I left Dublin? Has there been any fresh development there since I left?

Please give my cordial greetings to your sons and daughters and accept my warmest regards.

Yours very sincerely
Subhas C. Bose.

BIBLIOGRAPHY

Primary sources

Republic of Ireland

National Archives of Ireland, Dublin
Bureau of Military History
Cabinet Minutes
Department of Foreign Affairs
Department of Justice
Department of the Taoiseach
Office of the Secretary of the President

National Library, Dublin
Joseph H. Fowler papers
Joseph McGarrity papers
Art O Brien papers
Hanna Sheehy Skeffington papers
Woods family papers

University College Dublin Archives
Frank Aiken papers
Eamon de Valera papers
Sighle Humphreys papers
Moss Twomey papers
Michael Hayes papers
Desmond Fitzgerald papers
Seán MacEntee papers

Military Archives, Dublin
G2 Intelligence files

Britain and Northern Ireland

Public Records Office, London
Cabinet Committee Papers
Dominions Office
Foreign Office
Government Code and Cipher School
Metropolitan Police
Security Service

BIBLIOGRAPHY

The British Library, Oriental and India Office Collection
Indian Political Intelligence
India Office Records
Shapurji Saklatvala papers

Women's Library, University of London
Charlotte Despard papers

Hull University Archives
Reginald Bridgeman papers
League Against Imperialism papers

Public Record Office of Northern Ireland, Belfast
Charlotte Despard papers

India

National Archives of India
Home Political Section
Ministry of External Affairs
Private Papers Collection

Nehru Memorial Library
Private Papers Collections

Online archives
The diaries of William Lyon Mackenzie King: http://king.collectionscanada.ca/
Franklin D. Roosevelt papers: www.fdrlibrary.marist.edu
Foreign Relations of the United States series: www.state.gov/r/pa/ho/frus/
The Avalon Project, Yale Law School: www.yale.edu/lawweb/avalon/20th.htm

Parliamentary and official publications
Dáil Debates
Hansard Debates
Constitutional relations between Britain and India: The Transfer of Power 1942–47, 12 vols
Documents in Irish Foreign Policy (vols 1–4)

Newspapers
Daily Mirror
Forward
The Hindu
The Hindustan Times
Irish Independent
Irish Press
The Irish Times
The Manchester Guardian

The New Leader
An Phoblacht
Republican Congress
Republican File
The Times
Workers Republic

Correspondence and interviews
Aideen Austen née Woods
Lalita Wright née Dey
Anna Austin
Eithne Frost

Secondary sources

Amery, Leo, *The Empire at Bay: The Leo Amery Diaries*, ed. J. Barnes and D. Nicholson (London, 1988).

Andrew, Christopher, *The Missing Dimension: Governments and Intelligence Communities in the Twentieth Century* (London, 1984).

—— *Secret Service: The Making of the British Intelligence Community* (London, 1985).

Babbington, Anthony, *The Devil to Pay: The Mutiny of the Connaught Rangers in India, July 1920* (London, 1991).

Bose, Arun Coomer, *Indian Revolutionaries Abroad, 1905–22: In the Background of International Developments* (Allahabad, 1971).

Bose, Mihir, *The Lost Hero: A Biography of Subhas Bose* (London, 1982).

Bose, Subhas Chandra, *Letters, Articles, Speeches and Statements, 1933–1937*, ed. S. K. Bose and S. Bose (Oxford, 1994).

—— *The Essential Writings of Netaji Subhas Chandra Bose*, ed. S. K. Bose and S. Bose (Oxford, 1997).

——*The Indian Struggle 1920–42*, ed. Sisir Kumar Bose and Sugata Bose (Oxford, 1997).

Bowman, John, *De Valera and the Ulster Question 1917–1973* (New York, 1982).

Brecher, Michael, *India and World Politics: Krishna Menon's View of the World* (Oxford, 1968).

Brockway, Fenner, *Inside the Left* (London, 1942).

Brown, Judith, *Modern India: The Origins of an Asian Democracy* (Oxford, 1994).

—— *Nehru: A Political Life* (London and New Haven, CT, 2003).

Brown, Judith and W. R. Louis (eds), *The Oxford History of the British Empire*, vol. 4: *The Twentieth Century* (Oxford, 1999).

Callaghan, John, *Ranjani Palme Dutt: A Study in British Stalinism* (London, 1993).

Canning, Paul, *British Policy Towards Ireland 1921–1941* (Oxford, 1985).

Carlton, David, *Churchill and the Soviet Union* (Manchester, 2000).

Carrol. F. M., *American Opinion and the Irish Question 1910–23: A Study in Opinion and Policy* (Dublin, 1978).

Chatterjee, Manini, *Do and Die: The Chittagong Uprising 1930–34* (New Delhi, 1999).

Chowdhury, R., *Ploughboy to President: Life-Story of V. J. Patel* (Calcutta, 1934).

Clarke, Peter, *The Cripps Version: The Life of Sir Srafford Cripps 1889–1952* (London, 2002).

Coogan, Tim Pat, *The IRA* (London, 1984).

Cook, S. B., *Imperial Affinities: Nineteenth Century Analogies and Exchanges between India and Ireland* (London, 1993).

Cronin, Sean, *Frank Ryan: The Search for the Republic* (Dublin, 1980).

Daly, Mary, 'Irish nationality and citizenship since 1922', *Irish Historical Studies*, 27 (May 2001).

De Valera, Eamon, *India and Ireland* (New York, 1920).

English, Richard, *Radicals and the Republic* (Oxford, 1994).

Feehan, John M., *The Shooting of Michael Collins: Murder or Accident?* (Cork, 1981).

Fisk, Robert, *In Time of War: Ireland, Ulster and the Price of Neutrality, 1939–45* (London, 1983).

Foster, Roy, *W. B. Yeats: A Life*, vol. 1 (Oxford, 1996).

Fraser, T. G., *Partition in Ireland, India and Palestine: Theory and Practice* (London, 1984).

French, Patrick, *Liberty or Death: India's Journey to Independence and Division* (London, 1998).

Garnett, David, *The Golden Echo* (London, 1970).

Gilmore, George, *Labour and the Republican Movement* (Dublin, 1966).

—— *The Irish Republican Congress*, 2nd edn (Cork, 1974).

Girvin, Brian and Geoffrey Roberts (eds), *Ireland and the Second World War: Politics, Society and Remembrance* (Dublin, 2000).

Gopal, Sarvepalli, *Jawaharlal Nehru: A Biography*, 3 vols (Oxford, 1975–1984).

—— *Jawaharlal Nehru: An Anthropology* (Oxford, 1983).

Gordon, Leonard, *Brothers Against the Raj: A Biography of Sarat and Subhas Chandra Bose* (New Delhi, 1990).

Griffiths, Sir Percival, *To Guard My People: The History of the Indian Police* (London, 1971).

Gupta, Partha Sarathi, *Imperialism and the British Labour Movement 1914–64* (London, 2002).

Haithcox, John Patrick, *Communism and Nationalism in India: M. N. Roy and Comintern Policy 1920–39* (New Jersey, 1971).

Hanley, Brian, *The IRA: 1926–36* (Dublin, 2002).

Harkness, D. W., *The Restless Dominion* (London, 1966).

Hartley, Stephen, *The Irish Question as a Problem in British Foreign Policy, 1914–18* (London, 1987).

Hasan, Mushirul, *India's Partition* (Oxford, 1993).

Haynes, John Earl and Harvey Klehr, *Venona: Decoding Soviet Espionage in America* (London, 1999).

Heehs, Peter, *Nationalism, Terrorism, Communalism* (Oxford, 1998).

Her Majesty's Government, *The Transfer of Power*, ed. P. N. S. Mansergh and E. W. R. Lumby, 12 vols (London, 1970–82).

Hoar, Adrian, *In Green and Red: The Lives of Frank Ryan* (Kerry, 2004).

Holmes, Denis and Michael Holmes (eds), *Ireland and India: Connections, Comparisons and Contrasts* (Dublin, 1997).

Howe, Stephen, *Ireland and India: Colonial Legacies in Irish History and Culture* (Oxford, 2002).

Hull, Mark, *Irish Secrets: German Espionage in Ireland, 1939–1945* (Dublin, 2003).

Jeffery, Keith (ed.), *An Irish Empire? Aspects of Ireland and the British Empire* (Manchester, 2000).

Jones, Jean, *Ben Bradley: Fighter For India's Freedom* (London, 1994).

—— *The League Against Imperialism* (London, 1996).

Kapur, Narinder, *The Irish Raj: Illustrated Stories about Irish in India and Indians in Ireland* (Antrim, 1997).

Kennedy, Michael and Joseph Morrison Skelly (eds), *Irish Foreign Policy 1919–66: From Independence to Internationalism* (Dublin, 2000).

Kenny, Kevin (ed.), *Ireland and the British Empire* (Oxford, 2004).

Lahiri, Shompa, *Indians in Britain: Anglo-Indian Encounters, Race and Identity, 1880–1930* (London, 2000).

Lal, Chaman, *The Vanishing Empire* (Tokyo, 1937).

Lee, J. J., *Ireland 1912–85* (Cambridge, 1985).

McCabe, Ian, *A Diplomatic History of Ireland 1948–49* (Dublin, 1995).

McCullagh, David, *A Makeshift Majority: The First Inter-Party Government, 1948–51* (Dublin, 1998).

MacEoin, Uinseann, *Survivors* (Dublin, 1980).

McDermott, Kevin and Jeremy Agnew, *The Comintern: A History of International Communism from Lenin to Stalin* (London, 1996).

McGarry, Fearghal, *Irish Politics and the Spanish Civil War* (Cork, 1999).

—— (ed.) *Republicanism in Modern Ireland* (Dublin, 2003).

—— *Frank Ryan* (Dundalk, 2004).

McLaughlin, Barry, 'Proletarian academics or party functionaries? Irish communists at the International Lenin School, Moscow, 1927–1937', *Saothar*, 22 (1997).

McMahon, Deirdre, *Republicans and Imperialists* (Yale, 1984).

Mansergh, Nicholas, *The Commonwealth and the Nations: Studies in British Commonwealth Relations* (London, 1948).

—— *Documents and Speeches on British Commonwealth Affairs 1931–52* (London, 1953).

—— *The Commonwealth Experience* (London, 1969).

—— *Prelude to Partition: Concepts and Aims in Ireland and India* (Cambridge, 1978).

—— *The Unresolved Question: The Anglo-Irish Settlement and its Undoing 1912–72* (London, 1991).

—— *Nationalism and Independence: Selected Irish Papers*, ed. Diana Mansergh (Cork, 1997).

—— *Independence Years: The Selected Indian and Commonwealth Papers of Nicholas Mansergh*, ed. Diana Mansergh (Oxford, 1999).

Milotte, Mike, *Communism in Modern Ireland: The Pursuit of the Workers' Republic since 1916* (Dublin, 1984).

Milton, Israel, *Communications and Power: Propaganda and the Press in the Indian National Struggle* (Cambridge, 1994).

Moon, Penderel (ed.), *Wavell: The Viceroy's Journal* (Oxford, 1978).

Nanda, B. R., *Three Statesmen: Gokhale, Gandhi and Nehru* (Oxford, 2004).

Nehru, Jawaharlal, *Glimpses of World History* (New York, 1942).

Norman, Dorothy, *Nehru: The First Sixty Years*, 2 vols (London, 1965).

O'Carroll, J. P. and John A. Murphy (eds), *De Valera and His Times* (Cork, 1983).

O'Connor, Emmet, *Red and the Green. Ireland, Russia and the Communist Internationals 1919–43* (Dublin, 2004).

O'Drisceoil, Donal, *Peadar O'Donnell* (Cork, 2001).

O'Grady, Joseph P., 'The Irish Free State passport and the question of citizenship, 1921–24', in *Irish Historical Studies* 104 (November, 1989).

O'Halpin, Eunan, 'Intelligence and Security in Ireland, 1922–45' in *Intelligence and National Security* 5 (1990).

—— *Defending Ireland: The Irish Free State and its Enemies since 1922.* (Oxford, 1999).

—— 'Small states and big secrets: understanding Sigint cooperation between unequal powers during the Second World War', *Intelligence and National Security*, 17 (2002).

—— (ed.), *MI5 and Ireland 1939–1945: The Official History* (Dublin, 2003).

O'Kelly, Seán T., *Ireland and India* (New York, 1924).

Pandey, B. N., *The Indian Nationalist Movement, 1885–1947: Selected Documents* (London, 1979).

Patel, Gordhanbhai L., *Vithalbhai Patel: Life and Times* (Bombay, 1951).

Patterson, Henry, *The Politics of Illusion: Republicanism and Socialism in Modern Ireland* (London, 1989).

Payne, Stanley G., *Politics and the Military in Modern Spain* (London, 1967).

Philips, C. H., and Mary Doreen Wainright (eds), *The Partition of India: Policies and Perspectives, 1935–1947* (London, 1970).

Popplewell, Richard, *Intelligence and Imperial Defence: British Intelligence and the Defence of the Indian Empire 1904–24* (London, 1995).

Ram, Janaki, *Krishna Menon: A Personal Memoir* (Oxford, 1997).

Read, Anthony and David Fisher, *The Proudest Day: India's Long Road to Independence* (London, 1998).

Roger, W. M., *In The Name of God, Go!* (London, 1992).

Ryan, Meda, *The Day Michael Collins Was Shot* (Dublin, 1989).

Sagar, Vidya, *Savarkar: A Study in the Evolution of Indian Nationalism* (London, 1967).

Said, Edward W., *Culture and Imperialism* (London, 1994).

Saklatvala, Sehri, *The Fifth Commandment: Biography of Shapurji Saklatvala* (Salford, 1991).

Silvestri, Michael, 'The Sinn Féin of India: Irish nationalism and the policing of revolutionary terrorism in Bengal', *Journal of British Studies*, 39 (2000).

—— 'Sir Charles Tegart and revolutionary terrorism in Bengal', *History Ireland* (winter, 2000).

Sloan, G. R., *The Geopolitics of Anglo-Irish Relations in the Twentieth Century* (London, 1997).

Stafford, David, *Churchill and Secret Service* (London, 1995).

Thorpe, Andrew, *The British Communist Party and Moscow, 1920–43* (Manchester, 2000).

Visram, Rozina, *Asians in Britain: 400 Years of History* (London, 2002).

INDEX

Note: numbers in italics refer to illustrations